ZAGATSURVEY®

1998/99

PARIS RESTAURANTS

**Edited by Alexander Lobrano,
François Simon, Mary Deschamps
and M.L. Lewis**

**Coordinated by
Elizabeth and Philippe d'Hémery**

**Published and distributed by
ZAGAT SURVEY, LLC
4 Columbus Circle
New York, New York 10019
Tel: 212 977 6000
E-mail: zagat@zagatsurvey.com**

**Distributed in France by
Flammarion
26, rue Racine
75006 Paris
Tel: 01 40 51 31 00**

Acknowledgments

We would especially like to thank the following people for their support:

Flore de Brantes and family, as well as Mathilde Casimir.

Astrid Aïdan, Michaël Aïdan, George Balkind, Axel Baum, Jean-Manuel Bourgois, Sabine and Patrick Brassart, Catherine Bret and Gilbert Brownstone, Jacques Dehornois, Karsten Diettrich, Alexandra Ernst and Dean Garret Siegel, Barbara and Peter Georgescu, Jack D. Gunther, Jr., Andrew Hibbert, Mark Kessel, Anne and Gérard Mazet, Michelle Moss, Amaury de la Moussaye, Anne de Ravel, Deirdre and Alfred J. Ross, Robert J. Sisk, Anne Thomas, Robert C. Treuhold, Virginia and Jean Perrette, Dagmar and François de la Tour d'Auvergne, Charlotte and Franck Ullmann, Yveline le Cerf Vaucher, Martine Vermeulen, Denise and Alexandre Vilgrain, Jennifer and Sebastien Vilgrain, Stephen R. Volk, Lawrence A. Weinbach.

Contents

Introduction

Here are the results of our first *Paris Restaurant Survey* covering 825 restaurants in Paris and its surroundings. The publication of this guide is a happy occasion for us, as it represents a return to the city where our *Survey* concept was born 30 years ago. As young, newly married lawyers working in Paris in 1968–69, we began listing our favorite restaurants and comparing notes on them with colleagues and friends. That list was the seed that grew into our guides to over 40 cities today.

By regularly surveying large numbers of local restaurant-goers, we think we have achieved a uniquely current and reliable guide. We hope you agree. More than 1,700 people participated. Since the participants dined out an average of 3.7 times per week, this *Survey* is based on about 330,000 meals per year – nearly 1,000 meals per day. Of the survey-ors, 96% are French, 4% are other nationalities; 71% are men, 29% are women. The breakdown by age is 11% in their 20s, 26% in their 30s, 23% in their 40s, 25% in their 50s and 15% in their 60s or above.

We want to thank each participant. They are a widely diverse group in all respects but one – they are food lovers all. This book is really "theirs."

To help guide our readers to Paris' best meals and best buys, we have prepared a number of top listings in the front of this guide. See, for example, Paris' Favorite Restaurants (page 9), Top Ratings (pages 10–15) and Best Buys (pages 16–18). On the assumption that most people want a quick fix on the places at which they are considering eating, we have also tried to be concise and to provide handy indexes.

We are particularly grateful to our coordinators, Elizabeth and Philippe d'Hémery, who pulled this project together, as well as to our editors: Alexander Lobrano, a food and travel writer; François Simon, a journalist and author of gastronomic guides; Mary Deschamps and M.L. Lewis, freelance writers specializing in lifestyle and cultural subjects.

We invite you to be a reviewer in our next *Survey*. To do so, simply send a stamped, self-addressed, business-size envelope to ZAGAT SURVEY, 4 Columbus Circle, New York, NY 10019, so that we may contact you. Each participant will receive a free copy of the next *Paris Restaurant Survey* when published.

Your comments and even criticisms of this *Survey* are also solicited. There is always room for improvement.

New York, NY   Nina and Tim Zagat
June 5, 1998

Key to Ratings/Symbols

This sample entry identifies the various types of information contained in your Zagat Survey.

(1) Restaurant Name, Address, Métro Stop & Phone Number

(2) Hours & Credit Cards

(3) ZAGAT Ratings

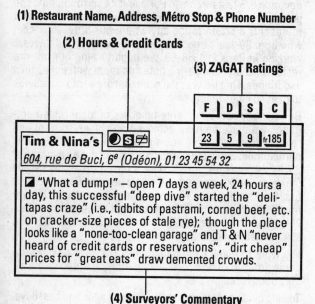

F	D	S	C
23	5	9	f185

Tim & Nina's ◖ Ⓢ ⌿

604, rue de Buci, 6ᵉ (Odéon), 01 23 45 54 32

■ "What a dump!" – open 7 days a week, 24 hours a day, this successful "deep dive" started the "deli-tapas craze" (i.e., tidbits of pastrami, corned beef, etc. on cracker-size pieces of stale rye); though the place looks like a "none-too-clean garage" and T & N "never heard of credit cards or reservations", "dirt cheap" prices for "great eats" draw demented crowds.

(4) Surveyors' Commentary

The names of restaurants with the highest overall ratings, greatest popularity and importance are printed in **CAPITAL LETTERS**. Address and phone numbers are printed in *italics*.

(2) Hours & Credit Cards

After each restaurant name you will find the following courtesy information:

◖ .... *serving after 11 PM*

Ⓢ .... *open on Sunday*

⌿ .... *no credit cards accepted*

(3) ZAGAT Ratings

Food, **Decor** and **Service** are each rated on a scale of **0** to **30**:

F	D	S	C

F .... *Food*
D .... *Decor*
S .... *Service*
C .... *Cost*

23	5	9	fr185

 0 - 9 .... *poor to fair*
10 - 15 .... *fair to good*
16 - 19 .... *good to very good*
20 - 25 .... *very good to excellent*
26 - 30 .... *extraordinary to perfection*

▽ 23	5	9	fr185

▽ .... *Low number of votes/less reliable*

The **Cost (C)** column reflects the estimated price of a dinner with one drink and tip. Lunch usually costs 25% less.

A restaurant listed without ratings is either an important **newcomer** or a popular **write-in**. The estimated cost, with one drink and tip, is indicated by the following symbols.

–	–	–	VE

I .... *below 200 Fr*
M .... *200 Fr to 350 Fr*
E .... *351 Fr to 500 Fr*
VE .... *more than 500 Fr*

(4) Surveyors' Commentary

Surveyors' comments are summarized, with literal comments shown in quotation marks. The following symbols indicate whether responses were mixed or uniform.

◪ .... *mixed*
◼ .... *uniform*

Paris' Favorites

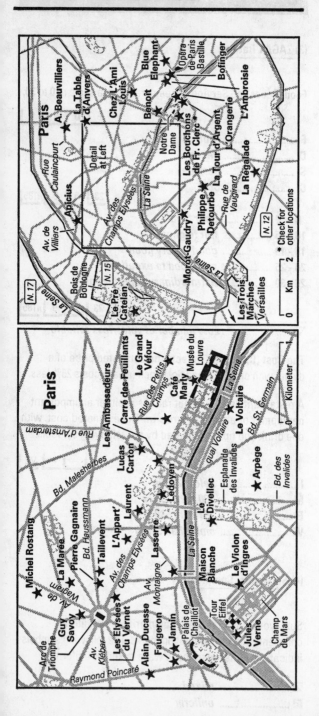

Paris' Favorite Restaurants

Each of our reviewers has been asked to name his or her five favorite restaurants. The 40 spots most frequently named, in order of their popularity, are:

1. Taillevent
2. Arpège
3. Ambroisie
4. Grand Véfour
5. Lucas Carton
6. Alain Ducasse
7. Tour d'Argent
8. Guy Savoy
9. Carré des Feuillants
10. Apicius
11. Pierre Gagnaire
12. Michel Rostang
13. Ambassadeurs
14. Jules Verne
15. Lasserre
16. Bouchons de Fr. Clerc
17. Maison Blanche
18. Laurent
19. Ami Louis
20. Ledoyen
21. Jamin
22. Faugeron
23. Orangerie
24. Appart'
25. Morot-Gaudry
26. Elysées du Vernet
27. Beauvilliers (A.)
28. Divellec
29. Violon d'Ingres
30. Pré Catelan
31. Voltaire
32. Table d'Anvers
33. Café Marly
34. Benoît
35. Régalade
36. Marée
37. Bofinger
38. Blue Elephant
39. Philippe Detourbe
40. Trois Marches

It's obvious that many of the restaurants on the above list are among the most expensive, but Parisians also love a bargain. Were popularity calibrated to price, we suspect that a number of other restaurants would join the above ranks. Thus, we have listed over 100 Best Buys on pages 16–18.

Top Ratings*

Top 40 Food Ranking

28 Taillevent
26 Ambroisie
   Arpège
   Guy Savoy
   Alain Ducasse
   Faugeron
   Lucas Carton
   Pierre Gagnaire
25 Michel Rostang
   Grand Véfour
   Violon d'Ingres
   Jamin
24 Ambassadeurs
   Apicius
   Trois Marches
   Carré des Feuillants
23 Bristol
   Rest. d'Eric Fréchon
   Duc (Le)
   Régence

   Gérard Besson
   Vivarois
   Divellec
   Pressoir
   Marée
   Goumard
22 Elysées du Vernet
   Espadon
   Jacques Cagna
   Philippe Detourbe
   Laurent
   Ami Louis
   Tour d'Argent
   Issé
   Amphyclès
   Kinugawa
   Paul Minchelli
   Lasserre
   Ledoyen
   Table d'Anvers

Top Spots by Cuisine
French Cuisine

Top Bistros (Contemporary)
25 Violon d'Ingres
23 Rest. d'Eric Fréchon
22 Philippe Detourbe
21 Epi Dupin
   Régalade
19 Bon Accueil

Top Bistros (Traditional)
22 Ami Louis
20 Benoît
   Petit Marguery
19 Voltaire
   Vieux Bistro
   Biche au Bois

Top Bouillabaisse
23 Goumard
19 Marius et Janette
18 Dôme
17 Augusta
   Marius
   Jarasse

Top Brasseries
18 Dôme
17 Pichet
15 Marty
14 Sébillon
   Brasserie Flo
   Bofinger

Top Breakfast
24 Ambassadeurs
23 Bristol
   Régence
18 Bar Vendôme
15 Savy
   Ladurée

Top Burgundy
19 Récamier
18 6 Bosquet
16 Ferme des Mathurins
15 Petite Auberge
   Bourguignon
14 Ma Bourgogne

---

* Excluding restaurants with low votes.

Top Cassoulet
21 Trou Gascon
    Sousceyrac
20 Benoît
    Quincy
18 Chez Eux
17 Truffière

Top Caviar
20 Maison Prunier
19 Caviar Kaspia
18 Cochon d'Or
17 Maison du Caviar
14 Comptoir du Saumon Fumé
    Daru

Top Classic Haute Cuisine
28 Taillevent
26 Ambroisie
    Alain Ducasse
    Faugeron
25 Michel Rostang
    Grand Véfour

Top Confit
19 Paul Chêne
    Lous Landès
18 Cazaudehore La For.
    Chez Eux
17 Deux Canards
16 Bascou

Top Contemporary
26 Arpège
    Guy Savoy
    Lucas Carton
    Pierre Gagnaire
24 Apicius
    Trois Marches

Top Hotel Dining
24 Ambassadeurs
    Hôtel de Crillon
23 Bristol
    Hôtel Bristol
    Régence
    Hôtel Plaza-Athénée
22 Espadon
    Hôtel Ritz
20 Montparnasse 25
    Méridien-Montparnasse
    Meurice
    Hôtel Meurice

Top Late-Night
19 Caviar Kaspia
    Villaret
18 Dôme
17 Denise
15 Ladurée
14 Brasserie Flo

Top Lyons
20 Bellecour
17 Saint Vincent
    Bistrot d'Alex
16 Moissonnier
    Parc aux Cerfs
15 Auberge Bressane

Top Newcomers/Rated
25 Violon d'Ingres
20 Detourbe Duret
    C'Amelot
19 Repaire de Cartouche
17 Bistro d'Hubert
    Macéo

Top Newcomers/Unrated
    A et M Le Bistrot
    Astor
    Avant Goût
    Fogón Saint Julien
    Fumoir
    Stella Maris

Top Provence
22 Elysées du Vernet
20 Casa Olympe
    Campagne et Provence
19 Olivades
18 Bastide Odéon
    Petit Niçois

Top Seafood
23 Duc (Le)
    Divellec
    Goumard
22 Paul Minchelli
21 Ecaille et Plume
20 Maison Prunier

Top See and Be Seen
18 Stresa
16 Relais Plaza
15 Anahï
14 Omar
13 Brasserie Lipp
11 Costes

11

Top Shellfish
- 19 Michel
- 15 Ty Coz
- 14 Sébillon
  Brasserie Flo
  Bofinger
- 13 Brasserie Lutétia

Top Southwest
- 21 Comte de Gascogne
  Trou Gascon
  Sousceyrac
- 19 Rest. du Marché
- 18 Chez Eux
  Baracane

Top Steakhouses
- 18 Cochon d'Or
  Relais de Venise
- 17 Denise
  Rôtisserie d'en Face
  Bœuf Couronné
- 16 Bistrot du Cochon d'Or

Top Sunday Dining
- 26 Arpège
  Pierre Gagnaire
- 24 Ambassadeurs
  Trois Marches
- 23 Bristol
  Régence

Top Tea & Desserts
- 15 Mariage Frères
  Ladurée
- 13 Angelina
- — Hôtel de Crillon
  Hôtel Plaza-Athénée
  Hôtel Ritz

Top Wine Lists*
- 30 Taillevent
- 29 Bouchons de Fr. Clerc
- 28 Lucas Carton
  Ambroisie
- 27 Alain Ducasse
  Tour d'Argent

Other Cuisines

Top Chinese
- 20 Mirama**
- 18 Tsé-Yang
  Chen**
  Ngo
  Diep
- 17 Foc-Ly (Neuilly)

Top Indian
- 20 Ravi**
- 19 Yugaraj
- 17 Indra
  Vishnou
- 16 Annapurna

Top Italian
- 21 Grand Venise
  Sormani
- 19 Romantica
  Fellini
  Conti
  Paolo Petrini

Top Japanese
- 22 Issé
  Kinugawa
- 21 Tsukizi**
  Suntory
- 18 Benkay
- 17 Orient-Extrême

Top Mediterranean
- 19 Mavrommatis
  Délices d'Aphrodite
- 17 Fakhr el Dine
  Al Diwan
- 16 Al Dar
- 15 San Valero

Top North African
- 20 Mansouria
- 19 Oum el Banine
- 18 404
  Wally Le Saharien
  Timgad
- 17 Atlas

Top Thai
- 19 Erawan
  Blue Elephant
- 18 Foch-An**
- 17 Chieng Mai
  Foc-Ly (Neuilly)
- 16 Sawadee

Top Vietnamese
- 21 Kim Anh**
  Lac Hong**
- 20 Tan Dinh
- 19 Baie d'Ha Long
- 18 Foch-An**
  Ngo

* Rated for their wine lists.
** Low votes.

12

Tops by Arrondissement

1st & 2nd
25 Grand Véfour
24 Carré des Feuillants
23 Gérard Besson
    Goumard
22 Espadon
    Issé

3rd & 4th
26 Ambroisie
22 Ami Louis
20 Benoît
19 Marais-Cage
    Vieux Bistro
18 Hangar

5th & 6th
22 Jacques Cagna
    Tour d'Argent
21 Relais Louis XIII
    Epi Dupin
20 Timonerie
    Campagne et Provence

7th
26 Arpège
25 Violon d'Ingres
23 Divellec
22 Paul Minchelli
21 Ecaille et Plume
    Jules Verne

8th
28 Taillevent
26 Lucas Carton
    Pierre Gagnaire
24 Ambassadeurs
23 Bristol
    Régence

9th & 10th
22 Table d'Anvers
20 Rest. Opéra
    Casa Olympe
19 Châteaubriant
    Michel
18 Muses

11th, 12th & 13th
23 Pressoir
21 Trou Gascon
    Sousceyrac
20 Quincy
    Petit Marguery
    C'Amelot

14th & 15th
23 Duc (Le)
22 Philippe Detourbe
21 Dînée
    Grand Venise
    Régalade
20 Montparnasse 25

16th
26 Alain Ducasse
    Faugeron
25 Jamin
23 Vivarois
21 Pré Catelan
20 Maison Prunier

17th
26 Guy Savoy
25 Michel Rostang
24 Apicius
22 Amphyclès
21 Faucher
    Sormani

18th, 19th & 20th
23 Rest. d'Eric Fréchon
20 Beauvilliers (A.)
18 Cochon d'Or
    Allobroges
    Vincent
17 Bœuf Couronné

Outlying Areas
24 Trois Marches (Versailles)
21 Comte de Gascogne (Boulogne)
20 Camélia (Bougival)
19 Carpe Diem (Neuilly)
    Romantica (Clichy)
    Truffe Noire (Neuilly)

Top 40 Decor Ranking

28	Grand Véfour	23	Bristol
	Tour d'Argent		Maison Blanche
27	Ambassadeurs		Ledoyen
26	Train Bleu		Beauvilliers (A.)
	Jules Verne		Bar Vendôme
25	Maxim's		Café Marly
	Taillevent		Buddha Bar
	Meurice		Maison de l'Amérique Latine
	Lucas Carton		404
	Espadon		China Club
	Grande Cascade		Trois Marches
	Lasserre	22	Costes
	Pré Catelan		Elysées du Vernet
24	Ambroisie		Orangerie
	Alain Ducasse		Rest. du Musée d'Orsay
	Régence		Pavillon Montsouris
	Laurent		Domarais
	Blue Elephant		Maison Prunier
	Toupary		Jardins de Bagatelle
	Lapérouse	21	Sud

Top Gardens

Bar Vendôme	Maison de l'Amérique Latine
Grande Cascade	Pavillon Montsouris
Laurent	Pré Catelan
Ledoyen	Trois Marches

Top Historic

Ambassadeurs	Lucas Carton
Grand Véfour	Maxim's
Lapérouse	Train Bleu

Top Romantic

Beauvilliers (A.)	Jardins de Bagatelle
Bûcherie	Orangerie
Coupe-Chou	Pauline

Top Rooms

Alain Ducasse	Lasserre
Ambassadeurs	Lucas Carton
Ambroisie	Maxim's
Grand Véfour	Meurice
Jules Verne	Taillevent
Lapérouse	Train Bleu

Top Terraces

Café Les Deux Magots	Fouquet's
Closerie des Lilas	Guirlande de Julie
Fontaine de Mars	Jardins de Bagatelle

Top Views

Café Marly
Jules Verne
Maison Blanche

Morot-Gaudry
Toupary
Tour d'Argent

Top Waterside

Cap Seguin
Guinguette de Neuilly
Pavillon Panama

Petit Poucet
Quai Ouest
River Café

Top 40 Service Ranking

27 Taillevent
25 Alain Ducasse
Ambassadeurs
24 Ambroisie
Grand Véfour
Lucas Carton
Espadon
23 Tour d'Argent
Bristol
Faugeron
Michel Rostang
Laurent
Guy Savoy
Lasserre
Arpège
Meurice
Jamin
Régence
21 Trois Marches
Bar Vendôme

Ledoyen
Pierre Gagnaire
Carré des Feuillants
Elysées du Vernet
Gérard Besson
20 Goumard
Pré Catelan
Quincy
Rest. Opéra
Jacques Cagna
Pressoir
Apicius
Jules Verne
Marée
Violon d'Ingres
Grande Cascade
Relais Louis XIII
Deux Canards
Maxim's
19 Amphyclès

Best Buys

This list reflects the best dining values in our *Survey*. It is produced by dividing the cost of a meal into the combined ratings for food, decor and service.

1. Cosi
2. Germaine
3. Chartier
4. Lina's
5. Deux Abeilles
6. Flèche d'Or Café
7. Mathusalem
8. Crêperie de Josselin
9. Café de l'Industrie
10. Agape
11. Entrepôt
12. Mariage Frères
13. Dame Tartine
14. Clown Bar
15. Camille
16. 404
17. Temps des Cerises
18. Perraudin
19. Lescure
20. Polidor
21. Bouillon Racine
22. Biche au Bois
23. Délices d'Aphrodite
24. Angelina
25. Café de la Musique
26. Baracane
27. Jacques Mélac
28. Café Beaubourg
29. Relais de Venise
30. Ay!! Caramba!!
31. Auberge Etchégorry
32. Al Mounia
33. Marais-Cage
34. Pied de Chameau
35. Petit Prince de Paris
36. Viaduc Café
37. Omar
38. Thanksgiving
39. New Nioullaville
40. Alsaco
41. Dos de la Baleine
42. China Club
43. Café Runtz
44. Chieng Mai
45. Allobroges
46. Café Marly
47. Paul
48. China Town Belleville
49. Marianne
50. Bon Accueil
51. Astier
52. Hangar
53. Mansouria
54. Deux Canards
55. Nouveau Village Tao Tao
56. Coco de Mer
57. Ebauchoir
58. Denise
59. C'Amelot
60. Café du Commerce
61. Rest. du Palais Royal
62. Impatient
63. Chicago Pizza Pie Factory
64. Epi Dupin
65. Café des Lettres
66. Rendez-vous/Camionneurs
67. Driver's
68. Ladurée
69. Chardenoux
70. Brasserie de l'Isle St-Louis
71. Bistro de la Grille
72. Grizzli
73. Ferme de Boulogne
74. Studio
75. Mavrommatis
76. Bistrot d'à Côté Neuilly
77. Juvenile's
78. Square Trousseau
79. Bistro du 17
80. Président

Additional Good Values

(A bit more expensive, but worth it.)

Amazigh	Kim Anh
Androuët	Kinugawa
Atlas	Lac Hong
Bamboche	Macéo
Bar Vendôme	Maison de l'Amérique
Béatilles	Latine
Bellecour	Maison du Valais
Bertie's	Maître Paul
Bistro d'Hubert	Marie et Fils
Blue Elephant	Marlotte
Braisière	Maupertu
Café du Passage	Michel Courtalhac
Campagne et Provence	Monsieur Lapin
Carpe Diem	Obélisque
Carré Kléber	Oeillade
Cartes Postales	Pavillon Montsouris
Cercle Ledoyen	Petit Marguery
Châteaubriant	"Pierre" à la Fontaine
Cote d'Amour	Gaillon
Da Mimmo	P'tit Troquet
Dariole de Viry	Quercy
Dînée	Quincy
Excuse	Ravi
Ferme St-Simon	Relais du Parc
Fermette Marbeuf 1900	René
Gabriel	Rest. du Marché
Gallopin	Romantica
Gastroquet	Saudade
Gaya, Estaminet	Sud
Gaya Rive Gauche	Tan Dinh
Glénan	Timgad
Graindorge	Troyon
Il Cortile	Tsé-Yang
Indra	Vishnou
Julien	Vong
Kambodgia	Zygomates

Good Values by Arrondissement
(100–250 francs)

1st & 2nd
Denise
Epi d'Or
Café Runtz
Crus de Bourgogne
Lescure
Bistrot Gambas

3rd & 4th
Marais-Cage
Hangar
404
Baracane
Bascou
Camille

5th & 6th
Epi Dupin
Mavrommatis
Délices d'Aphrodite
Fontaines
Chieng Mai
Bistrot d'à Côté St-Germain

7th
Bon Accueil
Petit Niçois
Ambassade du Sud-Ouest
Affriolé
Deux Abeilles
Auberge Bressane

8th
Al Diwan
Mariage Frères
Ladurée
Yvan, Petit
Ecluse
Cou de la Girafe

9th & 10th
I Golosi
Alsaco
Da Mimmo
Cave Drouot
Bacchantes
Terminus Nord

11th, 12th & 13th
C'Amelot
Mansouria
Villaret
Biche au Bois
Astier
Anacréon

14th & 15th
Os à Moelle
Agape
Erawan
Vin et Marée
Sawadee
Il Barone

16th
Baie d'Ha Long
Al Mounia
Mathusalem
Vin et Marée
Al Dar
Noura

17th
Impatient
Relais de Venise
Bistrot de l'Etoile Troyon
Bistrot de l'Etoile Niel
Huîtrier
Bistrot d'à Côté Villiers

18th, 19th & 20th
Allobroges
Vincent
Marie Louise
Café de la Musique
Ay!! Caramba!!
Flèche d'Or Café

Outlying Areas
Foc-Ly (Neuilly)
Ferme de Boulogne (Boulogne)
Bistrot d'à Côté Neuilly (Neuilly)
Coco d'Isles (Neuilly)
Petit Poucet (Levallois)
Cap Seguin (Boulogne)

Alphabetical Directory of Restaurants

Absinthe (L') ☻   13 | 14 | 13 | fr243
24, place du Marché St-Honoré, 1ᵉʳ (Tuileries), 01 49 26 90 04
☑ Under the direction of chef Michel Rostang, this trendy, upscale bistro with a "pleasant" terrace overlooking the new Marché Saint-Honoré serves "inventive" cuisine with "Mediterranean charm" at "reasonable prices" to rock stars and fashion mavens; while purists call the food "ridiculously modern" and cite "uneven" service, others rank it among the "neighborhood's best" buys.

A et M Le Bistrot   – | – | – | M
136, bd. Murat, 16ᵉ (Porte de St-Cloud), 01 45 27 39 60
New and very handsome, this venture from Jean-Pierre Vigato of Apicius and François Grandjean of Marius offers traditional French fare from an à la carte menu as well as a reasonable prix fixe; the crowd is as stylish as the ambiance.

Affriolé (L')   16 | 9 | 14 | fr247
17, rue Malar, 7ᵉ (Invalides/La Tour-Maubourg), 01 44 18 31 33
☑ There's "good food in a cozy atmosphere" at this Left Bank bistro near Les Invalides featuring traditional French fare with a modern touch; diners praise the "good value" but have less kind words for the sometimes "humorless" service from an "overwhelmed staff."

Agape (L')   19 | 9 | 14 | fr165
281, rue Lecourbe, 15ᵉ (Boucicaut/Lourmel), 01 45 58 19 29
☑ This "friendly neighborhood place" in the 15th is "unbeatable" for the price say fans of its "inventive" French fare; alas, the decor cries out for a face-lift: "what a shame – you hesitate to invite guests here because of the setting."

Ailleurs ☻   10 | 16 | 12 | fr204
26, rue Jean Mermoz, 8ᵉ (Franklin Roosevelt), 01 53 53 98 00
☑ As the name suggests (it means 'elsewhere'), this newcomer off the Champs-Elysées offers a "mix of cultures" in its "inventive" International menu and decor; but since many find the food "bland", the ambiance "noisy" (hear those "cell phones ring"), the tables "close" and service "robotic", critics say "you're better off eating *ailleurs*."

ALAIN DUCASSE   26 | 24 | 25 | fr950
59, av. Raymond Poincaré, 16ᵉ (Trocadéro/Victor Hugo), 01 47 27 12 27
■ "A great moment" awaits diners at this "gastronomic mecca" in a "sublime" townhouse in the 16th, where the Classic French cuisine of Alain Ducasse (the man with six Michelin stars) is deemed the "closest thing to heaven on earth" and well worth the two-month wait for a reservation; though a few find it "disappointing compared with Ducasse in Monaco", and many wail about the wallop to their wallet, for the majority it's "worth every penny" – this is "as good as it gets."

Al Dar ◐ⓢ
$$16 \quad 10 \quad 14 \quad \text{fr}216$$
8, rue Frédéric Sauton, 5ᵉ (Maubert-Mutualité), 01 43 25 17 15
93, av. Raymond Poincaré, 16ᵉ (Victor Hugo), 01 45 00 96 64
■ "Authentic" Lebanese cuisine that "respects" Middle Eastern traditions draws a "chic" crowd to this eatery near the Place Victor Hugo; respondents praise the couscous and "grand variety" of maza (first courses) at reasonable prices, plus the "fast" service and "warm welcome", but it's thumbs down for the "ordinary" setting; takeout available.

Al Diwan ◐ⓢ
$$17 \quad 13 \quad 14 \quad \text{fr}240$$
30, av. George V, 8ᵉ (Alma-Marceau/George V), 01 47 23 45 45
■ "You can bring a Lebanese without his camel" to this "luxurious, pleasant but pricey" Middle Eastern in the heart of the posh 8th district, where voters salute the "authentic" cuisine, hearty maza ("a whole meal"), "excellent" pastries and schwarma sandwiches; "exotic" dining guaranteed.

Alisier (L')
$$\triangledown \quad 20 \quad 11 \quad 19 \quad \text{fr}229$$
26, rue de Montmorency, 3ᵉ (Rambuteau), 01 42 72 31 04
■ A "personalized welcome" and "creative nouvelle" French cuisine "respecting the flavors of the finest, freshest ingredients" make this a best bet in the neighborhood near the Pompidou Center; it's also a "good value", with luncheon prix fixe menus and, at night, a four-course 'discovery' degustation that changes weekly.

Allard ◐
$$16 \quad 14 \quad 13 \quad \text{fr}310$$
41, rue St-André-des-Arts, 6ᵉ (Odéon), 01 43 26 48 23
◪ "Living off its reputation" gripe some longtime patrons of this "traditional", "touristy" Latin Quarter bistro famed for its duck with olives (and critics claim even that "isn't what it used to be"); but defenders still swear by the "comfort" food served in "big-enough-for-two" portions (plan "a nap after lunch"), declaring "this is what a Left Bank restaurant should be."

Allobroges (Les)
$$18 \quad 13 \quad 15 \quad \text{fr}223$$
71, rue des Grands-Champs, 20ᵉ (Maraîchers/Nation),
01 43 73 40 00
■ "An oasis of gastronomic freshness in an urban desert" say fans of this classic bistro tucked in a working-class neighborhood near Nation featuring "very good cuisine" and friendly, "provincial" atmosphere in a setting decorated by Pierre-Yves Rochon.

Al Mounia
$$17 \quad 19 \quad 15 \quad \text{fr}234$$
16, rue de Magdebourg, 16ᵉ (Trocadéro), 01 47 27 57 28
■ "Attentive waiters" serve some of the city's "best couscous" and other refined Moroccan dishes in an "authentic" *"Arabian Nights"* setting near Trocadero where diners sit on couches and leather poufs ("avoid miniskirts"); "very chic, very expensive", but exoticism is "guaranteed" at what some crown the top Moroccan in Paris.

Alsaco (L')
17 | 12 | 16 | fr211

10, rue Condorcet, 9ᵉ (Anvers/Poissonnière), 01 45 26 44 31

■ "Best choucroute in Paris" say fans of this Alsatian brewery-style pub offering hearty dishes and a 200-bottle list of Alsatian wines; foes claim service can be "nonexistent" and feel the "smoky", "stuffy" ambiance detracts from what many consider the city's "most authentic" Alsatian cuisine.

Altitude 95 ⓢ
▽ **11 | 19 | 14 | fr226**

Tour Eiffel, Champ-de-Mars, 1st fl., 7ᵉ (Champ-de-Mars), 01 45 55 20 04

☑ Cynics say "for the view" only, but others call this French Regionalist perched in the Eiffel Tower a "superb location for a reasonable meal"; "ignore the tourists" (or bring one along) and focus on the "exceptional" scenery, but don't plan to linger too long: "the elevator stops early, so dinner is always rushed."

Amazigh
▽ **21 | 18 | 21 | fr300**

2, rue de La Pérouse, 16ᵉ (Boissière/Kléber), 01 47 20 90 38

■ Expect "high-class", "consistently" good Moroccan cuisine at this "elegant" (coat and tie required) spot in the posh 16th; respondents say if it's "upscale exoticism" you're after, this is it, complete with some of the "best", "airiest" couscous in Paris served in a "calm", friendly atmosphere.

Ambassade d'Auvergne ⓢ
16 | 15 | 15 | fr251

22, rue du Grenier-St-Lazare, 3ᵉ (Rambuteau), 01 42 72 31 22

■ "Old-fashioned, richer-than-Croesus" regional dishes ("bring your appetite") are "nothing short of heaven" say fans of this "affordable" Auvergnat bistro near the Pompidou Center; special mention goes to the "rustic, comfortable" atmosphere and the "amazing" aligot (a potato-cheese dish), "a true delicacy" that's "worth the detour."

Ambassade du Sud-Ouest ⓢ
17 | 12 | 14 | fr230

46, av. de la Bourdonnais, 7ᵉ (Ecole Militaire), 01 45 55 59 59

■ Toast bread at your table and savor what some deem the "best foie gras in Paris" at this "small", "unpretentious", farm-style Regional French bistro near the Ecole Militaire, which also scores as a "good destination for duck lovers"; the decor may be "sparse" but the welcome is "very warm."

AMBASSADEURS (LES) ⓢ
24 | 27 | 25 | fr705

Hôtel de Crillon, 10, place de la Concorde, 8ᵉ (Concorde), 01 44 71 16 16

■ "By far the best of the city's hotel restaurants" say admirers of this "luxurious" Classic French with a "fairy-tale" 18th-century setting in the Crillon overlooking the Place de la Concorde; surveyors rate the room one of Paris' "most beautiful" (complete with mini-stools for ladies' purses) and salute the "consistently fine" cuisine and "exceptional" service; expensive, of course, but "deserving of its name – an ambassador of French gastronomy."

AMBROISIE (L')
26 | 24 | 24 | fr849

9, place des Vosges, 4ᵉ (Bastille/St-Paul), 01 42 78 51 45

■ "A dream" to dine at but often a nightmare to book (call months ahead) describes this "perfect but pricey" French overlooking the Place des Vosges in the Marais; Bernard Pacaud's creative cooking, which earns the *Survey*'s No. 2 food rating, is "deliciously refined", and though some find the setting (newly enlarged by two rooms) "elegant" but "cold" and service "impersonal", for devotees a meal here is "equivalent to an evening at the opera."

AMI LOUIS (CHEZ L') ●S
22 | 14 | 16 | fr545

32, rue du Vertbois, 3ᵉ (Arts-et-Métiers/Temple), 01 48 87 77 48

☑ The cholesterol is "intense" and so are the prices at this renowned old bistro near République overflowing with tourists, occasional Hollywood types and "big eaters" downing "enormous portions" of "hearty" fare (including "excellent" foie gras and roast chicken); fans find it "marvelous" right down to the "wonderful nondecor", while foes call it a case of faded magic, citing "variable" quality and "haughty" waiters.

Ami Pierre (A l') ●
▽ 17 | 12 | 14 | fr360

5, rue de la Main d'Or, 11ᵉ (Bastille/Ledru-Rollin), 01 47 00 17 35

■ Tucked behind the trendy Bastille district, this casual bistro doubles as an "unpretentious" wine bar featuring "authentic" Southwestern French fare and a wide selection of "good wines" in a "relaxed", "very Parisian" atmosphere.

Amognes (Les)
18 | 9 | 12 | fr256

243, rue du Faubourg St-Antoine, 11ᵉ (Faidherbe-Chaligny), 01 43 72 73 05

☑ Most surveyors love the 'new look' gastronomic bistro fare "full of original ideas" whipped up by a "talented and promising" chef at this "bustling" eatery in the 11th, even if they grumble about "slow" service; it offers "rustic" simplicity and "excellent value", making it a "pleasant" "surprise for the neighborhood"; N.B. there's been a post-*Survey* decor spruce-up.

Amphyclès
22 | 16 | 19 | fr600

78, av. des Ternes, 17ᵉ (Porte Maillot), 01 45 74 31 57

☑ Philippe Groult (who learned from Joël Robuchon) and his Classic French near the Porte Maillot pleases partisans who describe it as "pocket-sized but providing maximum emotion"; but while most praise its "inventive" blend of French flavors with "subtle" "fragrances of the Orient", critics bemoan a "disappointing gourmet adventure", calling it "uneven" and "outrageously overpriced"; a "change of decor" is also suggested.

Amuse Bouche (L') ▽ | 20 | 13 | 15 | fr265

186, rue du Château, 14ᵉ (Gaîté/Mouton-Duvernet), 01 43 35 31 61
■ Definitely "in", this "minuscule", casual neighborhood spot in the 14th is "charming" and "cozy", with "inventive, flavorful" French fare enhanced by "great desserts daily" and a "good wine cellar" – in short, all the makings for "a fun evening" at an affordable cost.

Anacréon 18 | 9 | 15 | fr236

53, bd. St-Marcel, 13ᵉ (Les Gobelins), 01 43 31 71 18
◪ Not far from the Place d'Italie, this quiet "neighborhood restaurant" (now run by a former chef from La Tour d'Argent) serves "excellent", "refined" cuisine (the canard au sang is singled out for praise) in a simple, "old-fashioned" setting; for devotees it's "a must", but a few outvoted dissenters find it "disappointing."

Anahï ●🅂 15 | 14 | 13 | fr241

49, rue Volta, 3ᵉ (Arts-et-Métiers/Temple), 01 48 87 88 24
■ Calling all "carnivore" "snobs" to this "trendy" Argentine-style steakhouse set in a former butcher shop not far from the Place de la République, where "artists, hipsters" and the like enjoy what supporters call some of the "best beef in Paris" along with "excellent Spanish wines"; the welcome is warm and the back room provides plenty of privacy.

Anahuacalli 🅂 – | – | – | I

30, rue des Bernardins, 5ᵉ (Maubert-Mutualité), 01 43 26 10 20
An oasis of calm and good eating in the Latin Quarter, this authentic Mexican in an attractively converted bistro is a delicious alternative to the local profusion of mediocre Tex-Mex places; reasonable prices add to its popularity.

André (Chez) ●🅂 13 | 11 | 14 | fr241

12, rue Marbeuf, 8ᵉ (Franklin Roosevelt), 01 47 20 59 57
■ "A Paris brasserie at its best: great food, long waits and superb wines" say fans of this "noisy", "crowded" hot spot behind the Champs-Elysées catering to "le tout Paris" and the fashion crowd; "no surprises" here, but that's fine with those who love the "friendly, efficient" staff, summer terrace and a tab that's "not too expensive" given the neighborhood.

Androuët 16 | 13 | 14 | fr308

6, rue Arsène Houssaye, 8ᵉ (Charles de Gaulle-Étoile), 01 42 89 95 00
■ A "fantastic orgy" awaits cheese lovers at this "unique" restaurant near the Etoile filled with the pungent aromas of cheeses from France and elsewhere; "Androuët is to cheese what Paris is to gastronomy", a "feast for the nose and palate", "pure satisfaction" are typical accolades; standouts include the one-of-a-kind tasting menu and "superb Roquefort soufflé."

Angelina **S**   13 | 18 | 10 | fr177
226, rue de Rivoli, 1er (Tuileries), 01 42 60 82 00

☑ Famed for its "thick-as-mud" hot chocolate and "to-die-for mont blanc" served by not always friendly staff, this "pretty" if rather "faded" tea salon facing the Tuileries Gardens caters to tourists, "well-heeled grannies" and others who enjoy its yesteryear ambiance; critics dismiss it as an "overrated", "overpriced" anachronism, but even they can't deny it's fine for "people-watching."

Ange Vin (L')   ▽ 13 | 11 | 13 | fr179
168, rue Montmartre, 2e (Rue Montmartre), 01 42 36 20 20

☑ A "neighborhood bistro" off the Grands Boulevards appealing especially to wine lovers, this solid newcomer earns modest ratings but encouraging words for owner Jean-Pierre Robinot's "sincerity and exceptional wine expertise", "good" cuisine and "pleasant" service.

Annapurna ◗   16 | 15 | 14 | fr286
32, rue de Berri, 8e (George V), 01 45 63 91 56

☑ Enthusiasts say this Indian off the Champs-Elysées is still one of the "best in Paris", noting that the "sounds of the sitar" add to the "memorable evening"; but some find the ambiance "gloomy", and naysayers insist it's best for people who want to "die of boredom in a dark place."

APICIUS   24 | 18 | 20 | fr586
122, av. de Villiers, 17e (Pereire), 01 43 80 19 66

☑ "Divinely creative" fare ("foie gras with chocolate!") and a "warm welcome" are what most find at this pricey bastion of nouvelle cuisine near the Place Pereire; for fans, chef Jean-Pierre Vigato's "exceptional" cuisine captures "the grandeur of gourmet dining", even if the "soberly chic" decor strikes some as "cold" (or even "boring") and service can be "slow"; dissenters label it "undeserving of its reputation" and "mediocre", but they're outvoted.

APPART' (L') ◗ **S**   13 | 18 | 13 | fr239
9-11, rue du Colisée, 8e (Franklin Roosevelt), 01 53 75 16 34

■ "Amusingly" designed to resemble an apartment, this "trendy" "wanna-be" hangout off the Champs-Elysées feels so much "like home" you don't mind even if you have to "wait" for French food rated from "good" to "insipid", served by "indifferent" but "ravishing" waitresses; most enjoy the "chic" ambiance and "good value" for the neighborhood.

Arbuci ◗ **S**   11 | 12 | 12 | fr204
25, rue de Buci, 6e (Odéon/St-Germain-des-Prés), 01 44 32 16 00

☑ "What a shame the service and meat dishes leave much to be desired" sigh critics of this "animated" brasserie near Saint-Germain famous for its Tuesday-Saturday jazz soirees; but the "all you can eat" oyster menu is still a draw and music lovers find the jazz dinners "good value", making it a nice "place to take out-of-town guests."

Ardoise (L')   – – – I
28, rue Mont-Thabor, 1ᵉʳ (Concorde/Tuileries), 01 42 96 28 18
One of the best values in the 1st arrondissement, this modest French between the rue de Rivoli and the Place Vendôme offers a reasonable prix fixe menu that's carefully done from start to finish, enhanced by service that's particularly attentive and an engaging wine list; the clientele is as well put together as the food.

Armand au Palais Royal   15 | 16 | 14 | fr317
6, rue de Beaujolais, 1ᵉʳ (Bourse/Palais-Royal), 01 42 60 05 11
☑ This tiny haven with a vaulted ceiling near the Palais-Royal is "so comfortable, you don't want to leave", and admirers also have warm feelings about the "good food" (especially the "great crêpes") from a traditional French kitchen; but it's not cheap and "parking is tough."

Armoise (L')   – – – I
67, rue des Entrepreneurs, 15ᵉ (Charles-Michels/Commerce), 01 45 79 03 31
"Simple but good" is the consensus on this "calm" French in the 15th district serving family-style fare (with an emphasis on fish) to locals; some call the decor "cold", but others find it a "cozy" match for the proprietor's "kindness"; the "good choice of wines" and modest prices also earn praise.

ARPÈGE (L') ⑤   26 | 20 | 23 | fr792
84, rue de Varenne, 7ᵉ (Varenne), 01 45 51 47 33
■ "If there were a Nobel Prize for gastronomy", many surveyors would nominate Alain Passard for his "flawless", "imaginative" French cuisine featuring equal parts "intelligence" and "audacity"; given its lofty reputation – and break-the-bank prices – it's perhaps inevitable that some diners feel let down, grumbling about "uneven" cooking and the "minimalist", "Zen-like" setting in the 7th, but its ranking as Paris' No. 2 favorite restaurant says a lot.

Arthur (Chez) ⑤   ▽ 15 | 13 | 18 | fr223
51, bd. Garibaldi, 15ᵉ (Sèvres-Lecourbe), 01 45 67 97 91
☑ With a facade hidden by supports for the overhead Métro tracks, this Lebanese-Armenian in the middle of the 15th arrondissement is known by only a few surveyors; they report "very good" food, but it's a bit "heavy" and the decor more or less consists of a roof overhead.

Assassins (Aux) ◑⌗   7 | 9 | 10 | fr185
40, rue Jacob, 6ᵉ (St-Germain-des-Prés), no telephone
■ Off-color humor and bawdy songs offset what most rate as "mediocre" bistro fare at this St.-Germain "curiosity" catering to the "bachelor party" crowd and student types looking to share a "simple meal among friends"; forget about calling to reserve – there's no phone.

Assiette (L') §
18 | 9 | 11 | fr381
*181, rue du Château, 14ᵉ (Gaîté/Mouton-Duvernet/Pernety),
01 43 22 64 86*
■ This simple-looking bistro in an old butcher shop behind
Montparnasse attracts "incognito" movie stars, writers,
politicians and others who appreciate "excellent" food
made from the "freshest seasonal ingredients" by Lulu,
the "very original" chef-owner; it's "a party every time",
but you pay the price.

Astier
18 | 10 | 13 | fr203
44, rue J.P. Timbaud, 11ᵉ (Oberkampf/Parmentier), 01 43 57 16 35
■ The equivalent of "down-home" French cooking and
"the real Paris" say loyalists of this unpretentious, "noisy"
dive with no decor to speak of nestled in a corner of the
working-class 11th district behind République; it's popular
for its "extraordinary value", "great cheese platter" and
good, low-cost wines.

Astor (L')
– | – | – | E
Hôtel Astor, 11, rue d'Astorg, 8ᵉ (St-Augustin), 01 53 05 05 20
Accolades such as "already one of the best in Paris" aren't
surprising, given that Joël Robuchon directs the kitchen of
this hotel dining room not far from the Madeleine, where a
former Robuchon student turns out "very creative" French
fare from a menu that shows the 'retired' culinary wizard's
touch; the Frédéric Mechiche–designed decor is stylish
and service is "very good", but the bill isn't cheap.

Atelier Gourmand
17 | 12 | 15 | fr258
20, rue de Tocqueville, 17ᵉ (Villiers), 01 42 27 03 71
■ "Carefully prepared, refined, elegant" French from a
menu created by Philippe Billy (formerly with Bocuse and
Lenôtre) draws praise from respondents who also note the
"charming welcome" from the missus; there's "no pressure
on the heart, stomach or wallet", though some find the
pale yellow setting "sad."

Atelier Maître Albert
14 | 18 | 13 | fr254
1, rue Maître Albert, 5ᵉ (Maubert-Mutualité), 01 46 33 13 78
■ "Comfortable and cozy" with a 15th-century fireplace
burning in winter, this Left Bank standby is perfect "for out-
of-town guests" thanks to its "serious", "uncomplicated"
French cuisine and "friendly atmosphere"; however, parking
is a nightmare and the less impressed say it's most useful
as a "rainy night destination for people who live nearby."

Atlas (L') §
17 | 14 | 17 | fr253
12, bd. St-Germain, 5ᵉ (Maubert-Mutualité), 01 46 33 86 98
■ "Lovely service and good food" but on the "expensive"
side complain respondents who go to this Moroccan for
high-style couscous and other specialties served amidst
exotic decor a stone's throw from the Institute of the Arab
World; "one of the warmest welcomes in Paris" is a bonus.

Auberge (L') S   15 | 15 | 15 | fr257
86, av. J.B. Clément, Boulogne-Billancourt (Billancourt/ Pont de Sèvres), 01 46 05 67 19

■ Admirers say there's good hospitality and "quality food" in a "pleasant" setting at this Classic French on the southwestern edge of Paris that was recently taken over by the son of TV host Jacques Martin; though a few doubters label the cooking "average", supporters salute signs of "progress" with a "bravo."

Auberge Bressane (L') S   15 | 13 | 14 | fr236
16, av. de La Motte-Picquet, 7ᵉ (La Tour-Maubourg), 01 47 05 98 37

■ What every Parisian brasserie should offer – "generous" portions of "good regional [Lyons] dishes" in a "relaxed", "friendly" atmosphere at "reasonable" cost say fans of this "chic" 'country inn' in the posh 7th district near Les Invalides; the "original", "medieval setting" adds to the charm, but doesn't diminish the noise or clear the smoke.

Auberge Dab (L') S   13 | 12 | 13 | fr255
161, av. de Malakoff, 16ᵉ (Porte Maillot), 01 45 00 32 22

◪ This "unpretentious", "well-located" brasserie near the Porte Maillot earns praise for its choucroute, seafood platters and fish dishes, but the rest is "just ordinary" say some diners; still, supporters call it fine for a "classic business lunch" and handy because it's "open late."

Auberge des Dolomites   13 | 12 | 16 | fr220
38, rue Poncelet, 17ᵉ (Ternes), 01 42 27 94 56

◪ Fans say there's "good value" and a "friendly" welcome awaiting the "solid middle-class" locals who frequent this small, "cozy" French in the upscale 17th district; though some call the food "reliable", others hand down a "can do better" verdict.

Auberge du Champ de Mars   ▽ 14 | 13 | 14 | fr234
18, rue de l'Exposition, 7ᵉ (Ecole Militaire), 01 45 51 78 08

◪ "Satisfactory but not outstanding" say locals who frequent this "pretty", inn-style French near the Eiffel Tower; even if the prix fixe offerings "don't change much", regulars consider it a good buy.

Auberge Etchégorry   16 | 16 | 15 | fr215
41, rue Croulebarbe, 13ᵉ (Corvisart/Les Gobelins), 01 44 08 83 51

◪ "Great food at a great price" are what admirers find at this Basque specialist a stone's throw from the Gobelins Tapestry works in the 13th district ("an opportunity to go to the middle of nowhere"); "wines by the glass adapted to" the menu are also appreciated, but sensitive ears complain that it's "noisy."

Auberge Landaise ▽ | 12 | 10 | 11 | fr269
23, rue Clauzel, 9ᵉ (St-Georges), 01 48 78 74 40
☑ Though faultfinders complain of a "glacial" atmosphere "lacking charm" and note a sharp decline in recent years coupled with "high prices", defenders praise this Regional French near the quaint Place Saint-Georges for its "quality" dishes and the owner's "friendly" personality", saying they'd "recommend" it to friends.

Augusta | 17 | 10 | 16 | fr442
98, rue de Tocqueville, 17ᵉ (Malesherbes/Villiers), 01 47 63 39 97
■ Respondents hail the "generous" portions of "excellent bouillabaisse" as well as the "lovely fresh produce" and "constant quality" at this Classic French seafood specialist near Villiers; but it also generates a few grumbles about high prices and a "lack of personality."

Avant Goût (L') | – | – | – | I
26, rue Bobillot, 13ᵉ (Place d'Italie), 01 53 80 24 00
Though in a slightly out of the way part of town near the Place d'Italie, this prix fixe bistro in a renovated cafe is packed nightly with knowing types who come for the first-rate *cuisine du marché* of young chef Christophe Beaufront; it's often noisy, but offers great value for the money.

Avenue (L') ◐⑤ | 11 | 13 | 12 | fr286
41, av. Montaigne, 8ᵉ (Franklin Roosevelt), 01 40 70 14 91
☑ This "trendy", upscale brasserie "well located" on the Avenue Montaigne in the heart of the city's chicest shopping district is best for "people-watching" ("fashion and media" types) or a "business lunch"; otherwise, most agree the "ordinary" food is hardly worth "long waits and arrogant service."

Ay!! Caramba!! ◐⑤ | 11 | 16 | 12 | fr179
59, rue de Mouzaïa, 19ᵉ (Pré St-Gervais), 01 42 41 23 80
☑ A majority loves the "real change of scenery" provided by this "authentic" Mexican in the far reaches of the 19th district, praising its live music, "honest" if "simple" cuisine and "great" margaritas and calling it a step up from "run-of-the-mill Tex-Mex"; dissenters say "noisy", "nothing special", but it's "fun for groups."

Bacchantes (Les) ◐ | 14 | 10 | 10 | fr189
21, rue de Caumartin, 9ᵉ (Auber/Madeleine/Opéra), 01 42 65 25 35
■ "Good any time of day" say those who appreciate this "noisy, smoke-filled" bistro/wine bar near the Opéra for its "congenial" ambiance, "friendly" owner (Raymond Pocous) hovering over customers and "well-priced" wine list; if some have experienced "offhand service", most have no complaints.

Baie d'Ha Long (La)
19 | 11 | 14 | fr248

164, av. de Versailles, 16ᵉ (Porte de St-Cloud), 01 45 24 60 62

■ "Refined" Asian fare in the southwestern corner of the city is what most find at this "pricey" purveyor of Vietnamese dishes à la française; service is "fast and unpretentious" – if only they'd spruce up the "gloomy decor."

Bains (Les)
– | – | – | M

7, rue du Bourg l'Abbé, 3ᵉ (Etienne-Marcel/Réaumur Sébastopol), 01 48 87 01 80

Regularly, this restaurant in the famed nightclub near the Pompidou Center recreates itself, perhaps in an attempt to overcome its mediocre culinary reputation; this time it's offering reasonably successful Thai food amidst decor reworked in tones of ocher and red, but the main appeal remains the beautiful people crowd and sexy atmosphere.

Ballon des Ternes (Le) ◑⑤
13 | 11 | 12 | fr230

103, av. des Ternes, 17ᵉ (Porte Maillot), 01 45 74 17 98

■ A "standard French brasserie" in funky art deco digs near the Porte Maillot serving "very good" oysters and seafood platters "even in the heat of summer"; it's fine for "no surprises" dining, though wildly divergent opinions on service ("excellent" to "awful") might make you think twice.

Bamboche (Le)
18 | 15 | 16 | fr322

15, rue de Babylone, 7ᵉ (Sèvres-Babylone), 01 45 49 14 40

■ A "revelation" exclaim admirers of this "small", "dynamic" French near the Bon Marché department store, hailed for its "imaginative, perfectly prepared" cuisine and "lovely", yellow-toned modern decor; reaction to the cost ("overpriced" vs. "excellent value") may depend on whether one dines à la carte or via the prix fixe.

Baracane ◑
18 | 9 | 15 | fr184

38, rue des Tournelles, 4ᵉ (Bastille), 01 42 71 43 33

☑ Homestyle Southwestern French fare keeps surveyors coming back to this discreet cousin of L'Oulette, located near the Place des Vosges, despite reservations about the "dark decor" and "elbow-to-elbow" room that can be "suffocatingly hot" in summer; fans appreciate the owner's "warm welcome" and "good value", especially at lunch.

Bar à Huîtres (Le) ◑⑤
13 | 10 | 12 | fr233

33, bd. Beaumarchais, 3ᵉ (Bastille), 01 48 87 98 92
33, rue St-Jacques, 5ᵉ (Cluny-La Sorbonne/Maubert-Mutualité), 01 44 07 27 37
112, bd. Montparnasse, 14ᵉ (Raspail/Vavin), 01 43 20 71 01

☑ "Excellent shellfish platters" (but some claim their size is "shrinking") are the draw at this "noisy" oyster bar chain with cold, modern decor; complaints aside ("lacks soul", "slightly expensive", "overbooks" to "cram you in like sardines"), bivalve buffs rate it "good" for an oyster nosh, especially late at night or "seated at the bar."

Bar au Sel (Le) 🅂
16 | 15 | 13 | fr294

49, quai d'Orsay, 7ᵉ (Invalides), 01 45 51 58 58

■ "A treat" for fish lovers, this small, stylish, ultrachic spot near Les Invalides lures "lawyers", "fashion writers" and others with "fresh, high-quality" fish dishes served in "generous" portions; faultfinders note the menu is "limited" ("no meat – unacceptable" say carnivores) and service is "friendly" but not always swift.

Bar des Théâtres ◗🅂
11 | 10 | 12 | fr223

6, av. Montaigne, 8ᵉ (Alma-Marceau), 01 47 23 34 63

☑ Though the steak tartare earns kudos, most voters agree that this "happening" bistro on Avenue Montaigne is "better for people-watching than dining"; its location (across from the Théâtre des Champs-Elysées) and "fast" service make it a natural "pre/post-theater" and celebs/models still abound, but to detractors it's just a "stuffy, noisy" "has-been."

Barfly 🅂
7 | 17 | 7 | fr237

49, av. George V, 8ᵉ (George V), 01 53 67 84 60

☑ "For the gastronomically ignorant" is one reaction to the "overpriced" mixed-bag menu (French with some American dishes and sushi) at this "trendy", "snobby" "scene" near the Champs-Elysées; even if some find the food "not bad", insiders advise "stick to the bar" and check out the "New York–style" decor and "show-off" model/show biz crowd.

Barrail (Le)
▽ 18 | 8 | 15 | fr215

17, rue Falguière, 15ᵉ (Falguière), 01 43 22 42 61

■ Most respondents rate this "cozy" hangout in the 15th as among the neighborhood's best, citing "excellent" value for generous portions of "inventive", "refined" French cuisine; still, some cite "mediocre" decor and report a "decline in quality" in recent years.

Barrière de Clichy (La)
17 | 12 | 15 | fr328

1, rue de Paris, Clichy (Porte de Clichy), 01 47 37 05 18

☑ This "historic" spot north of Paris is where some of France's greatest chefs (including Guy Savoy) earned their stripes; admirers say the food is still "excellent" and the attitude "sincere", even if the setting is on the "depressing" side and the location "too far from my center of gravity"; to naysayers it's just "a classic bore."

Bar Vendôme 🅂
18 | 23 | 21 | fr356

Hôtel Ritz, 15, place Vendôme, 1ᵉʳ (Concorde/Madeleine), 01 43 16 33 63

■ "Absolutely outrageous prices" don't scare away enthusiasts of this famed Place Vendôme hotel cocktail lounge and legendary Hemingway destination, now serving lunch and tea to "the power crowd"; "warm, comfortable, calming", it's "the perfect place to take a pretty date" or recover after "stressful shopping"; the summer terrace wins applause, as do the "discreet" waiters.

Bascou (Au)
16 | 13 | 15 | fr242

38, rue Réaumur, 3ᵉ (Arts-et-Métiers), 01 42 72 69 25

■ "One of the city's best bistros" "deserves a better setting" say surveyors about this "unpretentious" neighborhood place near the Place de la République serving "good Basque fare" to locals; the wines (featuring a big selection of Irouléguy) are "outstanding", the owner (Jean-Guy Loustau) "colorful" and the whole experience "a ray of sunshine."

Basilic (Le) S
11 | 14 | 12 | fr246

2, rue Casimir Perier, 7ᵉ (Invalides/Solférino), 01 44 18 94 64

◪ Perfect for a "lover's tête-à-tête", this small bistro overlooking the church of Sainte-Clothilde wins points for its "classic" decor and "delightful" terrace, even if many find the food "irregular"; the leg of lamb is recommended.

Bastide Odéon (La)
18 | 12 | 15 | fr257

7, rue Corneille, 6ᵉ (Odéon), 01 43 26 03 65

■ "Delicious" Provençale cuisine in a Mediterranean setting makes this "a find" say enthusiasts who also appreciate its proximity to the Odéon theater, "relaxed" ambiance and "good value for the quality"; others complain of "impersonal" service ("maybe we were transparent") and cuisine on the decline, but they're outvoted.

Batifol ◐S
– | – | – | I

15, place de la République, 3ᵉ (République), 01 48 04 02 12
1, bd. St-Germain, 5ᵉ (Jussieu), 01 43 54 49 05
76, av. des Champs-Elysées, 8ᵉ (Charles de Gaulle-Etoile/St-Philippe-du-Roule), 01 45 62 64 93
36, bd. des Italiens, 9ᵉ (Opéra), 01 45 23 09 34
3, place Blanche, 9ᵉ (Blanche), 01 48 74 39 37
8, rue Denain, 10ᵉ (Gare du Nord), 01 42 80 34 74
117, av. Général Leclerc, 14ᵉ (Porte d'Orléans), 01 45 41 19 08
154, rue St-Charles, 15ᵉ (Charles-Michels/Lourmel), 01 45 54 52 09
6, place du Maréchal Juin, 17ᵉ (Pereire), 01 43 80 01 41
29, av. Corentin Cariou, 19ᵉ (Corentin Cariou), 01 40 36 12 36
143, bd. Jean Jaurès, Boulogne (Marcel Semblat), 01 46 04 80 44

This bistro chain has built its reputation by offering rustic classics at moderate prices in lively, old-fashioned settings; while handy for an occasional meal, it has also been knocked for the usual chain faults: mass-produced food, lack of personality, uneven service; in what may be a telling sign, seven branches were recently sold to the Loli cafes.

Baumann Ternes ◐S
13 | 12 | 12 | fr256

64, av. des Ternes, 17ᵉ (Charles de Gaulle-Etoile/Ternes), 01 45 74 16 66

◪ As far as "updated brasseries" go, this one near the Place des Ternes is among "the best", with a fish choucroute that's "a sheer delight" and "lovely Alsatian white wines" enjoyed by a "bourgeois" business crowd; dissenters call it "much ado about nothing", but regulars say it's a "sure bet" when you're "short on ideas."

Bauta (La)
17 | 13 | 15 | fr255

129, bd. Montparnasse, 6ᵉ (Vavin), 01 43 22 52 35

■ "Excellent Venetian cuisine" featuring "unexpected" flavors delight diners thrilled to find a "genuine", "warm" Italian tucked among the myriad restaurants in this busy corner of Vavin; but "ridiculously small portions" raise some eyebrows, as do the limited menu and "kitsch" decor.

Béatilles (Les)
19 | 13 | 16 | fr283

11 bis, rue Villebois-Mareuil, 17ᵉ (Ternes), 01 45 74 43 80

■ The setting may be a little "cold", but surveyors say it doesn't detract from the "festival of flavors" served in this small, "pleasant" French off the Avenue des Ternes; besides the "good, orginal" food, patrons like the "personalized" (if sometimes "slow") service and "good choice of wines."

Beato
16 | 13 | 14 | fr291

8, rue Malar, 7ᵉ (Invalides), 01 47 05 94 27

■ Catering to "Ferrari" owners, among others, this "classy" Italian in the 7th district pleases most with its "refined" cuisine ("best tiramisu in Paris") and "agreeable" service, but not everyone likes the neo-Pompeiian decor ("pretty" vs. "average") and some find it "very expensive" – the "pasta costs nearly as much as caviar."

Beaujolais d'Auteuil ⑤
11 | 11 | 13 | fr188

99, bd. de Montmorency, 16ᵉ (Porte d'Auteuil), 01 47 43 03 56

◪ This 1920s-style bistro near Roland Garros Stadium at the Porte d'Auteuil is deemed useful for an "inexpensive" "family" night out or Sunday lunch; however, some voters report a "decline in quality" and "pursed-lip" welcome.

BEAUVILLIERS (A.) ⑤
20 | 23 | 18 | fr486

52, rue Lamarck, 18ᵉ (Lamarck Caulaincourt), 01 42 54 54 42

◪ There's "romance" in the air at this flower-bedecked Classic French in Montmartre, called a "splendid place to celebrate a special event" by fans of its "sumptuous" decor and "delicious" food; but it's not for everyone: "pretentious", "doesn't live up to its reputation", "expensive"; service can be "irreproachable" – "if they know you."

Bellecour (Le)
20 | 13 | 16 | fr348

22, rue Surcouf, 7 e (Invalides/La Tour-Maubourg), 01 45 51 46 93

◪ "Good Lyonnaise cuisine" means "rich but refined" to respondents who appreciate the "good value" prix fixe menu, "quiet" dining room and "good wine list" at this bistro near Les Invalides; dissenters dislike the "gloomy" ambiance and complain that this "bourgeois" haven "lacks soul."

Bellini
15 | 12 | 14 | fr271

28, rue Le Sueur, 16ᵉ (Argentine), 01 45 00 54 20

■ There's "good Franco-Italian" fare in a "pleasant" setting with a relaxed ambiance at this upscale restaurant between Etoile and the Porte Maillot; "excellent – keep going" urge supporters.

Benkay (Le) S
18 | 15 | 15 | fr428

Hôtel Nikko, 61, quai de Grenelle, 15ᵉ
(Bir-Hakeim/Charles-Michels), 01 40 58 21 26
☑ "Japanese tourists who don't want to go out" aren't the only ones to frequent this "pricey" hotel restaurant overlooking the Seine; fans say the food is as tasty as it is "beautiful to behold", praising the "very fresh" sushi and grilled meats; but others berate small portions and say it's "bland" to "anyone who's been to Japan."

Benoît S
20 | 18 | 19 | fr426

20, rue St-Martin, 4ᵉ (Châtelet), 01 42 72 25 76
■ This "authentic," old-fashioned" bistro is nothing less than "a classified historic monument" for devotees of its "country-style" dishes served by "attentive" waiters in a cozy, Belle Epoque setting in central Paris near the Pompidou Center; for many it's "a must", but some note "frighteningly" high prices and a proprietor who sometimes acts like a "star"; N.B. it finally takes credit cards (AE).

Bermuda Onion S
10 | 17 | 11 | fr241

16, rue Linois, 15ᵉ (Charles-Michels), 01 45 75 11 11
☑ This "trendy", "noisy" eatery in Beaugrenelle with trompe l'oeil decor boasts a "superb" view of the Seine and the Statue of Liberty plus some of Paris' "sexiest" waitresses, so who cares if opinions on the French food veer from "zippy" to "ok"?; critics call it a "has-been '80s holdover", but it's hard to fault the terrace or "great brunch fare."

Bernica (Le) S
– | – | – | M

4, Impasse de la Gaîté, 14ᵉ (Edgar-Quinet), 01 43 20 39 02
"A little corner of island paradise" in the 14th district where surveyors enjoy "spicy, nuanced" food from Réunion in a "warm ambiance" with "efficient", "discreet" service; a tasty vanilla coffee rounds out a fun evening that doesn't leave you bankrupt.

Berry's ◑
13 | 9 | 11 | fr211

46, rue de Naples, 8ᵉ (Villiers), 01 40 75 01 56
■ In this bourgeois neighborhood near Villiers respondents say it's "nice" to find a Regional French that's "pleasant" and affordable, with "good" food that gives patrons "a chance to get back to their roots."

Berthoud (Le)
14 | 13 | 13 | fr234

1, rue Valette, 5ᵉ (Maubert-Mutualité), 01 43 54 38 81
■ You'll "rediscover the joys of simple pleasures like good mashed potatoes" at this Left Bank bistro near Maubert-Mutualité where the "freshest ingredients" are used to whip up "delicious", "good quality" "family-style" fare; "egg lovers" are especially happy here.

Bertie's S
17 | 18 | 18 | fr321

Hôtel Baltimore, 1, rue Léo Delibes, 16ᵉ (Boissière),
01 44 34 54 34

■ "The best British food in Paris" can be found at the Hotel Baltimore's clubby English-style dining room off the posh Avenue Kléber; besides "surprisingly" good cuisine, surveyors praise the "well-executed" service, "calm", "pretty" setting and excellent, "reasonably priced" wine list; "too bad it's never this good across the Channel."

Beudant (Le)
∇ 16 | 11 | 15 | fr272

97, rue des Dames, 17ᵉ (Villiers), 01 43 87 11 20

■ A "chic", quiet hideaway for "lovers" is how some respondents view this small French near Villiers; while the majority applauds "excellent" dishes made from "seasonal produce", the "dependable" service and "pleasant" ambiance, a few find it "pricey."

Biche au Bois (A la)
19 | 11 | 15 | fr193

45, av. Ledru-Rollin, 12ᵉ (Gare de Lyon), 01 43 43 34 38

■ One of the city's most "surprising" secrets say reviewers who aren't anxious to spread the word about this "fabulous", "reasonably priced" bistro specializing in game near the Gare de Lyon; the waiters are "efficient" and "nice", the ambiance a bit "rowdy"; only the decor needs improvement.

Bistro 121 ◐ S
16 | 13 | 15 | fr316

121, rue de la Convention, 15ᵉ (Boucicaut/Convention),
01 45 57 52 90

◪ Most diners appreciate this small bistro in the 15th district for its "solid traditional food" ("excellent foie gras") that offers "no surprises, good or bad", calling it "nice with the family or en tête-à-tête"; but a few note "indifferent" service and high-ish prices, claiming it "lives off its reputation."

Bistro de Gala (Le) ◐
∇ 12 | 10 | 13 | fr234

45, rue du Fbg. Montmartre, 9ᵉ (Le Peletier), 01 40 22 90 50

■ This unpretentious bistro run by a cinema buff in the bustling Faubourg Montmartre offers "inventive" French cuisine and a "charming reception" in a neighborhood where "you'd be hard pressed to find something better"; "good value" and "friendly service" boost its appeal.

Bistro de la Grille ◐ S
13 | 13 | 13 | fr199

14, rue Mabillon, 6ᵉ (Mabillon), 01 43 54 16 87

◪ "Good fare", "excellent value" and a "congenial" atmosphere make this "typical" Saint-Germain bistro a "Parisian jewel" "worth the detour" according to partisans; a few doubters say "nothing outstanding", but for most it "never disappoints"; late hours are a plus.

Bistro des Deux Théâtres (Le) ◐ ⓢ   12 | 10 | 13 | fr196
18, rue Blanche, 9ᵉ (Trinité), 01 45 26 41 43

▣ Catering to theatergoers and the clock-watching lunch crowd, this "crowded", "noisy, smoke-filled bistro" near Trinity church is fine "for a simple meal among friends"; supporters consider it an "excellent value" with "satisfying" food and "good service", but it doesn't impress everyone: "disappointing", "mediocre."

Bistro d'Hubert (Le) ⓢ   17 | 15 | 15 | fr259
41, bd. Pasteur, 15ᵉ (Pasteur), 01 47 34 15 50

▣ "Balanced, tasty" dishes are whipped up before your eyes at this "charming" (if sometimes "noisy") new bistro on the Boulevard Pasteur; regulars tout the "daily specials" and admire the "country chic" decor and lively ambiance, with some calling it "one of the best bargains of the year."

Bistro du 17 (Le) ⓢ   13 | 11 | 13 | fr191
108, av. de Villiers, 17ᵉ (Pereire), 01 47 63 32 77

▣ This busy bistro on the Place Pereire offers well-heeled locals who are "too lazy to make dinner" a "great value" prix fixe menu that fans call "the best by far in its category"; while "nothing out of the ordinary", it's "reliable" and "honest"; "noise" and "tight seating" are drawbacks, but "things calm down" after 10 PM.

Bistro Melrose ◐ⓢ   ▽ 13 | 12 | 12 | fr181
5, place Clichy, 17ᵉ (Place Clichy), 01 42 93 61 34

▣ An "unpretentious, cheap" bistro on the bustling Place Clichy where locals "dine among friends"; "ok, no surprises" sums it up, but it's "pleasant" and easy on the pocketbook.

Bistrot d'à Côté Flaubert ◐ⓢ   16 | 13 | 14 | fr290
10, rue Gustave Flaubert, 17ᵉ (Ternes), 01 42 67 05 81

▣ "Excellent food", "old bistro" ambiance, "intimacy and charm" are "exactly what you want in Paris" rave fans of this jammed bistro behind the Place des Ternes owned by Michel Rostang (whose classy eponymous venue is next door); it helped pioneer the trend towards lower-priced bistro annexes from great chefs, but mixed in with praise are gripes about elbow-to-elbow seating, high-ish prices and service that may favor regulars.

Bistrot d'à Côté Neuilly   16 | 14 | 14 | fr226
4, rue Boutard, Neuilly-sur-Seine (Pont de Neuilly), 01 47 45 34 55

▣ Another Rostang venture, which means "good food, end of story" for devotees of the renowned chef; this Neuilly outpost is lauded for its "solid" bistro fare and decor, "good service" and "reasonable prices", as well as its valet parking ("fantastic" given the area's jammed streets), with a few complaints about "tables too close together."

Bistrot d'à Côté Saint-Germain   16   13   14   fr242
*16, bd. St-Germain, 5ᵉ (Cardinal Lemoine/Maubert-Mutualité),
01 43 54 59 10*
■ This Rostang bistro in Saint-Germain draws "tourists" and
chic locals looking for "correct" "provincial-style bistro fare"
that's deemed especially "good for the neighborhood";
"noise" and "slow" service draw complaints (some call it a
"victim of its own success"), and a few just find it "average."

Bistrot d'à Côté Villiers   14   13   14   fr238
16, av. de Villiers, 17ᵉ (Villiers), 01 47 63 25 61
■ Though it earns lower scores than its siblings, this
Rostang bistro near Villiers catering to locals and a
lunchtime business crowd earns equal praise for its
"traditional" bistro cooking updated by a master, "friendly
service" and "excellent value"; "bravo Rostang!"

Bistrot d'Alex   17   13   17   fr251
2, rue Clément, 6ᵉ (Mabillon/Odéon), 01 43 54 09 53
■ This unpretentious bistro near Odéon, a lunchtime
hangout for the publishing world, is well rated for its half-
Lyonnais, half-Provençal menu, "attentive" service and
"delightful" proprietors who greet you like an old friend
even on your first visit; the only hitch is the decor – "cozy"
to some, "depressing" to others.

Bistrot d'André (Le)   ∇ 13   13   13   fr202
232, rue St-Charles, 15ᵉ (Balard), 01 45 57 89 14
■ Surveyors like this simple, turn-of-the-century bistro off
the beaten path in the 15th district; named after French car
mogul André Citroën and decorated with posters of old
Citroën cars (the company's main factory was once nearby),
it offers "excellent steaks and desserts" plus other bistro
fare at reasonable prices; fine for "a business lunch" too.

Bistrot de Breteuil (Le) ◐S   12   11   13   fr208
3, place de Breteuil, 7ᵉ (Duroc/Sèvres-Lecourbe), 01 45 67 07 27
☑ This comfy bistro in the quiet, upscale 7th district is
perhaps "nothing special", but its "economical" prix fixe
menus won't leave you bankrupt and it's "great in summer"
with a "pleasant" terrace; diners also like the "warm"
welcome and "family" ambiance, especially Sundays.

Bistrot de l'Etoile Lauriston ◐   16   13   15   fr297
*19, rue Lauriston, 16ᵉ (Charles de Gaulle-Etoile/Kléber),
01 40 67 11 16*
■ "Out of the ordinary dishes" dreamed up by top chef Guy
Savoy and "good value" prices please most diners at
this Savoy spin-off near the Etoile, one of his six satellite
restaurants; a daily changing menu, "friendly service" and
long list of inexpensive wines are pluses, but some find the
"modern" setting "cramped" and "noisy"; critics call it a
"fake bistro", but they're outvoted.

Bistrot de l'Etoile Niel ◗🅢   16 | 12 | 14 | fr251
75, av. Niel, 17ᵉ (Pereire), 01 42 27 88 44
■ Similar ratings but mixed comments go to this member of Guy Savoy's Bistrot de L'Etoile trio; in the posh 17th district, it pleases most with its "refined cuisine" and "casual" ambiance ("ideal for lunch with a friend" or Sunday dinner "after a weekend" away), but others report "disappointing service and food" and a "snooty" welcome.

Bistrot de l'Etoile Troyon 🅢   16 | 10 | 14 | fr247
13, rue Troyon, 17ᵉ (Charles de Gaulle-Etoile), 01 42 67 25 95
☑ The oldest of Guy Savoy's Bistrot de L'Etoile trio is a "chic, discreet" spot across from his eponymous flagship, near the Etoile; while some feel it falls short of its cousins, supporters say it's "a sure bet" for "imaginative" bistro fare – if you don't mind eating on your neighbor's lap in a "noisy, cramped" setting.

Bistrot de Marius (Le) ◗🅢   15 | 12 | 12 | fr264
6, av. George V, 8ᵉ (Alma-Marceau), 01 40 70 11 76
☑ While most agree that the fish and seafood are "always fresh" at this lower-cost offshoot of neighboring Marius et Janette near the Place de l'Alma, opinion is divided on the cost ("good value" vs. still "too pricey") and service ("efficient" vs. "slow"); the setting is "ordinary" but there's a "pretty view" from the large terrace.

Bistrot de Paris (Le) 🅢   15 | 13 | 13 | fr288
33, rue de Lille, 7ᵉ (Rue du Bac), 01 42 61 16 83
☑ Though famed chef Michel Oliver is no longer at the helm, some say new owners "are breathing new life into" this slightly "snobby" Left Bank bistro; however, respondents aren't so keen on the "nonchalant" service and pan the decor as still "gloomy even after renovations" – "what a shame" since the food can be "excellent."

Bistrot d'Henri (Le) ◗⌀   16 | 11 | 17 | fr264
16, rue Princesse, 6ᵉ (Mabillon/St-Germain-des-Prés), 01 46 33 51 12
■ In a little street "typical of Saint-Germain-des-Prés", this French "for artists" serves "completely honest food in an unforgettably droll atmosphere" with moleskin banquettes and walls plastered with souvenirs; "kind" service is another reason why admirers call this "a good, solid bistro the way we like them."

Bistrot du Cochon d'Or   16 | 15 | 15 | fr275
192, av. Jean Jaurès, 19ᵉ (Porte de Pantin), 01 42 45 46 46
■ "A good alternative" if you can't afford the Cochon d'Or say fans of this fabulous "annex" to one of the "best steakhouses" in Paris; it may be a trek out to the Villette, but "low prices for very fine food" make it worth the trip.

Bistrot du Dôme (Le) 🅂
16 | 14 | 14 | fr258

2, rue de la Bastille, 4ᵉ (Bastille), 01 48 04 88 44 ◗
1, rue Delambre, 14ᵉ (Vavin), 01 43 35 32 00

■ "Flawless fish" at "reasonable prices" are what most surveyors find at these Le Dôme offsprings at the Bastille and in Montparnasse; the sole, bouillabaisse and shellfish are winners and the "original" decor adds to the pleasure, but they can be "noisy" with "blasé", "inconsistent" service.

Bistrot du Sommelier
16 | 10 | 15 | fr365

97, bd. Haussmann, 8ᵉ (St-Augustin), 01 42 65 24 85

◪ "Ah, if only the food were as good as the wines" sums up the majority view on this classy wine-oriented French on the Boulevard Haussmann, run by master sommelier Philippe Faure-Brac; the food may strike some as "mediocre and pricey", but with a "superb" wine list it's "*the* place to learn about marrying wines" with cuisine.

Bistrot Gambas (Le)
14 | 11 | 13 | fr215

40, r. Notre-Dame-des-Victoires, 2ᵉ (Bourse), 01 42 36 37 35
4, rue du Débarcadère, 17ᵉ (Argentine/Porte Maillot),
01 45 72 22 55

◪ "You have to be a shrimp lover" to go to these bistros (one near the Bourse, the other behind Porte Maillot) specializing in shrimp dishes with a Provençal accent; but even then you may find the idea "interesting" but the execution less than successful, with critics citing "meager" portions of "ordinary", "overpriced" fare, plus "nonexistent" service.

Bistrot Mazarin ◗🅂
11 | 11 | 12 | fr183

42, rue Mazarine, 6ᵉ (Odéon/St-Germain-des-Prés),
01 43 29 99 01

◪ "Why is it so hard to find a table?" ask those who find the bistro food just "ok" and the service "unfriendly" at this "cheap" hangout for students and local art dealers near Odéon; the key to its appeal: a "relaxed" "Left Bank" ambiance and a terrace that's "very pleasant" in summer.

Bistrot Papillon (Le)
▽ 20 | 12 | 15 | fr190

6, rue Papillon, 9ᵉ (Cadet/Poissonnière), 01 47 70 90 03

■ Tucked on a quiet street between the Gares du Nord and de l'Est, this little Belle Epoque eatery "frequented by locals" earns high marks for its "refined" French fare and "warm" ambiance; the prix fixe menu is a good value, and classics like foie gras and duck breast with cherries ensure the loyalty of a large crowd of regulars.

Bistrot St-James
▽ 13 | 11 | 13 | fr235

2, rue Général Henrion-Berthier, Neuilly-sur-Seine (Pont de Neuilly), 01 46 24 21 06

■ Surveyors like this bistro near the Pont de Neuilly for its "inventive" seasonal bistro fare, "very friendly service", "well-spaced tables" and "very good Bordeaux wines"; only a few sniff that it's "overrated."

Blue Elephant ●S
19 | 24 | 16 | fr309

43, rue de la Roquette, 11ᵉ (Bastille), 01 47 00 42 00

■ The "sumptuous decor" of plants, tropical woods and bamboo conjures up "Thailand in all its splendor" at this "charming", "refined" eatery near the Bastille; add "good cooking" and you have what some call "the best Thai in Paris" – "the Royal Menu is worth the trip if you can find a place to park"; just be prepared for "slow service" and a bill that many find "expensive."

Bœuf Couronné (Au) ●
17 | 13 | 15 | fr296

188, av. Jean Jaurès, 19ᵉ (Porte de Pantin), 01 42 39 44 44

■ Calling all carnivores to this "meat lovers' paradise" on the site of the old slaughterhouses at the Villette; it's "hard to get there" and parking's a nightmare, but the beef is "top quality" and the ambiance "convivial" at this "pricey" "institution" that keeps alive "the history" of the area.

Bœuf Gros Sel (Le)
▽ 14 | 12 | 13 | fr212

120, rue des Grands-Champs, 20ᵉ (Maraîchers), 01 43 73 96 58

■ "Adorable" waiters serve "simple" but "good" French fare (including the namesake dish) at this popular eatery in the remote 20th district; the "extraordinary" terrace is a hit, but some find the decor kitsch and the bill a bit hard on the wallet.

Bœuf sur le Toit (Le) ●S
13 | 17 | 13 | fr251

34, rue du Colisée, 8ᵉ (St-Philippe-du-Roule), 01 53 93 65 55

☑ Take earplugs to this fashionable '30s-style brasserie (part of the Flo chain) off the Champs-Elysées where "the welcome is warm even when the place is jammed"; most diners enjoy the "lively" ambiance and find the food "satisfactory for the price", but dissenters complain of assembly-line service and "pre-fab" fare, offering the ultimate putdown: a "place to take American tourists."

Bofinger ●S
14 | 21 | 14 | fr272

5, rue de la Bastille, 4ᵉ (Bastille), 01 42 72 87 82

☑ The "superb" turn-of-the-century decor at this legendary brasserie near the Bastille dazzles diners more than what's on their plates; still, it's a "great late-night address" ("ideal after the Opéra Bastille") for "good choucroute", shellfish and such in a "noisy", "dynamic" ambiance; naysayers note "declining quality", increasing tourists; N.B. the pretty main dining room is no-smoking.

Bon Accueil (Au)
19 | 12 | 15 | fr226

14, rue de Monttessuy, 7ᵉ (Alma-Marceau), 01 47 05 46 11

■ "The find of the year" rave admirers of this "simple, old-fashioned" bistro near the Eiffel Tower serving "interesting" contemporary fare and "well-chosen wines" at "reasonable cost" to chic locals; the tables are a bit cramped and service can be "overwhelmed", but most cheer "bravo! – if only more [restaurateurs] were as nice."

Bon St. Pourçain (Au) ⌦   14 | 11 | 13 | fr226
10 bis, rue Servandoni, 6ᵉ (Odéon/St-Sulpice), 01 43 54 93 63
■ Tucked away in a cobbled lane just off the Place Saint
Sulpice, this pint-sized bistro is "a real neighborhood
restaurant" with "good, simple" "family-style" cooking
served in an "amiable", "homely" atmosphere.

Bookinistes (Les) ◑⑤   15 | 13 | 13 | fr264
53, quai des Grands-Augustins, 6ᵉ (St-Michel), 01 43 25 45 94
☑ Guy Savoy's "trendy" Left Bank bistro overlooking the
Seine at Saint-Michel divides surveyors; while supporters
praise its "refined", "original" nouvelle cuisine, "cheery"
contemporary decor ("feels like New York") and "pleasant"
staff, detractors find the food "unremarkable", the ambiance
"cold" and service lacking; your call.

Botequim Brasileiro ◑⑤   ▽ 17 | 9 | 13 | fr201
1, rue Berthollet, 5ᵉ (Censier-Daubenton), 01 43 37 98 46
■ "Reservations are a must" (especially weekends) at
this purveyor of what many call the city's "best Brazilian
food", set in a small street in the 5th; the cost is reasonable
and the welcome "pleasant"; "even Brazilians eat here!"

Bouchon Beaujolais (Le)   ▽ 13 | 9 | 12 | fr250
27 ter, bd. Diderot, 12ᵉ (Gare de Lyon), 01 43 43 62 84
■ Surveyors say this "authentic", "congenial" little
brasserie dishing up Lyonnaise cuisine is a fine choice
across from the Gare de Lyon "where good dining options
are rare"; the 1908-vintage setting is simple, but there's a
nice "family-style" ambiance.

BOUCHONS DE FR. CLERC (LES) 16 | 14 | 14 | fr277
*12, rue de l' Hôtel Colbert, 5ᵉ (Maubert-Mutualité),
01 43 54 15 34*
22, rue de la Terrasse, 17ᵉ (Villiers), 01 42 27 31 51
7, rue du Boccador, 8ᵉ (Alma-Marceau), 01 47 23 57 80
32, bd. du Montparnasse, 15ᵉ (Duroc/Falguière), 01 45 48 52 03
■ "A must for wine lovers", this innovative concept created
by the chef François Clerc offers the "rare" opportunity to
drink "high-class wines at cost"; some quibble over the
French fare ("satisfactory" vs. "too complicated, doesn't
always work") and several prefer the "wine-cellar" setting
of the 5th district branch, but all applaud a "vintastique"
bargain; P.S. try the "superb cheese tray."

Bouillon Racine ◑⑤   12 | 20 | 13 | fr197
3, rue Racine, 6ᵉ (Cluny-La Sorbonne/Odéon), 01 44 32 15 60
☑ Surveyors adore the "fabulous" art nouveau setting
(classified as a French historical monument) but are less
enthusiastic about the Belgian beer-based cuisine at this
brasserie near Odéon; still, the food is "solid" and "not
expensive", there's a "wide variety of beers" and the
atmosphere is "fun" and "relaxing."

Boule d'Or (La) 🆂   14 | 12 | 14 | fr311
13, bd. de La Tour-Maubourg, 7ᵉ (Invalides),
01 47 05 50 18
■ "A comfortable place with no surprises" say those who head to this "classy" French near Les Invalides; "eating here is always a happy occasion" according to admirers.

Bourguignon (Au)   ▽ 15 | 15 | 14 | fr259
52, rue François Miron, 4ᵉ (Pont Marie/St-Paul),
01 48 87 15 40
■ Burgundy buffs say this "unpretentious" but stylish wine bar in the Marais lives up to its name, offering a "good selection" of the best Burgundies plus "simple but excellent" French food; some find the menu "limited", but the cheese ("what cheese!") is recommended; service can be "warm" or "cold", "depending on the day."

Braisière (La)   21 | 13 | 16 | fr321
54, rue Cardinet, 17ᵉ (Malesherbes), 01 47 63 40 37
■ Surveyors are enthusiastic about this "excellent" place in the residential 17th district near Malesherbes serving high-class French classics with special flair created by a chef who is "passionate" about cuisine and French wines; "discreet" and "relaxing", it's "pleasant for a quiet business dinner" and "affordable" given the quality.

Brasserie Balzar ◐🆂   13 | 16 | 15 | fr240
49, rue des Ecoles, 5ᵉ (Cluny-La Sorbonne), 01 43 54 13 67
◪ In the heart of the Latin Quarter lies what many view as "the most Parisian" brasserie of all, dishing up "honest" French classics to "the Sorbonne crowd" and tourists eager to hobnob with them; while some say the food has slipped, others call the menu "timeless" and hope new owners (the Flo group) "don't change a thing" – except perhaps long waits and service that can be "distant", bordering on "surly."

Brasserie de la Poste ◐🆂   10 | 12 | 12 | fr226
54, rue de Longchamp, 16ᵉ (Trocadéro), 01 47 55 01 31
◪ Right out of a "Toulouse-Lautrec painting", this chic brasserie near Trocadéro with "elbow-to-elbow" seating has plenty of critics who stamp it "noisy, ordinary" and "not what it was"; but defenders like its "fast" service and "reasonable" prices, which may be why it's "always full."

Brasserie de l'Isle St-Louis ◐🆂   12 | 14 | 14 | fr204
55, quai de Bourbon, 4ᵉ (Cité/Pont Marie), 01 43 54 02 59
◪ Surveyors praise this "agreeable" Ile Saint-Louis brasserie for its "honest" fare, "cold beer", "lovely" terrace and "great location" near Notre Dame; but they also complain about "noise" and "tourists", advising "take out-of-towners" or people "with whom you don't want to converse."

Brasserie du Louvre ◗S
13 14 12 fr218

Hôtel du Louvre, place André Malraux, 1er (Palais-Royal), 01 44 58 38 38

■ This "comfortable" brasserie in the Hotel du Louvre near the museum is recommended as a good place to "recharge your batteries after an afternoon of shopping" in the area; the food's "honest" and "less expensive" than at some "less luxurious" spots in the neighborhood.

Brasserie Flo ◗S
14 18 14 fr269

7, cour des Petites-Ecuries, 10e (Château d'Eau), 01 47 70 13 59

◪ The "exceptional" turn-of-the century decor with stained glass windows and "typical brasserie ambiance" earn high praise at this "landmark" in a "picturesque alley" near the Porte Saint-Denis; however, it's "noisy", the tables are "too close" and opinions on the food range from "correct", "good value" to "much ado about cuisine in decline."

Brasserie Le Stella ◗S
11 8 12 fr240

133, av. Victor Hugo, 16e (Victor Hugo), 01 47 27 60 54

◪ This "lively", "16th district institution" attracting wealthy locals and a smattering of celebs is "a classic" according to fans of its signature oysters and steak tartare; dissenters deplore the "sad decor" and lack of elbow room ("you're part of your neighbor's conversation, like it or not") and say it's "overpriced" for what you get.

Brasserie Lipp ◗S
13 18 13 fr281

151, bd. St-Germain, 6e (St-Germain-des-Prés), 01 45 48 53 91

◪ This "pricey" Left Bank "institution" still draws politicians, intellectuals and wanna-bes looking "to see and be seen" while enjoying its "old-fashioned" brasserie ambiance, art nouveau tiles and "mythic" "charm"; partisans insist it's "best in its class", but to foes it's "a place for snobs", doling out "mediocre food" and a cool reception to unknowns.

Brasserie Lorraine ◗S
10 11 10 fr287

2-4, place des Ternes, 8e (Ternes), 01 42 27 80 04

◪ "Not what it used to be" is the verdict on this "aging" brasserie on the Place des Ternes; a change of owners hasn't swayed surveyors who lambaste it for "expensive", "mediocre" food served by "slow" waiters to wealthy locals and expense-accounters; still, fans say its "impeccable" oysters work for a "late-night meal after a show."

Brasserie Lutétia S
13 13 14 fr259

Hôtel Lutétia, 23, rue de Sèvres, 6e (Sèvres-Babylone), 01 49 54 46 76

◪ Reaction is lukewarm to this spacious, "well-located" brasserie in the Left Bank hotel of the same name featuring basic French fare that some rate "not bad" and others dismiss as "boring"; the "impersonal" decor and "noise" also take some hits, but the kids' menu (a rarity in Paris) and "patient" service are pluses.

Brasserie Mollard ◑ S
13 | 17 | 12 | fr269

115, rue St-Lazare, 8ᵉ (St-Lazare), 01 43 87 50 22

◪ This "classic brasserie" with a "very handsome" art nouveau interior near the Gare Saint-Lazare is a sleeping beauty that's "aging badly" according to critics who cite "ordinary" food and service; but many like its "traditional" ways and say it still serves "very good shellfish" and "one of the best steak tartares in Paris."

Brasserie Munichoise ◑
▽ 11 | 13 | 11 | fr199

5, rue Danielle Casanova, 1ᵉʳ (Opéra), 01 42 61 47 16

◪ Supporters say this German-style pub near the Opéra "remains faithful to the cuisine and ambiance of Munich", serving some of the "best sausages in Paris" in a "warm" setting; but critics simply dismiss it as a "has-been."

BRISTOL (LE) S
23 | 23 | 23 | fr599

Hôtel Bristol, 112, rue du Fbg. St-Honoré, 8ᵉ (Miromesnil), 01 53 43 43 40

◼ Chef Michel del Burgo has brought about a "lovely resurrection" of this "elegant" hotel restaurant on the Faubourg Saint-Honoré say voters who describe the "creative nouvelle" French fare as "sheer perfection"; while the service and "sublime" patio also win praise, views are mixed on the decor: "magical" vs. "sanitized, lacking charm"; it's also "costly, but you get what you pay for."

Bûcherie (La) ◑ S
13 | 15 | 12 | fr314

41, rue de la Bûcherie, 5ᵉ (St-Michel), 01 43 54 24 52

◪ Admirers of this "cozy", upscale French with a wood-burning fireplace and view of Notre Dame call it an ideal place "for a romantic dinner", praising its "good food" and "warm", "intimate" atmosphere; however, faultfinders call it "overpriced" and say service could be better.

Buddha Bar ◑ S
11 | 23 | 9 | fr301

8, rue Boissy-d'Anglas, 8ᵉ (Concorde), 01 53 05 90 00

◪ It's "all in the decor" – and that means the "beautiful people" and "celebs" as well as the "eye-catching" (some say "gaudy") Asian-themed surroundings, including a giant gold-painted Buddha – at this "trendy", "New York–style" "see and be seen" scene near the Place de la Concorde; given "uneven", pricey Asian fusion food, "slow" service and "a long wait to get in", "once is enough" for some.

Butte Chaillot (La) ◑ S
15 | 13 | 13 | fr274

110 bis, av. Kléber, 16ᵉ (Trocadéro), 01 47 27 88 88

◪ Most surveyors give high marks to the "excellent", updated bistro fare and "modern" decor at this Guy Savoy venture near Trocadéro; don't miss the poulet de Bresse and mashed potatoes ("savor the smell before you devour"); a few find the ambiance "very 16th" and "cold", but the staff is "young and attentive" and the whole package is welcome "in an underserviced neighborhood."

Café Beaubourg ◑🅂
9 17 11 fr168

100, rue St-Martin, 4ᵉ (Châtelet), 01 48 87 63 96

■ The Costes brothers' cafe "for trendies" facing the busy plaza of the Pompidou Center is considered the perfect spot to meet for a drink or snack "after viewing an exhibition"; its modern decor and crowd make it a show in its own right, and if the food is "disappointing", the ambiance is "relaxed" and the terrace ideal for "watching the world go by."

Café Bennett 🅂
- - - I

40, place du Marché St-Honoré, 1ᵉʳ (Opéra/Pyramides), 01 42 86 04 24

Surveyors don't see eye to eye over this "in" place near the Opéra Garnier; some find it "affordable" and praise the "adorable" waiters, while others balk at "bistro fare at restaurant prices" and complain that quality has slipped.

Café Bleu Lanvin
11 13 12 fr195

15, rue du Fbg. St-Honoré, 8ᵉ (Concorde), 01 44 71 32 32

☑ "Good for a quick lunch in the neighborhood" but only if you're not "claustrophobic" say patrons of this "chic" oasis in the Lanvin boutique on the elegant Faubourg Saint-Honoré catering to wealthy shoppers and "kept women"; it may be "expensive for a trendy salad" but most think it works for a "business lunch on the run."

Café de Flore ◑🅂
- - - I

172, bd. St-Germain, 6ᵉ (St-Germain-des-Prés), 01 45 48 55 26

Though one of the world's best-known cafes (hence a tourist magnet), the Flore still maintains its Left Bank allure, drawing the smart set and what remains of the local intellectual scene (philosopher Bernard-Henri Lévy, for example, is often found on the second floor, the location preferred by brainy types); prices are nervy but the coffee's excellent and one can have a simple but appealing light meal; catch breakfast on the weekends for a high-voltage power scene.

Café de la Musique ◑🅂
12 19 13 fr186

213, av. Jean Jaurès, 19ᵉ (Porte de Pantin), 01 48 03 15 91

■ Surveyors are in harmony when it comes to this Costes brothers creation, a new wave French cafe a stone's throw from the Villette exhibition center; its "modern-day light" cuisine is modestly priced, but it's the cheery, contemporary decor, "delightful" staff and sunny terrace that keep diners coming back.

Café de la Paix (Le) ◑🅂
11 17 13 fr243

12, bd. des Capucines, 9ᵉ (Auber/Opéra), 01 40 07 30 20

☑ "A tourist trap to be avoided" is one way of looking at this "legendary" brasserie "ideally situated" across from the Opéra; but the Charles Garnier setting is "magnificent" and the "world parades before you" when seated on the terrace, so you may not care if the food is "variable" and served by waiters "who've forgotten how to smile."

Café de l'Industrie ●⑤ 　　10 | 18 | 11 | fr147
16, rue St-Sabin, 11ᵉ (Bastille/Bréguet Sabin), 01 47 00 13 53
■ "One of the cooler spots" near the Bastille, this "congenial" cafe draws a "hip crowd" that comes more for the "neat", "exotic" colonial-style decor, "lively" ambiance and "superb" waitresses than for the "simple" bistro fare (with a few Caribbean accents), which some call a "good value" and others dismiss as "uneven", so-so.

Café de Mars ●⑤ 　　11 | 11 | 12 | fr196
11, rue Augereau, 7ᵉ (Ecole Militaire), 01 47 05 05 91
☑ This "trendy" bistro near the Ecole Militaire featuring American-style cuisine with a French twist may be "in", but it's on the outs with critics who call it "a pseudo good address" that's "expensive" for what it is; fans, meanwhile, praise the "excellent daily specials with exotic, original flavors" and say it does the trick if "you're lost in the 7th."

Café des Lettres ⑤ 　　10 | 15 | 13 | fr196
53, rue de Verneuil, 7ᵉ (Rue du Bac/Solférino), 01 42 22 52 17
■ Most surveyors appreciate this "original" Scandinavian in the quiet 7th district near Solférino even if they find the menu "expensive" and "repetitive"; what wins them over are the "beautiful", "efficient" waitresses and "marvelous" outdoor dining in the cobblestone courtyard.

Café des Théâtres ● 　　▽ 13 | 12 | 14 | fr189
17, rue de Choiseul, 2ᵉ (Quatre-Septembre), 01 42 65 77 40
■ Surveyors applaud the decor ("unusual", "sweet") as well as the "exceptional menu" at this bistro in central Paris that's popular with stockbrokers at noon, but quieter at night; some even consider it one of the city's "best values", with several prix fixe menus offering crowd-pleasers like filet mignon with morel mushrooms and rouget in vanilla sauce.

Café du Commerce (Le) ●⑤ 　　9 | 14 | 10 | fr163
51, rue du Commerce, 15ᵉ (Emile Zola/La Motte-Picquet Grenelle), 01 45 75 03 27
☑ An institution in the 15th, this vintage 1920s tri-level brasserie built around an atrium is blasted by foes as a "noisy" "factory" churning out "mediocre", "reheated" food, but others call it a "good value" and enjoy the "original" decor and roof that slides open in summer; it's definitely a "curiosity" and "a must if you live in the neighborhood."

Café du Passage (Le) ●⑤ 　　▽ 18 | 15 | 17 | fr242
12, rue de Charonne, 11ᵉ (Bastille), 01 49 29 97 64
■ The working-class Bastille neighborhood has gone upscale in recent years, hence the birth of places like this wine-oriented bistro, appreciated for its "tasty little" dishes tailored to its "extensive wine list"; the ambiance is "cozy" and "warm", as is the "real welcome" you get at the door.

Café Indochine ◗ · · · · · · · · · · · 13 | 15 | 11 | fr258
195, rue du Fbg. St-Honoré, 8ᵉ (Charles de Gaulle-Etoile),
01 53 75 15 63

◪ Admirers of this "trendy", "nouvelle" Asian across from
the Salle Pleyel like its Vietnamese fare and "pretty colonial
decor" recalling "Saigon in the '30s"; however, many gripe
about "high prices" ("for Vietnamese"), "small portions"
and "aloof" service, and conclude it's "resting on its laurels."

Café la Jatte ⑤ · · · · · · · · · · · 12 | 17 | 12 | fr246
60, bd. Vital Bouhot, Neuilly-sur-Seine (Pont de Levallois),
01 47 45 04 20

◪ Headquarters for the ad world, yuppies and celebs ("a
temple for snobs" sniff some), this "trendy", upscale French
on the Ile de la Jatte scores higher for its "amusing" modern
decor (a dinosaur skeleton hangs over the "barn"-sized,
"noisy" room) than its food ("antiseptic but satisfactory",
"overpriced"); the summer terrace is "pleasant."

Café Les Deux Magots ◗⑤ · · · · · 10 | 18 | 11 | fr223
6, place St-Germain-des-Prés, 6ᵉ (St-Germain-des-Prés),
01 45 48 55 25

■ "The spirit of the Left Bank" pervades this "legendary"
and "unavoidable" cafe in Saint-Germain-des-Prés where
Sartre and de Beauvoir used to linger; most "come here
for a drink and to talk, not eat", and even at that some find
it "ridiculously expensive", but it's definitely a "place to
be seen"; insiders recommend "breakast on the terrace in
summer" to avoid the "tourist crush" later on.

Café Louis Philippe · · · · · · · · ▽ 13 | 13 | 14 | fr200
66, Quai de l'Hôtel de Ville, 4ᵉ (Pont Marie), 01 42 72 29 42

■ This "romantic spot next to the Seine" on the edge of the
Marais "hasn't changed much in 20 years"; it still serves
"good" bistro cooking at easy prices in the upstairs dining
room or on the "appealing", if sometimes "noisy", terrace.

Café Marly ◗⑤ · · · · · · · · · · · · 11 | 23 | 11 | fr221
93, rue de Rivoli, 1ᵉʳ (Louvre/Palais-Royal), 01 49 26 06 60

■ One of the "most beautiful settings in Paris", the Louvre,
explains why the Costes brothers' "chic" French is a
"magical place" for fans who say "long waits", "indifferent"
waiters and "mediocre" food don't matter given the stylish
dining rooms and the terrace's view of I.M. Pei's pyramid; it's
a "people-watching" paradise and "lovely early or late."

Café Pancrace · · · · · · · · · · · · ▽ 13 | 11 | 11 | fr195
38, rue d'Aguesseau, Boulogne-Billancourt (Boulogne
Jean Jaurès), 01 46 05 01 93

■ This French "off the beaten" path caters mainly to
young locals and reminds respondents of the "'20s and '30s";
most like its "traditional" fare based on seasonal ingredients,
"pleasant" service and setting, declaring "this is what a
restaurant should be, and there aren't enough of them."

Café Runtz ◑   15 16 15 fr218
16, rue Favart, 2ᵉ (Richelieu-Drouot), 01 42 96 69 86
■ Near the Drouot auction house, this Alsatian brasserie is rated among "the neighborhood's best" by those who like its "solid" cuisine, old-fashioned decor, "charming" proprietor in typical Alsatian dress and "warm" service; a few grumble about the "limited" wine list.

Cafetière (La)   15 14 13 fr249
21, rue Mazarine, 6ᵉ (Odéon), 01 46 33 76 90
☑ For admirers, this Franco-Italian standby near the Odéon ranks among the city's "most original Italians", offering "refined" cuisine in a "cozy" setting decorated with old-fashioned coffeepots; foes call it "nothing exceptional" and "pricey for what you get", but they're outvoted; "friendly" service is a plus.

Caffé Bini   12 10 11 fr201
34, rue des Saints-Pères, 7ᵉ (St-Germain-des-Prés), 01 42 84 28 95
☑ This Tuscan cafe/bar behind Saint-Germain-des-Prés featuring Italian-style sandwiches is "overrated" according to some surveyors who also grumble about "too much money for too much bread"; but others say it works for a "fast lunch" or late snack "after the movies."

Caffé Foy (Le)   ▽ 13 12 15 fr214
165, rue St-Honoré, 1ᵉʳ (Palais-Royal), 01 42 86 06 96
☑ Regulars appreciate the proprietor's "warm" reception, "service with a smile" and the tranquil terrace at this historic literary cafe overlooking the Comédie Française at Palais-Royal; most find the brasserie fare "correct" and "the prices right", but a few say "uninteresting"; the lively crowd and views of this busy crossroads through large windows outshine the nondescript decor.

Cagouille (La) ⬛   19 9 13 fr324
10, place C. Brancusi, 14ᵉ (Gaîté), 01 43 22 09 01
☑ "Excellent", "fresh" fish "to die for" served in a "glacial", "uncomfortable" setting "to cry for" is the majority opinion on this starkly modern "temple of fish" in a redeveloped part of the 14th district; dissenters call it "overpriced" and "overrated" and blast "student-type" waiters; but "the lovely terrace makes you think you're on vacation."

Calèche (La)   ▽ 14 10 13 fr249
8, rue de Lille, 7ᵉ (Musée d'Orsay/Rue du Bac/St-Germain-des-Prés), 01 42 60 24 76
■ Respondents recommend this simple country French set in an 18th-century private villa across from the Musée d'Orsay for its "excellent value" fixed price menus and "nice" waiters, calling it "pleasant" for a "business lunch."

Caméléon (Le) 17 | 12 | 15 | fr257
6, rue de Chevreuse, 6ᵉ (Vavin), 01 43 20 63 43
■ By most accounts, this "charming" Montparnasse hideaway is a source of "great, old-fashioned" country-style bistro fare served "without affectation" by a "friendly", "attentive" staff; while a few see it differently ("pricey", "tourist trap", "little service"), they're soundly outvoted.

Camélia (Le) S 20 | 17 | 17 | fr419
7, quai G. Clémenceau, Bougival (RER La Défense), 01 39 18 36 06
☑ "Unfortunately, it's a trek" to this elegant Nouvelle French beyond the western edge of the city where admirers give high marks to the creative food and appreciate its "reasonable prices" for the quality; however, dissenters rate the food "fair" and cite "slow" service; N.B. a post-*Survey* takeover by the Blanc brothers may mean changes.

C'Amelot (Au) 20 | 8 | 15 | fr212
50, rue Amelot, 11ᵉ (Chemin Vert), 01 43 55 54 04
■ "The best value" in Paris say enthusiasts of this hole-in-the-wall between the Bastille and Place de la République; there's no regular menu, just daily specials featuring "copious" portions of "grand", "inventive" cuisine enhanced by "easy-priced wines" and the staff's "warm welcome"; despite the "depressing" setting, most call it a "pure joy."

Camille S 15 | 14 | 16 | fr190
24, rue des Francs-Bourgeois, 3ᵉ (St-Paul), 01 42 72 20 50
■ According to respondents, this Marais bistro features "very satisfactory" traditional fare brought by "a-do-ra-ble" waiters in a "typically Parisian setting"; the "fabulous" reception also earns praise.

Campagne et Provence 20 | 14 | 15 | fr263
25, quai de la Tournelle, 5ᵉ (Maubert-Mutualité), 01 43 54 05 17
■ "Interesting" Provençale food and "low-priced" wines please surveyors who say this restaurant along the quais near Notre Dame is a "delight for the eyes and palate", at "reasonable prices"; "you feel transported down South."

Canard Laqué Pékinois ◑S – | – | – | I
34, bd. Bonne-Nouvelle, 10ᵉ (Bonne-Nouvelle), 01 47 70 31 65
It may not be much on decor, but the price "can't be beat" (especially for the namesake dish) at this no-nonsense Chinese in the 10th district.

Cantine des Gourmets (La) S 19 | 15 | 17 | fr429
Le Bourdonnais Hôtel, 113, av. de La Bourdonnais, 7ᵉ (Ecole Militaire), 01 47 05 16 54
☑ Discord runs deep over this fancy French in the well-heeled 7th district catering to 'le tout Paris' and celebs; while some call it "exceptional on all counts" with "excellent", "elaborate" cuisine, others pan it as "pretentious" and "overpriced", and resent the "cold" reception given to "ordinary folk"; ratings suggest fans are in the majority.

Cap Seguin (Le)
12 | 17 | 12 | fr230

Quai le Gallo, Boulogne-Billancourt (Pont de Sèvres),
01 46 05 06 07

☑ This "trendy" houseboat with "a Californian look" serves "unpretentious" French fare to the likes of "ad execs and tourists" enjoying its "marvelous" location on the Seine opposite Mount Valérien in Boulogne-Billancourt; if many rate the food "so-so", the "on-vacation" ambiance and scenery compensate – just don't "fall overboard."

Cap Vernet (Le) ⑤
14 | 13 | 13 | fr269

82, av. Marceau, 8ᵉ (Charles de Gaulle-Etoile), 01 47 20 20 40

☑ "Good seafood" and "yummy oysters" are winners with admirers of Guy Savoy's modern brasserie near Etoile; some object to the "noise", crowded tables (you can "eat out of your neighbor's plate") and "fancy" prices, but most agree it's one of the neighborhood's "best addresses" for fish.

Caroubier (Le) ⑤
▽ 18 | 9 | 16 | fr210

122, av. du Maine, 14ᵉ (Gaîté/Montparnasse), 01 43 20 41 49

■ The "copious" couscous dishes are among the "best in Paris" say fans of this Montparnasse North African, and the tagines (fragrant stews) and service also win high marks; while the setting is simple, enthusiasts simply "love it."

Carpe Diem
19 | 13 | 16 | fr296

10, rue de l'Eglise, Neuilly-sur-Seine (Pont de Neuilly),
01 46 24 95 01

☑ "Good but pricey" is how a majority judges this "intimate" Neuilly French, where "carefully prepared" fare is served in portions that some find "undersized"; a few harsher critics label the food "ordinary", but "very good service" is a plus.

CARRÉ DES FEUILLANTS
24 | 21 | 21 | fr615

14, rue de Castiglione, 1ᵉʳ (Concorde/Opéra/Tuileries),
01 42 86 82 82

☑ "A brush with perfection" rave devotees of Alain Dutournier's "elegant" bastion of French gastronomy between the Tuileries and the Place Vendôme; among the city's top 10 favorites, it's praised for its "accomplished" Southwestern French–style cuisine, "outstanding" wine cellar, "exceptional" tasting menu and "attentive" service; it's "costly" and doesn't awe everyone ("disappointing", "irregular"), but most rate it "one of the best."

Carré Kléber (Le)
15 | 12 | 14 | fr290

Paris K. Palace, 11 bis, rue Magdebourg, 16ᵉ (Trocadéro),
01 47 55 82 08

☑ This "calm" hotel restaurant overlooking the garden courtyard of this dramatic Ricardo Bofill–designed building pleases most surveyors with its "inventive, varied" menu of "good" Provençale cuisine and large wine cellar; however, dissenters find the "modern" decor "cold", the atmosphere "snobby" and say service can be "slow."

Carr's S
9 | 13 | 11 | fr178

1, rue du Mont-Thabor, 1er (Tuileries), 01 42 60 60 26

■ "The city's best Irish" bar say admirers of this friendly spot not far from the Tuileries and the Place de la Concorde, offering better-than-average Hibernian pub grub including smoked salmon and lamb stew, as well as French dishes; with traditional Irish music most nights, it's a good "hangout" and a "fun place to celebrate St. Patrick's day", but wine-lovers be advised: "Guinness reigns" supreme here.

Cartes Postales (Les)
21 | 9 | 14 | fr325

7, rue Gomboust, 1er (Opéra/Pyramides), 01 42 61 02 93

■ "Admirable" Classic French fare prepared with "Japanese inspiration" by a chef from the Land of the Rising Sun merits high marks from surveyors who praise the "original" fish dishes at this "good little bistro" near the Marché Saint-Honoré; it's also called a "good value", but it's thumbs down for the "poor man's" decor.

Cartet ⌷
– | – | – | M

62, rue de Malte, 11e (République), 01 48 05 17 65

If it's "good, old-fashioned" Lyonnaise cuisine you're hankering for, surveyors say you'll find it at this "unknown" but "succulent" veteran "hidden" behind the Place de la République; the decor is faded and "outdated", but the service and price are right.

Casa Alcalde S
14 | 12 | 12 | fr240

117, bd. de Grenelle, 15e (La Motte-Picquet Grenelle), 01 47 83 39 71

◪ A "maximum number" of diners jam into this "tiny" Basque in the 15th near the Motte-Picquet for "excellent" paella and other specialties; naysayers feel "far, far from Spain", but they're outvoted by those who urge "reserve ahead: after five tries, we finally got to taste the divine gambas" under the watchful eye of the "kindly proprietor."

Casa Bini S
16 | 10 | 11 | fr267

36, rue Grégoire-de-Tours, 6e (Odéon), 01 46 34 05 60

◪ By most accounts, this "trendy" Left Bank Tuscan offers "expensive but great" pasta dishes and other "authentic" Northern Italian fare made with "perfect ingredients"; "small" portions may suit waist-watchers among the "snobs" and celebs crowd, but they irk critics who also blast the prices and find the whole package "pretentious."

Casa del Habano (La)
11 | 13 | 12 | fr268

169, bd. St-Germain, 6e (St-Germain-des-Prés), 01 45 49 24 30

◪ For "cigar lovers" "who don't mind the smoke", say surveyors about this Cuban in Saint-Germain-des-Prés featuring "very good meat" along with its famed selection of fat cigars; a few choke on the "high prices" and report "incompetent" service, but others find it a "friendly" place.

Casa Olympe
20 | 11 | 13 | fr273

48, rue St-Georges, 9ᵉ (St-Georges), 01 42 85 26 01

■ Voters are enthusiastic about this "discreet" hideaway "full of charm" near Saint-Georges serving a "delicious" blend of classic and Provençal bistro fare; to admirers it's one of the "best values" in town and "worth the detour if you can get in – Olympe still knows how to cook."

Casa Tina ●🛇🅂
12 | 11 | 12 | fr191

18, rue Lauriston, 16ᵉ (Charles de Gaulle-Etoile),
01 40 67 19 24

🗷 It's "olé olé" for this small Spanish near Etoile where fans flock for "good tapas" and "remarkable ambiance, despite the crowded space"; critics zero in on "noise", "high prices" and a menu which "doesn't vary."

Catounière (La)
▽ 15 | 9 | 17 | fr214

4, rue des Poissonniers, Neuilly-sur-Seine (Pont de Neuilly),
01 47 47 14 33

■ A clientele ranging from Neuilly "preppy types" to "retirees" frequents this cozy, "unpretentious" French that some regard as this ritzy suburb's "best bargain"; admirers appreciate the "excellent" cuisine, "warm" reception and "friendly professionals" who run it, recommending it for "a family outing or dinner with friends."

Caveau du Palais (Le)
13 | 14 | 13 | fr241

17-19, place Dauphine, 1ᵉʳ (Cité/Pont Neuf),
01 43 26 04 28

■ Lawyers hang out at this small, "restful" French tucked behind the Palais de Justice on the Place Dauphine; though a cynic claims "that shows lawyers aren't into food", others like the "whiff of flavors" blowing across its "marvelous" terrace in summer and appreciate its "well-chosen" wines.

Cave Drouot (La)
15 | 9 | 12 | fr241

8, rue Drouot, 9ᵉ (Richelieu-Drouot), 01 47 70 83 38

■ Ideally located near the Drouot auction house in central Paris, this "little bistro" catering to everyone from "art professionals" to "widows" pleases patrons with its "simple", "quality" food and "delicious wines" (chosen by owner Jean-Pierre Cachau) at "bargain" prices; "quick, let's have a meal before the sale begins"; no dinner.

Caves Pétrissans
14 | 12 | 13 | fr258

30 bis, av. Niel, 17ᵉ (Charles de Gaulle-Etoile/Ternes),
01 42 27 52 03

■ Admirers find this "very good little bistro" near the Place des Ternes "serious in all respects – food, service, setting" and, above all, wines, thanks to an "excellent" list featuring "marvelous little" choices to go with "tasty charcuterie"; dissenters say "it's nothing special", but they're outvoted by those who call it a "wine-tasting" "must."

Caves Solignac (Les) _ | _ | _ | M
9, rue Decrès, 14ᵉ (Plaisance), 01 45 45 58 59
There's good value for rustic cuisine at this "congenial"
eatery in the 14th; the food may be on the "heavy" side,
but there's "refinement on your plate", and the vintage-1900
decor of a former grocery with its original wooden counter,
shelves and lamps creates a warm, distinctive ambiance.

Caviar Kaspia ◐ 19 | 17 | 17 | fr453
17, place de la Madeleine, 8ᵉ (Madeleine), 01 42 65 33 52
■ Surveyors shower superlatives on this pricey Franco-
Russian on the Place de la Madeleine where "good caviar",
"quality smoked salmon and blinis" and "excellent vodka"
are served in a "marvelous setting" recalling 19th-century
Russia "in all its glory"; diners also praise the service and
call it "ideal" for a "a late-night" bite after a show.

Cazaudehore La Forestière 🖪 18 | 21 | 17 | fr433
*1, av. Kennedy, St-Germain-en-Laye (RER St-Germain-en-Laye),
01 30 61 64 64.*
☑ "Excellent" French fare in an "idyllic" setting overlooking
a lush garden next to the Saint-Germain-en-Laye forest rates
high with many who tout this "old classic" for a "summer
evening" or Sunday lunch; a few critics say it's "expensive"
and "nothing exceptional" apart from the scenery.

Céladon (Le) 🖪 19 | 17 | 19 | fr413
*Hôtel Westminster, 15, rue Daunou, 2ᵉ (Auber/Opéra/RER A),
01 47 03 40 42*
■ Near the Opéra Garnier, the Hotel Westminster's recently
redecorated restaurant comes up a winner among voters
who love the "chic, discreet" ambiance, lovely setting and
"delicate" French fare served by an "attentive" staff; it
works equally well "for a business lunch or romance."

Célébrités (Les) 🖪 19 | 17 | 18 | fr463
*Hôtel Nikko, 61, quai de Grenelle, 15ᵉ (Bir-Hakeim/
Charles-Michels), 01 40 58 21 29*
☑ Everyone loves the "beautiful" view of the Seine from this
Hotel Nikko restaurant (established by Joël Robuchon some
years ago), even if some find the decor "cold" and the
ambiance "impersonal"; most also applaud the "quality and
consistency" of the cuisine, with special praise for the "good
seafood", but a few feel it's "overpriced."

Cercle Ledoyen (Le) ◐ 16 | 18 | 16 | fr376
1, av. Dutuit, 8ᵉ (Champs-Elysées-Clémenceau), 01 53 05 10 02
☑ At this upscale, "modern" spot on the Champs-Elysées,
famed chef Ghislaine Arabian offers more affordable fare
than at her haute "big brother" upstairs; to many it's a top
gourmet "bargain" with "refined" food and lots of "class",
but critics grumble about "slow", "aloof" service ("unless
you're famous") and find the "spacious" room "lacking in
intimacy"; still, the terrace is "so pleasant in summer."

Chalet des Iles (Le) 🅂   10 | 20 | 12 | fr291
Lac du Bois de Boulogne, 16ᵉ (Rue de la Pompe),
01 42 88 04 69
▨ It's hard to beat the "bucolic" island setting (accessible only by boat) in the Bois de Boulogne, but while this French may be a "dream of romance", the food provokes such comments as "I had a nightmare I went back to eat there!"; "high prices" also draw fire, but "on a beautiful day" complaints fade away.

Champ de Mars (Le) 🅂   14 | 13 | 15 | fr254
17, av. de la Motte-Picquet, 7ᵉ (Ecole Militaire/La
Tour-Maubourg), 01 47 05 57 99
▪ This neighborhood brasserie near the Ecole Militaire proposes "very interesting menus" to locals who also appreciate its "traditional" fare (including oysters), "constant quality" and "good value."

Champs-Elysées Mandarin ●🅂   14 | 14 | 13 | fr376
1, rue de Berri, 8ᵉ (George V), 01 43 59 48 48
▪ Whether they call it a "real Chinese restaurant" or an "improved cafeteria", most surveyors like this Chinese off the Champs-Elysées attracting families and professionals to its "original" setting complete with a large dragon; "fast" service is a plus.

Chantairelle   - | - | - | M
17, rue Laplace, 5ᵉ (Maubert-Mutualité), 01 46 33 18 59
Surveyors love the "country" air that blows through this Regional French offering the best of Auvergne in the heart of the Latin Quarter; "original and authentic" at the same time, it offers "good food" and a "provincial" ambiance to match, complete with a little fountain and the taped sounds of babbling brooks and chirping birds.

Chardenoux   17 | 15 | 15 | fr247
1, rue Jules Vallès, 11ᵉ (Faidherbe-Chaligny), 01 43 71 49 52
▪ This "really pretty" bistro nestled among the narrow streets of a blue-collar district near Charonne strikes most respondents as "a real find" offering "hearty" portions of "well-prepared" food plus "good wines" and a "warm reception"; a few doubters find it "irregular" and "pricey", but they're outvoted by admirers who call it a charming "bit of old Paris."

Charlot - Roi des Coquillages ●🅂   15 | 13 | 13 | fr293
81, bd. de Clichy, 9ᵉ (Place de Clichy), 01 53 20 48 00
▨ Treasonous critics do their best to dethrone this 'king of shellfish', flinging zingers such as "a tourist rip-off", "falling quality"; but loyal defenders say this seafood institution at the bustling Place Clichy is still a good choice for "excellent" shellfish in a "pleasant" setting, though even they balk at the "high prices."

Charpentiers (Aux) S

12 | 12 | 11 | fr232

10, rue Mabillon, 6ᵉ (Odéon/St-Germain/St-Sulpice),
01 43 26 30 05

☑ Opinions diverge on this veteran bistro near Odéon attracting Left Bank intellectuals and tourists yearning for "the real thing"; admirers like its "generous portions of rustic cooking" and "authentic" "retro ambiance", while detractors say it's an "overpriced" "myth" "living off its reputation"; the ayes have a slight edge.

Chartier S

9 | 19 | 12 | fr124

7, rue Fbg. Montmartre, 9ᵉ (Rue Montmartre), 01 47 70 86 29

☑ This big old standby on the Rue Montmartre is beloved for its "inimitable" turn-of-the-century decor (an official landmark) and "congenial" family feel; but it's deemed "more institution than restaurant", with "old-fashioned" "assembly-line" French fare that's called "frankly mediocre"; still, when the "fast-moving" servers total the tab on your paper tablecloth it's a "great bargain", so it's "worth trying once."

Châteaubriant (Au)

19 | 14 | 15 | fr311

23, rue de Chabrol, 10ᵉ (Gare de l'Est/Poissonnière),
01 48 24 58 94

■ Partisans say they serve "the best pasta" in Paris at this Italian near the Gare de l'Est; though some find prices a bit "high", tables a "little close together" and the decor "ordinary" (despite some interesting artwork), fans consider it worth it because they "know about pleasing customers."

Chat Grippé (Le) S

17 | 11 | 15 | fr313

87, rue d'Assas, 6ᵉ (Port Royal/RER B), 01 43 54 70 00

■ Surveyors are enthusiastic about this "congenial" little neighborhood French near Port Royal serving "very good" Mediterranean-accented fare to well-heeled locals, even if some sigh "it won't go anywhere until it gets a face-lift"; "diligent", "considerate" service is another reason why regulars feel it deserves "to be better known."

Chaumière des Gourmets

▽ 15 | 11 | 14 | fr309

22, place Denfert-Rochereau, 14ᵉ (Denfert-Rochereau),
01 43 21 22 59

■ It may be "out of the way" but surveyors say this traditional French at Denfert-Rochereau is "worth the detour" for its "good" food and "tranquil", "quasi-provincial" atmosphere; however, some find it "pricey for what you get."

Chen ◐

▽ 18 | 13 | 15 | fr337

15, rue du Théâtre, 15ᵉ (Charles-Michels), 01 45 79 34 34

■ Near Beaugrenelle on the Seine in the 15th is a manicured mecca for Peking duck that raises the question: "Chen, the best Chinese in Paris"?; a majority affirms that it's "one of the best", even if a few find "the menu a bit limited, especially for appetizers", the prices "high" and the setting a bit dreary at the foot of a charmless high-rise.

Cherche Midi ◗🅂⊄   14 | 11 | 11 | fr233
22, rue du Cherche-Midi, 6ᵉ
(Sèvres-Babylone/St-Sulpice), 01 45 48 27 44

☑ Regulars say this trattoria in Saint-Germain-des-Prés is "authentic and fun", "especially on the terrace in summer"; the "pseudo-Italian" cuisine is "good", and though some cite "too many tables", "arrogant service" and a somewhat steep tab, it still "works fine in a pinch."

Chez Eux (D')   18 | 13 | 17 | fr337
2, av. Lowendal, 7ᵉ (Ecole Militaire), 01 47 05 52 55

■ This "temple of charcuterie" complete with red and white plaid tablecloths near the Avenue Lowendal is ideal "for foreign friends" or anyone looking for real "down-home" Southwestern French cuisine, including "excellent cassoulet", that will sate "hearty appetites" or help "break a diet"; while "nothing extraordinary" and a bit "pricey", it makes for a "pleasant" "big feast."

Chiberta   20 | 17 | 19 | fr503
3, rue Arsène Houssaye, 8ᵉ (Charles de Gaulle-Etoile),
01 45 63 77 90

☑ Near the Champs-Elysées, this sleek French with black lacquered decor has just changed hands, but still serves "high-class" food that impresses a majority of surveyors; naysayers who find it "excellent but boring" and "overpriced for its somber setting" also insist "service must be improved for it to rank among the top."

Chicago Meatpackers ◗🅂   8 | 12 | 10 | fr171
8, rue Coquillière, 1ᵉʳ (Châtelet-Les Halles/Louvre-Rivoli),
01 40 28 02 33

☑ With its miniature train running around the ceiling, this "real American" in Les Halles is a "good place to take kids", "especially Sunday AM"; but "there's plenty of ambiance" (i.e. "noise") and the food is "hearty but not very refined"; cynics say it reminds them "why they left the US."

Chicago Pizza Pie Factory ◗🅂   8 | 12 | 10 | fr149
5, rue de Berri, 8ᵉ (George V), 01 45 62 50 23

☑ "A must for American-style pizza" say fans of this popular place behind the Champs-Elysées; it may be something of a "noisy" "factory", but it's fun for "a dinner with friends" or to enjoy the servers' "birthday dance" performed along with cake and candles; critics find the pizza "a little heavy and not very crispy" and service "slow", claiming "they'd go bankrupt in Chicago."

Chieng Mai ◗🅂   17 | 9 | 14 | fr196
12, rue Frédéric Sauton, 5ᵉ (Maubert-Mutualité), 01 43 25 45 45

■ "One of Paris' secrets", this Thai in the heart of the Monge district wins approval for its "discreet, considerate service", "pleasant" ambiance and "excellent", "very reasonably priced" food; the only hitch: "ordinary decor."

China Club ◑ Ⓢ
12 **23** **13** fr231

50, rue de Charenton, 12ᵉ (Bastille/Ledru-Rollin), 01 43 43 82 02

■ In a setting reminiscent of "colonial" Hong Kong with a touch of "James Bond", this "cozy", club-style Chinese near the Bastille draws "young preppy/trendy types" who call it "snobby but pleasant"; "good cocktails" and the upstairs smoking lounge are keys to its appeal, since some say "have a drink but eat elsewhere" as it's "too expensive for ordinary food" and "inefficient" service.

China Town Belleville ◑ Ⓢ
12 **11** **10** fr161

27-29, rue du Buisson St-Louis, 10ᵉ (Belleville), 01 42 39 34 18

■ This "factory-sized" Chinese in Belleville may strike some as "lacking personality", but its cooking is judged "good" albeit "without great refinement" and its karaoke (more than 9,000 songs!) creates "a fun musical atmosphere, with or without a wedding party."

Chinatown Olympiades ◑ Ⓢ
14 **8** **8** fr170

44, av. d'Ivry, 13ᵉ (Porte d'Ivry), 01 45 84 72 21

■ The decor takes some flak ("makes you want to run away" or "scream") at this standby in the heart of the Chinese quarter, but what matters most to respondents is that it offers "real Chinese food", "traditional and down-to-earth", from a "varied menu prepared with care"; the fact that it's "frequented by Asians" is "a good sign."

Chope d'Alsace (La) Ⓢ
12 **11** **13** fr207

4, carrefour de l'Odéon, 6ᵉ (Odéon), 01 43 26 67 76

■ Choucroute aficionados say the version served at this "solid Alsatian brasserie" near the Odéon is "excellent", though some claim portions are "less generous than in the past"; the atmosphere is "warm", the quality of the meat is "good" and the "delicious seafood choucroute" comes highly recommended, even if "the whole thing seems a little old-fashioned."

Christine
▽ **15** **15** **13** fr267

1, rue Christine, 6ᵉ (Odéon/St-Michel), 01 40 51 71 64

■ Respondents say this little French near Saint-Michel is "perfect for dinner after the movies" nearby; if that isn't a convincing enough argument, there's also its "provincial charm", interior courtyard and above all, "freshly prepared" food served by "considerate" staff.

Cigale (La)
▽ **16** **7** **13** fr233

11 bis, rue Chomel, 7ᵉ (Sèvres-Babylone), 01 45 48 87 87

■ A former chef from Ledoyen is behind the stoves of this "tranquil" French next to the Bon Marché department store in the 7th arrondissement; it's "pleasant if not very modern – a good place to bring an old aunt", but despite the somewhat "sad" ambiance the food is "good" and the soufflés are "a dream."

Clément (Chez) ◐Ⓢ   `10` `14` `11` fr193

17, bd. des Capucines, 2ᵉ (Opéra), 01 53 43 82 00
21, bd. Beaumarchais, 4ᵉ (Bastille), 01 40 29 17 00
19, rue Marbeuf, 8ᵉ (Franklin Roosevelt), 01 53 23 90 00
123, av. des Champs-Elysées, 8ᵉ (George V), 01 40 73 87 00
106, bd. du Montparnasse, 14ᵉ (Vavin), 01 44 10 54 00
407, rue de Vaugirard, 15ᵉ (Porte de Versailles), 01 53 68 94 00
99, bd. Gouvion-Saint-Cyr, 17ᵉ (Porte Maillot), 01 45 72 93 00
47, av. de Wagram, 17ᵉ (Ternes), 01 53 81 97 00

◩ Opinion is mixed on this well-frequented chain of Paris bistros; while many appreciate its "good French food", "fast service", decent value and "original settings", calling them "ideal for groups", naysayers label the "pseudo-rustic" decor "ridiculous" and the food "banal"; on balance, it's "not bad and not expensive."

Clémentine   ▽ `13` `9` `10` fr187

62, av. Bosquet, 7ᵉ (Ecole Militaire), 01 45 51 41 16

■ A "good family bistro" in the 7th arrondissement near the Ecole Militaire that regulars appreciate for its "traditional", "carefully prepared" fare and "intimate" ambiance; admirers call it a "nice discovery for the neighborhood."

Cloche d'Or (La) ◐   ▽ `11` `13` `14` fr220

3, rue Mansart, 9ᵉ (Blanche/Pigalle), 01 48 74 48 88

■ "Night owls" love this French in Pigalle that's "perfect for dinner at any time of night", and others say it also works for a "fast business lunch" in a "warm setting"; critics may label it "overrated", but to loyalists it's still the "best spot in Paris for steak tartare at 3 AM."

Clocher Saint-Germain (Le) ◐Ⓢ▽ `12` `12` `14` fr215

22, rue Guillaume Apollinaire, 6ᵉ (St-Germain-des-Prés), 01 42 86 00 88

◩ There's no consensus on this bistro in the shadows of the Saint-Germain-des-Prés church; some call the menu "inventive and often rejuvenated", offering a "gastronomical Tour de France without ever leaving Paris", while others find "no surprises" here and say "you can leave happy, but also less so."

Closerie des Lilas (La) ◐Ⓢ   `13` `19` `13` fr336

171, bd. du Montparnasse, 6ᵉ (Raspail/Vavin), 01 40 51 34 50

■ Everyone has an opinion on this "lovely" landmark at Port Royal that once drew the likes of Verlaine, Baudelaire, Mallarmé, Hemingway and Fitzgerald; most prefer the brasserie, with one of the "best" steak tartares in Paris, a pleasant if rather "noisy" terrace and a bar where one can "pretend to be a poet"; as for the restaurant, many find it "disappointing", with "mediocre food" at "high prices"; "where have all the lilacs gone?" laments one diner, while another "wishes the new management well."

Clos Morillons (Le)
20 | 13 | 15 | fr317

50, rue des Morillons, 15ᵉ (Porte de Vanves), 01 48 28 04 37

◩ "After a long journey through the narrow streets of the 15th", diners "are well rewarded" by this "inventive" French that admirers praise for its good "marriage of spices and flavors" at "satisfactory" prices; however, a few doubters call the fare too "surprising" ("spices don't always make for good food"), and while some find the setting "intimate" and "exotic", others feel it's rather "sad."

Clovis (Le)
18 | 15 | 18 | fr400

Sofitel Arc de Triomphe, 2, av. Bertie Albrecht, 8ᵉ (George V), 01 53 89 50 53

■ Surveyors say it's a shame that the "good" Contemporary French food offered at the Sofitel Arc de Triomphe near the Etoile comes in "such an impersonal setting" ("impeccable but boring") with service that's sometimes "slow"; some also find it "too expensive", but even so it's deemed "worth trying" and "ideal for a business lunch."

Clown Bar ◖
12 | 20 | 13 | fr185

114, rue Amelot, 11ᵉ (Filles-du-Calvaire), 01 43 55 87 35

■ Tucked between the Bastille and République near the Cirque d'Hiver, this wine bar is famous for its landmarked art nouveau decor featuring clown-themed ceramics on the walls and ceiling; its "homestyle" French cooking is "often successful" and served by "down-to-earth people", but some find it "a little expensive" for what it is.

Club Matignon (Le) ⓢ
▽ 13 | 9 | 10 | fr251

1, av. Matignon, 8ᵉ (Franklin Roosevelt), 01 43 59 38 70

◩ Near the *rond-point* on the Champs-Elysées, this upstairs French doesn't wow everyone ("convenient, not much else"), but supporters say it serves tasty cooking including "excellent" fish at "good-value prices" in a setting that's simple but "light even in winter."

Cochon d'Or (Au) ⓢ
18 | 13 | 16 | fr380

192, av. Jean Jaurès, 19ᵉ (Porte de Pantin), 01 42 45 46 46

■ Near the site of the old slaughterhouses at La Villette, this "very good bistro" serves what many consider to be "the best red meat in Paris" along with "marvelous souffléd potatoes"; if the setting is "a bit tight" with grandmotherly, faded decor, solace can be found in the red Burgundies offered at a "reasonable cost."

Coco de Mer
19 | 17 | 14 | fr251

34, bd. St-Marcel, 5ᵉ (Les Gobelins/St-Marcel), 01 47 07 06 64

■ This may not be the liveliest part of the Latin Quarter, but fans say that what's on your plate makes up for it at this "veritable paradise" offering "excellent cuisine from the Seychelles" served in portions that are a bit "light" but "affordable"; "exoticism guaranteed, especially with the little 'beach'" at the entrance.

F | D | S | C

Coco d'Isles
14 | 7 | 9 | fr236
31, rue Madeleine Michelis, Neuilly-sur-Seine (Sablons),
01 46 40 17 21
◪ While critics claim this Caribbean in Neuilly serves "fake
Creole cuisine", admirers consider it "enticing, if a little
costly", with a "pleasant" reception; service can be "as
slow as in the islands", but "if you have time, it's a delight."

Coco et sa Maison
13 | 13 | 12 | fr249
18, rue Bayen, 17ᵉ (Charles de Gaulle-Etoile/Ternes),
01 45 74 73 73
◼ This newcomer in the 17th where diners "feel right at
home" gets encouraging words from surveyors who find the
"original" decor and "very good" reception on a par with
the "pleasing" French cuisine; some enjoy "hobnobbing
with the show biz types" who can be found here, but others
say that makes for a "snotty" ambiance.

Coconnas S
15 | 18 | 14 | fr300
2 bis, place des Vosges, 4ᵉ (Bastille/St-Paul), 01 42 78 58 16
◪ "The location and setting are the major attractions of this
restaurant" under the historic arches at the Place des
Vosges in the heart of the Marais; directed by Claude Terrail
(of La Tour d'Argent), it offers French cuisine that gets
mixed reviews, but prices are "relatively affordable" and
it's a "charming" place to lunch "like tourists."

Coffee Parisien ◑S
10 | 11 | 9 | fr175
4, rue Princesse, 6ᵉ (Mabillon), 01 43 54 18 18
◪ This "trendy" version of a "coffee shop for nostalgists"
draws plenty of brickbats from detractors who call it a "pale
imitation of an American restaurant" with "bland" food and
"unbearable music", judging it "forgettable apart from the
pretty waitresses"; but others find it "fun for a relaxing
Sunday brunch" or "to drink a Beck's" while "girl-watching."

Coin des Gourmets (Au) S
▽ 17 | 6 | 12 | fr189
5, rue Dante, 5ᵉ (Maubert-Mutualité), 01 43 26 12 92
◼ Given its minuscule setting and ordinary decor, this Asian
in the Monge area has "no ambiance except for the
kindness of the personnel", but its "real", "family-style"
Indochinese cuisine more than "makes up for" its looks.

Colette
– | – | – | M
213, rue St-Honoré, 1ᵉʳ (Tuileries), 01 13 31 55 35
One of the trendiest spots in Paris is this cafe in the
basement of Colette, the minimalist-chic store on the
elegant Rue Saint-Honoré, offering a menu as sleek as the
surroundings (asparagus tart, vegetarian lasagne, a salad
of *haricots verts*) along with 'power drinks'; the light fare
is appreciated by the fashion-conscious crowd.

60

Comptoir des Sports (Le)   ▽ 13 | 13 | 13 | fr193
3, rue Hautefeuille, 6ᵉ (St-Michel), 01 43 54 35 46

◼ It helps to be a sports fan, since there's often a "sports-loving crowd and terrible noise" at this bistro near the Odéon; that said, it's a "rustic, congenial" place for "good", "cheap" food; regulars say "try the chocolate cake."

Comptoir du Saumon Fumé   14 | 8 | 11 | fr222
60, rue François Miron, 4ᵉ (St-Paul), 01 42 77 23 08

☑ This smoked fish specialist is considered "good and simple" by those who appreciate its "fresh" salmon and "heaping platters of refined" Nordic delicacies; but even some who enjoy the food say that "tables are too tight" and find the ambiance a bit "formal" and "cold, like Sweden."

Comte de Gascogne (Le)   21 | 20 | 19 | fr486
89, av. J.B. Clément, Boulogne-Billancourt (Jean Jaurès), 01 46 03 47 27

◼ Though cynics suggest that this source of Southwestern French cuisine wouldn't stand out "if there were other restaurants in Boulogne", the vast majority finds it "divine" if "too expensive", serving "remarkable" food in a "superb" palm-decorated setting.

Congrès (Le) ◐S   11 | 9 | 11 | fr250
80, av. de la Grande Armée, 17ᵉ (Porte Maillot), 01 45 74 17 24

☑ It's "tough to find a table" at this solidly "classic" 24-hour brasserie at the Porte Maillot that's "popular with tourists" as well as "lovers of steak tartare" and "good seafood"; some find the decidedly 1970s decor "old-fashioned" and claim the food tastes best "at 3 AM", but most rate it "decent" and say the reception can be "excellent"; tip: "avoid peak hours."

Connivence (La) S   ▽ 21 | 11 | 19 | fr180
1, rue Cotte, 12ᵉ (Gare de Lyon/Ledru-Rollin), 01 46 28 46 17

◼ This little French near the Place d'Aligre run by a former student of famed chef Alain Senderens gets high marks for its cuisine made with fresh seasonal ingredients from the nearby market, served in a setting with little brick walls that ensure privacy; it offers "total satisfaction" and "excellent value" but "it's very small, so reserve in advance."

Conti   19 | 13 | 16 | fr401
72, rue Lauriston, 16ᵉ (Boissière), 01 47 27 74 67

☑ Run by Michel Ranvier (former chef on the Orient Express), this classy Italian in the quiet 16th district inspires enthusiastic praise from supporters – "excellent", "sublime", "the Michelangelo of Italian restaurants", "great wines . . . perfect" – but also provokes grumbles about "excessive" prices and decor in "need of a face-lift", with some saying it caters to "people who made their fortunes in the '50s."

Contre-Allée S   15 | 13 | 13 | fr238

83, av. Denfert-Rochereau, 14ᵉ (Denfert-Rochereau), 01 43 54 99 86

◪ "The only trendy place on the Avenue Denfert-Rochereau" is one reason why fans appreciate this French with sleek, contemporary decor; they call it "very good, not expensive and fun" with "intelligent" food and a "pleasant terrace", but some are more reserved in their reaction: "better in summer than winter", "overrated."

Copenhague   17 | 14 | 16 | fr352

142, av. des Champs-Elysées, 8ᵉ (Charles de Gaulle-Etoile/ George V), 01 44 13 86 26

■ In the middle of the Champs-Elysées, this Scandinavian is appreciated by most surveyors for its "excellent" salmon, and if some find the first-floor setting on the "sad side", it's at least "comfortable" and dishes like the salmon carpaccio with horseradish make devotees want to "roll on the floor" in ecstasy; stoics sum it up as "very good, but overpriced."

Coq de la Maison Blanche (Le)   18 | 11 | 15 | fr312

37, bd. Jean Jaurès, St-Ouen (Mairie de St-Ouen), 01 40 11 01 23

■ "A country inn in the heart of Saint-Ouen where they don't ration the portions", commended for its "good", and even "very good", Classic French food; despite a few nitpickers who cite slightly "boring, uncreative" presentations, satisfaction runs deep and "the proprietor is so entertaining, it saves you a trip to the movies."

Corniche (La)   – | – | – | I

77, bd. de Courcelles, 8ᵉ (Ternes), 01 42 27 38 97

There's praise for this relative newcomer on the Boulevard de Courcelles near the Place des Ternes specializing in "good" Tunisian-Jewish delicacies; respondents especially like the "Mediterranean atmosphere" and "high-quality" fish.

Cosi ◑S⇢   14 | 12 | 11 | fr96

54, rue de Seine, 6ᵉ (Odéon), 01 46 33 35 36

■ The "made-to-order" panini served at this sandwich shop in the Latin Quarter are judged "very good" and even "the best in Paris" by surveyors who also like the "calm, relaxing atmosphere" and opera music ("vive l'opéra!") playing in the background; it's an "original" formula that "works well."

Costes ◑S   11 | 22 | 11 | fr325

Hôtel Costes, 239, rue St-Honoré, 1ᵉʳ (Concorde/Madeleine/ Opéra), 01 42 44 50 25

◪ The latest in chic dining from the Costes brothers, this hotel hot spot near the Place Vendôme provokes debate: while some bash "mediocre" International fare ("people eat there?"), "arrogant service", "insane prices" and a "fashion victim" crowd, others adore the "people-watching", "sumptuous" rococo-kitsch decor and terrace; middle-grounders shrug "it's an in-place – we've seen worse."

Cote d'Amour (La) ▽ 18 | 14 | 16 | fr298

44, rue des Acacias, 17e (Charles de Gaulle-Etoile), 01 42 67 15 40

■ Set among the many restaurants on the Rue des Acacias near the Etoile, this Classic French doesn't generate much reaction from surveyors, but those who know it give it solid food scores and some even credit it with "the capital's best *pavé de boeuf* served in a dollhouse decor."

Côté 7ème (Du) S 12 | 12 | 13 | fr211

29, rue Surcouf, 7e (Invalides/La Tour-Maubourg), 01 47 05 81 65

◪ "Everything is fine, but nothing's special" is the general opinion on this typically Parisian bistro near Les Invalides; if offers "good value", a "copious, perhaps too copious" prix fixe formula, foie gras that's "not bad" and a pleasant welcome; still some find the whole package a little "boring."

Cottage Marcadet (Le) – | – | – | M

151 bis, rue Marcadet, 18e (Lamarck Caulaincourt), 01 42 57 71 22

Even if some find the neighborhood a "little dark and iffy", this tiny French tucked away in the 18th is worth the trip as the food is "excellent" ("classic but with remarkable finesse") and the setting "lovely"; smokers watch out: some claim "management doesn't care much for cigar smokers."

Cou de la Girafe (Le) 12 | 12 | 9 | fr223

7, rue P. Baudry, 8e (St-Philippe-du-Roule), 01 43 59 47 28

◪ Why is this Eclectic behind the Champs-Elysées "so popular" when the food is "good enough", but "similar to thousands of other trendy places"?; because the ambiance is "hip and young" (so "it's noisy too"), it draws a "beautiful people" crowd and the waitresses are "pretty" even if "slow and nonchalant"; in sum, "the show is in the dining room rather than on your plate."

Coupe-Chou (Le) ◐ S 13 | 21 | 13 | fr293

9, rue de Lanneau, 5e (Maubert-Mutualité), 01 46 33 68 69

■ Nostalgists searching for "old Paris" will find it at this centuries-old private villa near the Panthéon, where the "fantastic" setting, complete with fireplaces and cozy little rooms, is perfect for a "romantic", "candlelit dinner"; some find the French food "straightforward at best" and "a little pricey", but the decor makes up for it.

Coupole (La) ◐ S 13 | 19 | 13 | fr260

102, bd. du Montparnasse, 14e (Vavin), 01 43 20 14 20

◪ Long deemed the "the essence of the Parisian brasserie", this Montparnasse institution, now part of the Flo group, strikes some as having become "a factory" and "victim of its own fame"; but while critics bemoan a "magical place with assembly-line food", calling it "a myth that's lost its soul", loyalists say the "enormous art deco" room is still "infused with history" and "zest", so even if "the rest is only fair", it's "a must", and "a dream for out-of-towners."

Couronne (La)   ▽ 15 | 10 | 13 | fr369
Hôtel Warwick, 5, rue de Berri, 8ᵉ (George V), 01 45 61 82 08
■ Deep inside the Hotel Warwick just off the Champs-
Elysées, this dining room has decor that some find "lacking
in charm", but it's nonetheless appreciated for the "fine
technique" that goes into its French food as well as for
the "good value" of its "well-priced prix fixe menus."

Crêperie de Josselin (La) ●S≠   14 | 9 | 12 | fr135
*67, rue du Montparnasse, 14ᵉ (Edgar-Quinet/Montparnasse-
Bienvenue), 01 43 20 93 50*
■ According to admirers, "the best crêpes on the Rue du
Montparnasse" or even "in Paris" can be found at this tiny
crêperie offering "everything you could want": "warm
ambiance and nourishing food" that's "nicely served";
the only complaints: "they don't take credit cards" and
sometimes the food's "a little heavy."

Crus de Bourgogne (Aux)   15 | 13 | 15 | fr237
3, rue Bachaumont, 2ᵉ (Le Sentier/Les Halles), 01 42 33 48 24
■ "Now this is Paris!" exclaims an enthusiastic admirer of
this French near the Rue Montorgueil on the site of the old
Halles, a "secret address" that fans would like to keep for
themselves ("don't mention it"!); the "90-franc lobster" is a
big hit, the owner is "likable and savvy" and the ambiance
is "entertaining"; in sum, a "great neighborhood cafeteria."

Cuisinier François (Le) S   20 | 9 | 15 | fr286
19, rue Le Marois, 16ᵉ (Porte de St-Cloud), 01 45 27 83 74
■ The dining room may be a little "small" and the menu
"a little expensive" at this French near the Porte de Saint-
Cloud, but diners say that Thierry Conte, trained in some of
France's top kitchens (Marc Menau, Joël Robuchon, La
Tour d'Argent, Gérard Boyer), "makes great efforts" and
produces "original", "lovely results"; it's the "prototype of
the neighborhood standby" with an "extraordinary" wine list.

Dagorno ●S   15 | 13 | 14 | fr303
190, av. Jean Jaurès, 19ᵉ (Porte de Pantin), 01 40 40 09 39
☑ "Where has the Villette of my childhood gone?" wails one
diner nostalgic for the days when the old slaughterhouses
stood near this "very 19th century", "typical brasserie"
specializing in steak; though some complain that the "setting
and cuisine are out of date", supporter say it's "perfect for a
reconciliation with red meat" in a "congenial atmosphere."

Dame Jeanne   – | – | – | I
60, rue de Charonne, 11ᵉ (Ledru-Rollin), 01 47 00 37 40
The new kid on the block in the Bastille navigates a path
between trendiness and classicism, offering sincere French
fare based on seasonal ingredients in a pretty room with
sponged walls done in Provence-inspired tones of red and
yellow; it draws a neighborhood crowd that appreciates
both the good food and the good value of its prix fixe menu.

Dame Tartine ● S
12 | 10 | 11 | fr134

59, rue de Lyon, 12ᵉ (Bastille), 01 44 68 96 95

■ This "simple" sandwich specialist between the Gare de Lyon and the Opéra Bastille is more for "noshing than for eating a real meal", offering "pleasant snacks in a trendy neighborhood"; the tab is painless and it's "good for the price", especially "on the terrace"; even those who judge the food "not great" admit "we like it anyway."

Da Mimmo
16 | 6 | 11 | fr230

39, bd. de Magenta, 10ᵉ (Gare de l'Est/Jacques-Bonsergent), 01 42 06 44 47

■ Regulars keep coming back to this Southern Italian near the Gare de l'Est for its "very kitschy decor" (check out the frescoes and sculpted plaster moldings) and "traditional" Italian specialties; if the service is sometimes sloppy and the pizza doesn't please everyone, fans say the "main dishes are excellent", though "the bill mounts fast."

Dariole de Viry (La)
▽ 21 | 12 | 17 | fr308

21, rue Pasteur, Viry-Châtillon (RER Juvisy-sur-Orge), 01 69 44 22 40

■ Even if some surveyors "feel a bit lost in the middle of nowhere" in this southeastern suburb of Paris, they appreciate this "solid establishment" offering "imaginitive" French fare and "a very good reception" in a contemporary setting that "feels like the provinces."

Daru (Le)
14 | 10 | 12 | fr301

19, rue Daru, 8ᵉ (Courcelles), 01 42 27 23 60

◪ Not far from the Russian Orthodox church near the Place des Ternes, this "little Russian" has admirers who consider it "amusing but pricey", with "authentic" food and an "intimate" ambiance; but it also has a few critics who complain of "falling" quality.

Débarcadère ● S
11 | 14 | 10 | fr233

11, rue du Débarcadère, 17ᵉ (Porte Maillot), 01 53 81 95 95

◪ A "trendy" restaurant near the Porte Maillot with "handsome" decor and rather "loud music" as a backdrop for French food that's judged "not extraordinary" and "uneven"; critics say "you overpay for what you get" – if "they cooked as good as they look, things would be fine."

Délices d'Aphrodite (Les) ●
19 | 11 | 15 | fr193

4, rue de Candolle, 5ᵉ (Censier-Daubenton), 01 43 31 40 39

■ Little sister to Mavrommatis, this "real" Greek is "nothing like the cookie-cutter holes-in-the-wall lining the Rue de la Huchette in the Latin Quarter"; partisans praise its "excellent" food and the "exotic" ambiance on the "pleasant" terrace – "you feel as if you're on vacation."

Denise (Chez) ◐⬛
17 | 16 | 15 | fr245

(aka Tour de Montlhéry)

5, rue des Prouvaires, 1ᵉʳ (Les Halles), 01 42 36 21 82

■ "Unique in Paris" say devotees of this "genuine bistro for purists", open all night in the middle of Les Halles and serving "more-than-hearty cuisine" (tripe, pot-au-feu, boeuf gros sel) at "super value" prices to a "pleasant, joyful" clientele; "it never changes and that's what we like."

Dessirier ◐⬛
16 | 12 | 14 | fr365

9, place du Maréchal Juin, 17ᵉ (Pereire), 01 42 27 82 14

☑ Taken over by Michel Rostang a few years ago, this "satisfactory but expensive" fish specialist near the Place Pereire draws mixed reviews; some say it's "improved over the past three years" and praise its "excellent seafood", while others complain it "lives off its reputation in a 30-year-old setting", calling it "pretentious given average food" and a "gloomy" ambiance.

Detourbe Duret
20 | 12 | 15 | fr288

23, rue Duret, 16ᵉ (Argentine), 01 45 00 10 26

■ Admirers of this "modern, very creative" bistro near the Etoile praise its "refined" food, "romantic" ambiance and "considerate service", and if a few argue that it's "not as good as" older sibling Philippe Detourbe in the 15th, the fact that it's "always crowded" proves that most are impressed by the cooking of this "young chef to watch."

Deux Abeilles (Les) ◐
15 | 14 | 15 | fr158

189, rue de l'Université, 7ᵉ (Alma-Marceau/RER Pont de l'Alma), 01 45 55 64 04

■ A "very delightful tearoom" near the Pont de l'Alma catering to a "yuppie crowd" that considers it perfect for "lunch with the girls"; the desserts are "remarkable", but service is sometimes "slow" and it's "a little pricey for what you get."

Deux Canards (Aux)
17 | 14 | 20 | fr250

8, rue du Fbg. Poissonnière, 10ᵉ (Bonne-Nouvelle), 01 47 70 03 23

■ "You feel you're dining at a friend's home" say admirers of this inn-style French on the Grands Boulevards near the Rex cinema; the owner (a former dentist) is "very likable" as he touts the glories of his duck à l'orange (even "sharing the recipe with his customers"), so even if some find the food "a bit bland", his "enthusiasm" compensates.

Diamantaires (Les) ◐⬛
12 | 8 | 11 | fr207

60, rue La Fayette, 9ᵉ (Cadet), 01 47 70 78 14

☑ "My favorite Greek, even if it's not perfect" exclaims one admirer of this "amiable" Greco-Armenian in the Montholon area of the 9th arrondissement; if "the food isn't brilliant, it's enjoyable" and "good for a change of pace."

Diep (Chez) ◑ⓢ
`18 | 13 | 14 | f288`
55, rue Pierre Charron, 8ᵉ (Franklin Roosevelt), 01 45 63 52 76
■ This "trendy" Chinese off the Champs-Elysées offers "quality cuisine" at prices that can seem "high"; the setting is "sophisticated" to some, "somber" to others, but the menu includes some "really original dishes" plus what boosters call "the best ever Peking duck"; the "welcome is typically Asian: smiles and perfect diligence."

Dînée (La)
`21 | 12 | 17 | f343`
85, rue Leblanc, 15ᵉ (Balard), 01 45 54 20 49
■ Tucked in a remote corner of the 15th near Balard is an "excellent, unknown" French that admirers dub "a little gastronomic jewel"; surveyors praise the "very high-class" fare of chef Christophe Chabanel, who puts "lots of creativity into his cooking", but even so, some find the setting "too stark" and prices on the high side.

DIVELLEC (LE)
`23 | 16 | 19 | f586`
107, rue de l'Université, 7ᵉ (Invalides), 01 45 51 91 96
◪ This elegant restaurant on the esplanade of the Invalides reels in the rich and famous and draws waves of praise for its "excellent" fish: "the summit of seafood", "fantastic", "ah, the lobster"; but low tide washes in some criticism for "monstrously high prices" and a "pretentious" atmosphere.

Domarais (Le)
`12 | 22 | 13 | f328`
53 bis, rue des Francs-Bourgeois, 4ᵉ (Hôtel-de-Ville/ Rambuteau), 01 42 74 54 17
■ The setting is "stunning", in a centuries-old former auction house with a "superb" round dining room in the Marais near the Place des Vosges; "alas, it's noisy" and while the French food is "unpretentious", critics find it "too simple"; but the main draw is "amusing" entertainment (gospel music, cabaret, etc.) in a "unique" environment.

Dôme (Le) ◑ⓢ
`18 | 15 | 15 | f369`
108, bd. du Montparnasse, 14ᵉ (Vavin), 01 43 35 25 81
■ Sartre spent many an afternoon at this "classic, historic" Left Bank brasserie, one of the mythical sites for the postwar Montparnasse crowd; today, "excellent" fish is the star attraction, but while the quality is considered "exceptional", so is the bill: "pricey", "very pricey", "too pricey"; still, it's "a must for fish lovers."

Dominique ◑
`13 | 13 | 12 | f311`
19, rue Bréa, 6ᵉ (Vavin), 01 43 27 08 80
■ "A real Russian" in the heart of the "bustling" Vavin neighborhood behind Montparnasse, where admirers enjoy "excellent salmon and blinis" either at the bar or in the back room; the decor is "warm" and the ambiance "quiet and pleasant", and if some grumble that service is "much too slow", one can always pass the time by exploring the "extraordinary" vodka list.

Dos de la Baleine ⑤
14 12 14 fr186
*40, rue des Blancs-Manteaux, 4ᵉ (Hôtel-de-Ville/Rambuteau),
01 42 72 38 98*
◼ While most diners praise the "good, inventive" French
fare and "easygoing prices" at this restaurant near
Rambuteau not far from the Pompidou Center, a few find it
"uneven" and say the modern "decor is better than the
food"; still, "if you don't expect too much, you'll have a nice
time", especially since the "service is attentive."

Driver's ◗
13 12 13 fr191
6, rue Georges Bizet, 16ᵉ (Alma-Marceau), 01 47 23 61 15
◼ A "fun" "rendezvous for auto fans" in the 16th district that
pleases most with up-to-the-minute bistro cooking that's
"well prepared and generously served", even if the car-
themed decor doesn't get everyone's motor racing and some
complain that the service is "not always Formula One."

Drouant ⑤
20 19 19 fr528
18, rue Gaillon, 2ᵉ (Opéra/Quatre-Septembre), 01 42 65 15 16
◼ The site where the Goncourt jury decides the annual
winner of France's top literary prize, this historic French near
the Opéra "is a name that writers dream about", and so do
many diners; it earns honors for its ambiance ("elegant",
if a bit "stuffy") and "superb" art deco decor by Ruhlmann,
and if the "refined" food strikes some as "a little overrated",
service is "attentive" and the grill room is a "super value."

Drugstore Publicis
Champs-Elysées ◗⑤
6 7 8 fr192
*133, av. des Champs-Elysées, 8ᵉ (Charles de Gaulle-Etoile),
01 44 43 79 00*
◼ Everyone agrees that this legendary pub with '70s decor
and a "prime location" at the Etoile is "practical" if you're in
"a hurry" or looking for a late-night "snack" (it's open till
2 AM, along with the adjoining pharmacy and newsstand);
beyond that, many find "no soul" here, just lots of "noise."

DUC (LE)
23 14 19 fr546
243, bd. Raspail, 14ᵉ (Raspail), 01 43 20 96 30
◼ Praise is unanimous for this "fish paradise" near Vavin
with yacht-like decor and a power crowd: "a real pleasure",
"divine", "best in Paris", "the raw fish is exceptional"; while
"the food is fit for a king, so is the bill" but service is "friendly
and impeccable" and they serve "the best from the sea."

Durand Dupont ◗⑤
10 13 10 fr212
14, place du Marché, Neuilly-sur-Seine (Sablons), 01 41 92 93 00
◼ This "trendy" Neuilly eatery draws "dynamic execs" and
a sprinkling of TV "stars"; the French food is "only fair", but
regulars are forgiving since the ambiance is "fun", the
servers "pretty" and it's "very pleasant in summer" on the
front terrace or inside courtyard; there's a "good brunch"
too, but service sometimes flags: "please, hire some help!"

Ebauchoir (L')
15 | 8 | 11 | fr171

43-45, rue de Cîteaux, 12ᵉ (Ledru-Rollin), 01 43 42 49 31

■ Nestled between Bastille and Nation, this bistro taken over by a former hotel chef offers "well-prepared" "little dishes" that enthusiasts rate "divinely good", especially the "unbeatable" lunch menu; decor critics may point to "worn-out" banquettes, but most consider this a "tiny, quality spot for an evening among friends."

Ecaille de PCB (L')
16 | 11 | 12 | fr346

5, rue Mabillon, 6ᵉ (Mabillon), 01 43 26 12 84

☑ Located near the new Saint-Germain food market, this seafood specialist with ocean liner decor raises the question: "must fish be so expensive?"; the majority of reviewers rate it "excellent" nonetheless, and if some find the setting "cold" others note that the welcome is "nice."

Ecaille et Plume ◑
21 | 9 | 14 | fr325

25, rue Duvivier, 7ᵉ (Ecole Militaire), 01 45 55 06 72

■ Specializing in game and fish, this "minuscule" spot near the Ecole Militaire earns unanimous praise for its food: "remarkable", "grand dining in all simplicity", "original and full of poetry"; the picture cloud's a bit when it comes to the "shabby decor", but regulars say the ambiance can be "charming if the owner adopts you."

Echaudé St-Germain (L') 🅂
▽ 13 | 12 | 10 | fr251

21, rue de l'Echaudé, 6ᵉ (Mabillon), 01 43 54 79 02

■ While no one is shouting with joy over this restaurant catering mainly to tourists, surveyors do have kind words for its "good food", "charming enough Parisian decor" with beams and old stone walls, and "calm, intimate" atmosphere; in sum, a nice "refuge" for "simple meals."

Ecluse (L') ◑🅂
12 | 12 | 12 | fr226

15, quai Grands-Augustins, 6ᵉ (St-Michel), 01 46 33 58 74
64, rue François 1ᵉʳ, 8ᵉ (George V), 01 47 20 77 09
15, place de la Madeleine, 8ᵉ (Madeleine), 01 42 65 34 69
13, rue Roquette, 11ᵉ (Bastille), 01 48 05 19 12
1, rue d'Armaillé, 17ᵉ (Charles de Gaulle-Etoile), 01 47 63 88 29

☑ "A wine bar par excellence" say fans of this chain "specializing in Bordeaux"; some also get excited over the likes of "good foie gras" and steak tartare, while others find the food "ordinary" and the menu "not varied enough" and "pricey for what it is"; still, it works fine for "a light meal or nibble" with a "good glass of wine."

Elle (Chez)
– | – | – | M

7, rue des Prouvaires, 1ᵉʳ (Châtelet-Les Halles), 01 45 08 04 10

This bistro in Les Halles adorned with "old photographs of Paris brothels" draws a clientele of regulars who like its "good cuisine" with a classic accent (*pavé de boeuf sauce marchand*, for example) served amidst "charming decor."

ELYSÉES DU VERNET (LES)   22 | 22 | 21 | f587
*Hôtel Vernet, 25, rue Vernet, 8ᵉ (Charles de Gaulle-Etoile/
George V), 01 44 31 98 98*
■ Alain Solivérès "hasn't finished astonishing" respondents
with his "grand Provençale cooking" served in a "very
romantic" setting under a "beautiful" Gustave Eiffel glass
roof in this hotel near the Champs-Elysées; devotees say his
star is "rising" and he deserves "three from the Michelin
guide"; "if such perfection must be criticized, it's the slow"
service, but that's "understandable" given the results.

Emporio Armani Caffé   – | – | – | M
149, bd. St-Germain, 6ᵉ (St-Germain-des-Prés), 01 45 48 62 15
From the day it opened at the busy intersection of the
Boulevard Saint Germain and the Rue de Rennes in the
heart of Saint-Germain-des-Prés, this in-shop Italian with
modern Milanese decor has been the chicest place on the
Left Bank for the fashion crowd to lunch; though not cheap,
the food's good and service friendly; it's wise to reserve.

Enotéca (L') ●S   14 | 11 | 11 | f248
25, rue Charles V, 4ᵉ (St-Paul), 01 42 78 91 44
▨ Most surveyors enjoy this "excellent" Italian wine bar
in the Marais offering "at last, Italian food that's not just
pizza, but also pasta" along with "good wines"; though some
find the menu "limited" and service "uneven", the ambiance
is "warm" and "authentic" with its open beams and colorful
Murano chandeliers and the bill is "not too costly."

Entoto   ▽ 16 | 12 | 19 | f196
145, rue L.M. Nordmann, 13ᵉ (Glacière), 01 45 87 08 51
■ For "a change of scenery" and flavor, voters recommend
this Ethiopian in the 13th serving "original, good" food in a
setting adorned with lithographs recalling the splendor of
this East African nation; if some say it's "not extraordinary",
most find it "fun" and "exotic", with "attentive" service.

Entrepôt (L') ●S   10 | 16 | 11 | f150
7, rue Francis de Pressensé, 14ᵉ (Pernety), 01 45 40 60 70
■ This restaurant in a movie house behind Montparnasse
draws diners with its "original", "New York"–style movie-
themed decor and "simple" Eclectic-French fare at
"reasonable prices"; even if the food is judged "satisfactory,
but nothing great", there's plenty of ambiance and it's "fine
for a combo movie-and-meal."

Epicure 108   18 | 9 | 14 | f315
108, rue Cardinet, 17ᵉ (Malesherbes), 01 47 63 50 91
■ The setting may be "gloomy" and it's "tough to park"
around the Square des Batignolles in the 17th, but beyond
that "it's not bad at all" for a menu that, odd as it sounds,
"mixes Japanese and Alsatian" inspiration, yielding
"inventive", "good value" fare; enthusiasts go so far as to
gush: "time and space stop, the flavors wash over you."

Epi d'Or (L') ◑

15 | 12 | 14 | fr222

25, rue Jean-Jacques Rousseau, 1er (Louvre), 01 42 36 38 12

■ A "good, nothing fancy bistro" tucked between Palais-Royal and the Louvre that some consider one of the "neighborhood's best-kept secrets"; voters say it's a place to "go with friends" for "very good" Regional French cooking.

Epi Dupin (L')

21 | 12 | 15 | fr240

11, rue Dupin, 6e (Sèvres-Babylone), 01 42 22 64 56

■ A "culinary revelation" is how admirers view this "little neighborhood" bistro at Sèvres-Babylone where chef François Pasteau concocts a "remarkable" "blend of Mediterranean, sweet and sour, and nouvelle cuisine" that's judged an "excellent value"; hence it's no surprise that it's "always full" ("reserve way ahead") and the tables are a little "too close together."

Epopée (L')

– | – | – | M

89, av. Emile Zola, 15e (Charles-Michels), 01 45 77 71 37

According to fans, "quality, amiability and good value" team up at this French with a "tasteful setting" ("ideal for a business dinner") in a far corner of the 15th; as one regular puts it: "we rush there with choice guests and are never disappointed."

Erawan

19 | 12 | 15 | fr246

76, rue de la Fédération, 15e (La Motte-Picquet Grenelle), 01 47 83 55 67

■ It's thumbs up for the "remarkable Thai food" whipped up at this somewhat out of the way outpost near the above-ground métro in the 15th; service is "efficient" and the dishes are "beautifully presented"; "what a shame the decor is so tired."

Escargot Montorgueil (L') ⑤

13 | 18 | 12 | fr323

38, rue Montorgueil, 1er (Les Halles), 01 42 36 83 51

◪ This Les Halles institution is definitely "a must for snails" but beyond that it "lives off its reputation" according to many surveyors; while the "beautiful" setting is a virtual "museum", the food and reception are rated "mediocre" and the service "pretentious"; in short, "it ain't what it used to be."

Espace Sud-Ouest, Chez Papa ◑⑤

∇ 14 | 7 | 11 | fr149

6, rue Gassendi, 14e (Denfert-Rochereau), 01 43 22 41 19

■ Living up to its name, this French Regionalist provides plenty of foie gras, magret, tripoux and the like in a "good ambiance"; there may be "too long a wait", but the reward is "quality food in heaping portions" (including "salads the size of an entire meal") at prices that make it "ideal for students on a tight budget."

ESPADON (L') 🅂   22 | 25 | 24 | fr661
Hôtel Ritz, 15, place Vendôme, 1ᵉʳ (Concorde/Opéra),
01 43 16 30 80

■ "The Ritz is the Ritz" – "the perfection of classicism" typifies the praise showered on this "high-class" hotel oasis on the Place Vendôme; the "consistently good" Classic French fare "is fit for royalty", as is the service and "sumptuous decor worthy of the Sun King", right down to carpeting "so deep you sink in up to your ankles"; if some find it all "too classic", most revel in its "memorable opulence" and say lunch on the terrace is "a dream."

Etoile d'Or (L')   19 | 14 | 19 | fr393
Hôtel Concorde-La Fayette, 3, place du Gén. Koenig, 17ᵉ
(Porte Maillot), 01 40 68 51 28

■ In the Hotel Concorde-La Fayette at the Porte Maillot, this restaurant serves French cuisine worthy of a "grand hotel"; it's handy before or after shopping at the boutiques at the Palais des Congrès and "perfect for a business meal", even if this "gourmet fare is costly."

Etoile Marocaine (L') 🅂   ▽ 15 | 15 | 16 | fr235
56, rue Galilée, 8ᵉ (George V), 01 47 20 44 43

■ Though not far from the Champs-Elysées, diners feel miles away thanks to this Moroccan's exotic decor and "cozy ambiance"; some find the couscous "nothing special" while others call it the "best in Paris", but either way it's served "attentively."

Excuse (L')   ▽ 20 | 16 | 16 | fr261
14, rue Charles V, 4ᵉ (St-Paul), 01 42 77 98 97

◪ A "haven of peace" near Saint-Paul in the Marais with a "pretty setting" that leaves diners feeling "relaxed"; respondents also praise Michel Hache's "refined" French cuisine, but a few find it "repetitive and lacking imagination", as well as "pricey."

Fabrice (Chez)   ▽ 18 | 11 | 14 | fr283
38, rue Croix-des-Petits-Champs, 1ᵉʳ (Palais-Royal),
01 40 20 06 46

■ There's a "young restaurateur to encourage" working in this long, narrow dining room near the Place des Victoires; Fabrice Wolff executes "very fine" and "original" French fare at "gentle prices", offering prix fixe menus starting at 125 francs.

Fakhr el Dine ●🅂   17 | 12 | 15 | fr298
3, rue Quentin-Bauchart, 8ᵉ (George V), 01 47 23 44 42
30, rue de Longchamp, 16ᵉ (Iéna/Trocadéro), 01 47 27 90 00

■ Surveyors find a touch of "*Arabian Nights*" exoticism at the two branches of this "very good Lebanese" serving "very fresh" food including what fans call the "best maza in Paris"; some find the setting "a bit dismal" but say "bravo for the welcome."

Faucher
21 | 16 | 19 | fr434

123, av. de Wagram, 17ᵉ (Wagram), 01 42 27 61 50

■ "Gérard Faucher and his wife warmly greet guests in a pretty setting" at their well-respected French in an affluent residential section of the 17th, where they offer "lovely, original food" served with "efficiency and professionalism."

Fauchon - Le 30
18 | 15 | 15 | fr305

30, place de la Madeleine, 8ᵉ (Madeleine), 01 47 42 56 58

☑ The famed gourmet food store on the Place de la Madeleine gets mixed reviews for its upstairs restaurant: while admirers applaud "excellent" French food that's the "work of a pro", others feel it's "not up to the Fauchon reputation"; still, it's "ideal for a business meal given the location", and if the setting is a bit "dreary" at night, the "garden is pleasant" and there's a "warm welcome."

FAUGERON
26 | 18 | 23 | fr665

52, rue de Longchamp, 16ᵉ (Trocadéro), 01 47 04 24 53

■ Aside from decor that some call "a little old-fashioned", voters find "no false note" at this institution near Trocadéro beautifully run by Henri and Gerlindé Faugeron, "nicely helped out by perfect service and a sommelier who introduces diners to great wines at low prices"; compliments also abound for the "very classic and tasty" French fare, including a tasting menu that's "a moment of happiness."

Fellini
19 | 11 | 16 | fr251

47, rue de l'Arbre-Sec, 1ᵉʳ (Louvre-Rivoli), 01 42 60 90 66 ⓢ
58, rue de la Croix-Nivert, 15ᵉ (Commerce/Emile Zola),
01 45 77 40 77

■ "La dolce vita" at Les Halles or on a quiet street in the 15th; fans tout this duo for "real Italian cuisine" (the "pasta al vongole is delicious") enhanced by a very "Mediterranean welcome"; "simple" and "pleasant" sums it up.

Ferme de Boulogne (La)
16 | 12 | 17 | fr233

1, rue de Billancourt, Boulogne-Billancourt (Pont de St-Cloud),
01 46 03 61 69

■ A "little restaurant" near the Pont de Saint-Cloud "managed by a lovely couple" who create a "cozy" ambiance and offer "tasty" French food at "good value" prices to a subdued neighborhood clientele; they're so keen on "keeping their customers happy" that some say service can be a "little too much."

Ferme des Mathurins (La)
▽ 16 | 12 | 13 | fr248

17, rue Vignon, 8ᵉ (Havre-Caumartin/Madeleine), 01 42 66 46 39

☑ Near the Madeleine, this French immortalized by mystery writer Georges Simenon recalls bygone days, but some find the Burgundian food a little "heavy" and the rustic decor "boring"; still, it's "satisfactory" and "honest."

Ferme St-Simon (La) 18 | 14 | 16 | fr398

6, rue de St-Simon, 7e (Rue du Bac), 01 45 48 35 74

☑ This "good classic address" in a neighborhood full of government ministries is generally considered "excellent", with French food as appealing as the "lovely smile of the beautiful [owner] Denise"; though some say it "doesn't leave a lasting memory" and find the "tables cramped", it's "still a good place for a quiet business dinner."

Fermette Marbeuf 1900 (La) ●S 14 | 21 | 14 | fr298

5, rue Marbeuf, 8e (Alma-Marceau), 01 53 23 08 00

☑ The "sublime" vintage 1900 Belle Epoque setting (an official landmark) is "worth seeing" at this Classic French near the Champs-Elysées recently taken over by the Blanc brothers; alas, surveyors are less enthusiastic about the food ("ordinary", "industrial") and "impersonal" service; still, some find it "satisfactory" and "the setting saves it all."

Fernand (Chez)/ ▽ 15 | 6 | 12 | fr204
Les Fernandises ●

19, rue de la Fontaine au Roi, 11e (République), 01 48 06 16 96

■ "This really rustic restaurant" not far from République offers Norman cooking that earns mostly approval from surveyors, especially the "duck and Camembert cheese aged on the premises"; a few find the "hearty portions of down-home cooking a bit hard to digest", but "it's nice to see that Fernard has finally settled in . . . a man to watch."

Feuilles Libres (Les) 16 | 12 | 14 | fr302

34, rue Perronet, Neuilly-sur-Seine (Sablons), 01 46 24 41 41

■ Partisans "feel comfortable" at this "cozy" spot in Neuilly where the Classic French menu is enhanced by a touch of "inventiveness"; some find the setting a little "dreary" for a "very refined bourgeois restaurant", but it's deemed "ideal for a confidential business lunch."

Filoche (Le) ▽ 17 | 10 | 14 | fr270

34, rue du Laos, 15e (Cambronne/La Motte-Picquet Grenelle), 01 45 66 44 60

■ This "good little neighborhood place" near the Place Cambronne is liked for its "warm welcome and authentic" bistro fare (emphasizing fish and offal); but while the food is generally judged "excellent", some find the "rest just ok."

Finzi S 13 | 11 | 10 | fr245

24-26, av. George V, 8e (Alma-Marceau/George V), 01 47 20 09 94
182, bd. Haussmann, 8e (St-Philippe-du-Roule), 01 42 25 48 04 ●

☑ The Avenue George V branch of this "trendy" Italian duo is a place "to see and be seen" in a "modern, cold" setting where a "general hubbub" reigns and some diners feel "piled" on top of each other as they dig into food that's "not bad, but pricey"; those partial to the Boulevard Haussmann branch claim it's "more pleasant" and serves some of "the best pasta in Paris."

Flambée (La)/Bistrot du Sud Ouest – – – M
4, rue Taine, 12ᵉ (Daumesnil/Dugommier), 01 43 43 21 80
Surveyors say the food's "all pretty good" at this purveyor of
Southwestern French fare in a peaceful corner of the 12th;
though some pan the "inn-style" decor ("old-fashioned"),
the "good value" delights diners as does the "very good
cassoulet" and a menu that's becoming "more varied."

Flamboyant (Le) S ▽ 17 11 15 fr214
11, rue Boyer-Barret, 14ᵉ (Pernety), 01 45 41 00 22
■ Caribbean specialties are the draw at this "good, exotic"
change of pace near Pernety, a location that's "far from
everything" literally and figuratively thanks to "island food
served in a colonial setting"; surveyors also appreciate the
"warm reception" at this "pleasant getaway."

Flandrin (Le) ☾ S 11 10 11 fr272
80, av. Henri Martin, 16ᵉ (Rue de la Pompe), 01 45 04 34 69
◪ "Rolex watches, Lolitas and bourgeois cuisine" is
how some describe this eatery in an old train station in a
fashionable part of the 16th; the brasserie fare is "honest",
but the real draw here is watching patrons arrive "in the
most beautiful cars" and dining on the "sunny terrace
surrounded by pretty girls"; this "cafeteria for the rich"
"wouldn't be half bad without all the showing off."

Flèche d'Or Café S 8 20 8 fr131
*102 bis, rue de Bagnolet, 20ᵉ (Alexandre Dumas),
01 43 72 04 23*
◪ This "moderately priced" brasserie overlooking a bucolic
patch of the 20th district doesn't bowl anyone over with
its food, but that hardly matters since the main draw here
is the "astonishing decor" in a "superb old" train station,
with an ambiance described variously as "sinister",
"marginal", "trendy", "pleasant" and "colorful"; you get
the picture: an "original" place "for connoisseurs."

Flora Danica S 17 15 15 fr319
142, av. des Champs-Elysées, 8ᵉ (George V), 01 44 13 86 26
■ "More casual" but "just as good" as its big brother
Copenhague upstairs, this Scandinavian on the Champs-
Elysées offers "excellent varieties of salmon" and "sublime"
aquavit served by waiters "as placid as icebergs"; there's
also a "delightful indoor garden in summer", but "it's a
shame it's so costly."

Foch-An S ▽ 18 12 15 fr225
*142, av. Charles de Gaulle, Neuilly-sur-Seine (Pont de Neuilly),
01 47 22 96 46*
■ Admirers say this Pont de Neuilly Vietnamese serves
some "extraordinary" food in a setting where "privacy is
preserved thanks to panels between the tables"; what's
more, prices are "reasonable."

Foc-Ly 🅢
14 | 10 | 13 | fr241

71, av. de Suffren, 7ᵉ (La Motte-Picquet Grenelle), 01 47 83 27 12

■ This Chinese-Thai near the Champ-de-Mars prides itself on offering "simple Asian" cuisine including a "very good lemon chicken"; some find the decor "dull", others say it's on the "luxurious" side with "charming service."

Foc-Ly 🅢
17 | 12 | 15 | fr247

79, av. Charles de Gaulle, Neuilly-sur-Seine (Sablons), 01 46 24 43 36

■ "Hands down, the Peking duck is super" at this "simple but good" Chinese at Sablons which boosters regard as "a marvel for the price and quality"; a few say there are others "just as good", but that's not much of a complaint.

Fogón Saint Julien
– | – | – | I

10, rue St-Julien-Le-Pauvre, 5ᵉ (St-Michel/Maubert-Mutualité), 01 43 56 31 33

The city's latest Spanish entry, set in the former home of Colonies on the edge of the Latin Quarter, has a reasonably priced prix fixe menu (tapas, paëlla and dessert) and an ambiance that warms up as the evening goes on; it's one of the best deals to come along this year.

Fond de Cour ◑🅢
13 | 14 | 13 | fr258

3, rue Ste-Croix-de-la-Bretonnerie, 4ᵉ (Hôtel-de-Ville), 01 42 74 71 52

■ The main attraction at this "lively and gay" French in the heart of the Marais is the "pretty" inner courtyard that's "very pleasant in summer"; there's "good traditional" food too, making it an "agreeable" choice, especially for brunch.

Fontaine d'Auteuil (La)
17 | 12 | 15 | fr317

35 bis, rue La Fontaine, 16ᵉ (Jasmin), 01 42 88 04 47

■ A "nice surprise" in the Auteuil district of the 16th say admirers of this French restaurant that manages to be "traditional" at the same time that it displays "remarkable inventiveness"; it's "consistent and pleasant", with a "very homey" atmosphere and good value prices.

Fontaine de Mars (La) 🅢
14 | 14 | 14 | fr227

129, rue St-Dominique, 7ᵉ (Ecole Militaire), 01 47 05 46 44

■ A "picture-perfect but not touristy" bistro near the Ecole Militaire liked for its "family-style" Southwestern French fare, "warm service" and cozy setting with banquettes and copper railings; if a few critics find it a bit "overrated", fans retort "it's a *real* bistro – try it, the owner is charming."

Fontaines (Les)
18 | 8 | 14 | fr224

9, rue Soufflot, 5ᵉ (Maubert-Mutualité), 01 43 26 42 80

■ "The departure of the founder of this very good bistro" near the Panthéon "hasn't changed anything"; the setting may be "ordinary", but the food is "generous" (if sometimes "heavy"), the "quality is consistent" and it's an "excellent" value; "fun" and "likable" sums it up.

Fouquet's (Le) ◐⑤   12 | 16 | 12 | fr365
99, av. des Champs-Elysées, 8ᵉ (George V), 01 47 23 70 60
☑ "More a meeting place than a great restaurant" say surveyors about this "institution" "well situated" on the Champs-Elysées; come to "see and be seen", especially on the terrace, "but don't look for the least gastronomic thrill" from the French food at this "show biz" hangout that's also a "good central location for business lunches"; critics knock "slapdash service" and say "you pay a lot for pretense."

Fous d'en Face (Les) ◐⑤   13 | 10 | 13 | fr198
3, rue du Bourg-Tibourg, 4ᵉ (Hôtel-de-Ville), 01 48 87 03 75
☑ Diners delight in the "big choice" of "amusing" and "original" wines at this "crowded" place with a little terrace on the edge of the Marais, but opinions on the French cuisine are mixed: "delicious", "the food and setting are both enjoyable" vs. "airplane food", "average overall"; still, the atmosphere is "very pleasant."

Francis (Chez) ◐⑤   12 | 13 | 13 | fr324
7, place de l'Alma, 8ᵉ (Alma-Marceau), 01 47 20 86 83
☑ "The location is tops but alas, it's poorly used" say those who claim this brasserie at the Place de l'Alma serves "fairground food at absurd prices" and "isn't what it used to be"; but defenders find it "good" if "nothing special" and everyone enjoys the "terrace with its Eiffel Tower view" – too bad service can be "negligent" and "there are fewer and fewer pretty young things" among the "chic clientele."

Françoise (Chez) ⑤   15 | 13 | 15 | fr293
Aérogare Invalides, face 2, rue Fabert, 7ᵉ (Invalides), 01 47 05 49 03
■ Perhaps "you have to be a legislator" to really appreciate this "classic" (some say a "little old-fashioned") French in the *aérogare* of the Invalides near the Assemblée Nationale; yet even many who aren't part of the government crowd say it's "consistently good", with "simple but high quality" food, a "warm welcome" and "even parking."

Fred (Chez)   13 | 9 | 13 | fr247
190 bis, bd. Pereire, 17ᵉ (Porte Maillot), 01 45 74 20 48
☑ "Since the ownership change, the food is better but there's less ambiance" claim some habitués of this bistro overlooking the gardens of the Boulevard Pereire; fans "like to go often" for its "well-executed Lyonnaise specialties" even if some find them "hearty" but "without surprise."

Frézet (Chez) ◐⑤   ▽ 16 | 8 | 16 | fr259
181, rue Ordener, 18ᵉ (Guy Môquet/Jules Joffrin), 01 46 06 64 20
☑ Not far from the town hall in the 18th arrondissement, this French has specialized in fish and seafood for 50 years, and devotees say it's still "superb for an authentic, good" meal, with "excellent" foie gras to boot; but others see it differently: "it's slipped", "old-fashioned, needs renovation."

Friends ◑S
-|-|-|M

63, av. Franklin Roosevelt, 8ᵉ (St-Philippe-du-Roule), 01 45 63 21 22

In the former Marshal's space near the Champs-Elysées is a stylish newcomer with all the requisite trendy ingredients: neo-baroque decor, model-gorgeous servers, up-to-the-minute music, late-night dancing and food that follows the same format: Contemporary French fare plus touches like sushi; the crowd's trendy too.

Fumoir (Le) S
-|-|-|M

6, rue de l'Amiral Coligny, 1ᵉʳ (Louvre-Rivoli), 01 42 92 00 24

Arguably the most fashionable place to see and be seen in Paris at the moment is this cafe/restaurant facing the western facade of the Louvre; with a handsome interior that's a hybrid inspired by Viennese cafes, Irish pubs and deco-style New York bars, it offers Eclectic contemporary fare like herring in mustard and veal sautéed with sage and shallots; book ahead.

Gabriel (Chez)
▽ 18 | 13 | 18 | fr267

123, rue St-Honoré, 1ᵉʳ (Louvre-Rivoli), 01 42 33 02 99

■ With 36 years of experience under his belt, Serge Boullard knows how to offer "very inventive food and a charming reception" at this French near the Louvre des Antiquaires; surveyors appreciate the "very fresh ingredients and good salads" as well as the "owner's personality, which helps create an exceptional atmosphere."

Galerie (La)
-|-|-|I

16, rue Tholozé, 18ᵉ (Abbesses/Blanche), 01 42 59 25 76

"Too bad it's small and often full" say admirers of this prix fixe French at the foot of Montmartre, offering "light, refined" cuisine in a "sophisticated, intimate setting", all at a "modest price"; "it's good, and people know it."

Gallopin ◑
12 | 16 | 14 | fr263

40, rue Notre-Dame-des-Victoires, 2ᵉ (Bourse), 01 42 36 45 38

■ Facing the Bourse (stock exchange) is this "brasserie whose glory days were way back when"; a few say it's "in decline", but for most its "classic" menu (retained by new owners from Bofinger) is still a "sure bet", attracting "stockbrokers, financial journalists" and others who enjoy being "received like regulars" in an "authentic" old setting.

Galoche d'Aurillac (La) ◑
15 | 9 | 9 | fr245

41, rue de Lappe, 11ᵉ (Bastille), 01 47 00 77 15

☑ Fans find all the flavor and ambiance of the Auvergne in the heart of the Bastille at this regionalist that sates "hearty appetites"; though some grumble that the food "could be more varied" and "isn't always terrific", others say "you eat well here" and the ceiling hung with *galoches* (clogs) gives it an authentic touch.

Galopin (Le)

– | – | – | I

34, rue Ste-Marthe, 10ᵉ (Belleville/Colonel Fabien), 01 53 19 19 55
A "trendy bistro" in the Belleville area "frequented by
theater actors"; while some like its "good, everyday French
food", others find the cuisine more or less "nonexistent",
but the "wines are honest and the prices gentle."

Gare (La) ◗ ⑤

9 | 18 | 10 | fr227

19, chaussée-de-la-Muette, 16ᵉ (La Muette), 01 42 15 15 31
◪ The "unique setting" in the former Passy–La Muette
train station is the main appeal of this "deluxe cafeteria
for hipsters in the 16th"; supervised by Georges Blanc of
Vonnas, it specializes in rotisserie chicken and meats,
and though some find the menu "skimpy" and the food
"ordinary", the decor is "original", prices are reasonable
and the "terrace is tops in summer."

Gastronomie Quach ⑤

18 | 13 | 15 | fr292

47, av. Raymond Poincaré, 16ᵉ (Trocadéro/Victor Hugo),
01 47 27 98 40
◪ Most return enchanted by this Chinese-Vietnamese
between Trocadéro and the Place Victor Hugo: "out of the
ordinary", "best Peking duck in Paris", "some exceptional
dishes"; but not everyone is convinced: "disappointing",
"a little expensive", "impossible to park."

Gastroquet (Le)

▽ 18 | 11 | 19 | fr236

10, rue Desnouettes, 15ᵉ (Convention/Porte de Versailles),
01 48 28 60 91
■ The decor of this neighborhood bistro behind the Porte
de Versailles may be a little "depressing" and the street
"not very appealing", but "it's nice to be coddled there",
especially when "the owner sits down with you to tell you
about the daily specials"; the chef, trained at Benoît,
offers a classic repertoire (calves' kidneys, for example)
including a "good little cassoulet."

Gauloise (La) ⑤

14 | 12 | 13 | fr293

59, av. de La Motte-Picquet, 15ᵉ (La Motte-Picquet Grenelle),
01 47 34 11 64
◪ This traditional bistro at the Motte-Picquet keeps loyalists
satisfied with its "rustic, tasty" eats, served amidst
"appealing eclectic" decor in a "good atmosphere of
regulars"; a few find the "tables too close together" and
claim quality has "slipped a bit lately", but the terrace is
"pleasant on warm evenings."

Gavroche (Le) ◗

▽ 14 | 9 | 13 | fr237

19, rue St-Marc, 2ᵉ (Bourse/Richelieu-Drouot), 01 42 96 89 70
■ "One of the last of the old-time wine bars", complete with
a "chalkboard menu", near the Bourse (stock exchange);
the food can be "heavy" but fans note the "friendly"
reception, "super" Beaujolais, "real" *frites* and "excellent"
beef at a place where "you don't go to be seen, but to eat."

Gaya, Estaminet
17 | 15 | 16 | fr332

17, rue Duphot, 1er (Madeleine), 01 42 60 43 03

■ Behind the Place de la Madeleine, this former annex of Goumard offers "excellent, fresh seafood" to an "attractive clientele" that appreciates the "attentive service" and "original" decor featuring "pretty ceramic tiles"; it's also "nice for a business lunch."

Gaya Rive Gauche
18 | 14 | 17 | fr338

44, rue du Bac, 7e (Rue du Bac), 01 45 44 73 73

◪ Considered "trendier" than its big sister Gaya Estaminet by certain partisans, this seafooder draws waves of praise for its "remarkable" fish and "setting as elegant as the food"; a small critical faction finds it "disappointing for a supposed temple of the sea" and claims "neither the food nor service justifies the price", but they're outvoted.

Georges (Chez)
18 | 13 | 16 | fr302

1, rue du Mail, 2e (Bourse), 01 42 60 07 11

■ Flavorful fare "that tastes homemade" is served at this bistro behind the Place des Victoires with an "appealing, very Parisian" setting featuring a fresco at the entrance and a U-shaped curve of banquettes in the main room; considered one of the city's "best bistros", it's "classically good" with "unpretentious" service that helps to make its "cosmopolitan" clientele "feel good."

Georges Porte Maillot (Chez) ◖ S
15 | 11 | 14 | fr278

273, bd. Pereire, 17e (Porte Maillot), 01 45 74 31 00

◪ A "vigorous survivor from the grand bistro days" with a 1920s aura, this veteran near the Porte Maillot offers "no surprises", just "honest" food including an "excellent" leg of lamb sliced at the table; the main complaint: "too expensive."

Géorgiques (Les)
▽ 17 | 11 | 13 | fr360

36, av. George V, 8e (George V), 01 40 70 10 49

■ "Unjustly unknown" say devotees of Katsumaro Ishimaru, the Japanese chef-owner of this "discreet" French on the Avenue George V who intrigues diners with "exceptional" cuisine inspired by the classical repertoire as well as daily market offerings; the ambiance is "comfortable" though some find it "strangely calm."

GÉRARD BESSON
23 | 16 | 21 | fr569

5, rue Coq Héron, 1er (Louvre-Rivoli/Palais-Royal), 01 42 33 14 74

■ A "standout" between Les Halles and the Place des Victoires, where Gérard Besson (a "great talent") turns "high-quality ingredients" into "inventive, refined" Classic French fare; most rate it "excellent" all-around and appreciate its "discretion", though in this trendy area a few find it "a little boring" and others advise "don't look at the bill, it's indigestible" (the "good value" prix fixe lunch is easier to swallow).

Gérard (Chez)
13 | 10 | 10 | fr216

*10, rue Montrosier, Neuilly-sur-Seine (Porte Maillot),
01 46 24 86 37*

■ Some claim it "used to be better", but this "good" little bistro on the edge of Neuilly still makes locals purr with contentment: "very agreeable", with a "pleasant atmosphere, likable service" and "simple, flavorful" food.

Géraud (Chez) 🅂
15 | 14 | 14 | fr294

31, rue Vital, 16ᵉ (La Muette), 01 45 20 33 00

■ Surveyors salute this French for providing an "enjoyable gastronomic experience" in a peaceful area at the Muette, praising its "very good game in season", "the quality of the ingredients and the kitchen's technique", the wine list and, last but not least, the owner, who is missed when he's not around ("ah, if only Géraud were here!").

Germaine (Chez) ⇆
14 | 9 | 18 | fr108

30, rue Pierre Leroux, 7ᵉ (Duroc/Vaneau), 01 42 73 28 34

■ In an area of the 7th used to steeper prices, this French is a welcome surprise, offering a provincial atmosphere and straightforward fare (brandade, tripe, clafouti) at affordable prices; praise is unanimous for this "real food from a real restaurateur", served in a setting that's "spartan" but "just like home."

Gigot Fin (Au)
▽ 14 | 8 | 13 | fr228

*56, rue de Lancry, 10ᵉ (Jacques-Bonsergent/République),
01 42 08 38 81*

■ "To discover" say admirers of this "unpretentious" Southwestern French specialist in a little street near the Place de la République, serving "homestyle French fare", including what some nominate as "the best lamb in Paris", in a warm setting that hasn't changed since the '20s; a tip from regulars: "be hungry."

Gildo (Chez)
15 | 10 | 13 | fr328

153, rue de Grenelle, 7ᵉ (La Tour-Maubourg), 01 45 51 54 12

▨ Surveyors mix praise with complaints when it comes to this Italian at the Tour Maubourg: "delicious pasta at the price of caviar", "good but cramped", "go there to eavesdrop on your neighbors and eat Venetian-style calf's liver"; newcomers also gripe that the "owner only speaks to neighorhood regulars", but on balance, most are satisfied.

Gitane (La)
13 | 10 | 12 | fr199

*53 bis, av. de La Motte-Picquet, 15ᵉ (La Motte-Picquet Grenelle),
01 47 34 62 92*

■ "What more could you ask of a Parisian bistro?" muse devotees of this spot near the Champ-de-Mars; "nothing, it's that good" is the reply; though not fancy, it's a "likable" place that "resists trends", serving "honest if not always very refined" fare to a "young, lively crowd."

Giulio Rebellato
16 | 13 | 15 | fr325

136, rue de la Pompe, 16ᵉ (Victor Hugo), 01 47 27 50 26

■ "Excellent but pricey" is the consensus on this "trendy" Italian near the Place Victor Hugo; the "warm" welcome and "luxurious" setting inspired by Italy's famous Fenice theater help attract a "show biz" crowd.

Glénan (Les)
▽ 19 | 13 | 19 | fr324

54, rue de Bourgogne, 7ᵉ (Invalides/Varenne), 01 47 05 96 65

■ High marks go to this seafooder serving "always top-quality" food distinguished by "nicely balanced flavors" in an area of the 7th full of government offices; if some find the setting "incredibly dreary", they nonetheless applaud the "refined" food and find the experience "delightful."

Goldenberg Wagram ●⑤
10 | 8 | 10 | fr195

69, av. de Wagram, 17ᵉ (Ternes), 01 42 27 34 79

◪ Critics may blast it as a "terrible excuse" for a Jewish deli, but those "yearning" to "return to the Central Europe of yesteryear" trek to the Place des Ternes for gefilte fish, herring and other generally "good" fare (especially the "magnificent" smoked salmon); "ridiculously dainty portions", "arrogant" service and the decor also take a few knocks, but some tout it for Sunday brunch.

GOUMARD
23 | 20 | 20 | fr581

9, rue Duphot, 1ᵉʳ (Madeleine), 01 42 60 36 07

■ "A memorable meal at a memorable price" is what you can expect at this fish specialist (formerly Prunier) behind the Madeleine; "perfectly prepared dishes made from the freshest seafood" earn praise as do the "very lovely" contemporary decor and "excellent" reception and service; alas, the wines are "exorbitant" and some cite "endless waits"; P.S. "don't leave without visiting the bathrooms."

Gourmet de l'Isle ⑤
11 | 11 | 13 | fr219

42, rue St-Louis-en-l'Ile, 4ᵉ (Pont Marie), 01 43 26 79 27

◪ On the picturesque Ile Saint-Louis, this rustic French with an arched-ceiling, exposed-beam cellar room dating from the 17th-century is "mostly worth it for the decor"; beyond that, comments are mixed: "good value" vs. "for tourists", "so-so."

Gourmets des Ternes (Les)
17 | 8 | 10 | fr253

87, bd. de Courcelles, 8ᵉ (Ternes), 01 42 27 43 04

■ "Excellent, very tender" steaks, including one of the "best *pièces de boeuf* in Paris", are the draw at this old-fashioned bistro near the Place des Ternes catering to well-heeled locals and the occasional celeb; but even some fans beef about the owner's "moods."

Graindorge
20 | 13 | 15 | f310
15, rue de l'Arc de Triomphe, 17ᵉ (Charles de Gaulle-Etoile), 01 47 54 00 28
■ This tiny spot on an obscure street near the Etoile (its predecessor was called "The Unfindable") is "one of tomorrow's greats" according to admirers of its "refined Flemish cuisine" enhanced by "a wide choice of beers", served amidst 1930s decor by an "efficient, friendly" staff; regulars say you "feel good and eat well" here, recommending it for a "tête-à-tête or quiet business lunch."

Grand Café Capucines (Le) ◗ S
13 | 17 | 14 | f276
4, bd. des Capucines, 9ᵉ (Opéra), 01 43 12 19 00
☑ While everyone enjoys the "fabulous" Belle Epoque decor and "Parisian" (albeit "touristy") ambiance at this fashionable cafe in central Paris, they sour a bit on the French food: "on the decline", "overpriced"; it's "ideal after the theater" or Opéra nearby, but "you pay for the location."

Grand Chinois (Le) ◗ S
15 | 10 | 14 | f280
6, av. de New York, 16ᵉ (Alma-Marceau), 01 47 23 98 21
■ Most surveyors like the "good quality" traditional cuisine offered at this Chinese overlooking the Seine near Alma; some complain that the "location is noisy" and the ambiance "gloomy", but "smiling" waiters help compensate.

Grand Colbert (Le) ◗ S
13 | 19 | 15 | f263
2, rue Vivienne, 2ᵉ (Bourse), 01 42 86 87 88
■ This brasserie in the 18th-century Passage Vivienne near the Place des Victoires is famed for its "beautiful" old-fashioned decor that "corresponds to what foreigners think a French restaurant should look like"; the food is "honest" though "not exceptional", but "it's worth a visit for the atmosphere" and "ideal for a late-night steak tartare"; N.B. there's been a post-*Survey* change of owners.

Grande Cascade (La) S
20 | 25 | 20 | f542
Bois de Boulogne, allée de Longchamp, 16ᵉ (Porte d'Auteuil), 01 45 27 33 51
■ "A romantic dream" is how smitten surveyors view this "magical (especially in summer)" Napoleon III dining room in the middle of the Bois de Boulogne; while the setting outscores the French food, voters report a "marked improvement" since the arrival of an Alain Ducasse protégé, who has added a Riviera touch to the menu; it's lovely "for celebrations", but note that "prices are as lofty as the decor."

Grandes Marches (Les) ◗ S
13 | 14 | 15 | f297
6, place de la Bastille, 12ᵉ (Bastille), 01 43 42 90 32
■ "Convenient after an evening at the Opéra Bastille" next door, this "preppy, pricey" brasserie is a good spot to order "steak tartare and watch the stars"; it's "pleasant, if nothing more", with "superb oysters" and "very efficient service."

Grand Louvre (Le) **S** | 13 | 16 | 14 | fr298

*Musée du Louvre, under the pyramid, 1er (Palais-Royal),
01 40 20 53 41*

◪ Some are struck by the dichotomy between "Jean-Michel Wilmotte's cold decor and the warmth of the Southwestern French cuisine" at this restaurant under the pyramid at the Louvre; critics cite "ordinary food given the price", but others find it "a haven of relaxation in a luxurious ambiance."

GRAND VÉFOUR (LE) | 25 | 28 | 24 | fr681

17, rue de Beaujolais, 1er (Palais-Royal), 01 42 96 56 27

■ There's thunderous applause for this history-infused Classic French under the arches of the Palais-Royal; it's "a celebration on the plate, in the glass, for the eyes", with "mind-blowing Directoire decor" that's among the "most beautiful in Paris" (with ratings to match) and "superb" food by Guy Martin ("a great, a very great, chef"); despite a few reservations about "crowded" tables and the "formal" welcome, it's deemed a "gastronomic summit" and "a must, if you're ready to pay the price."

Grand Venise (Le) | 21 | 15 | 18 | fr454

171, rue de la Convention, 15e (Convention), 01 45 32 49 71

■ Everyone is happy with the "delicious" food served at this Italian with a "very floral" setting in the heart of the 15th, where "Mama turns herself inside out to satisfy your every whim"; but some diners get queasy from the bill: "extravagant", "crazy", "out of sight", "too much!"

Grange Batelière (A la) | 15 | 11 | 12 | fr279

*16, rue de la Grange Batelière, 9e (Richelieu-Drouot),
01 47 70 85 15*

■ With "inventive" French cuisine that represents "a happy marriage between modernism and tradition" and an authentic bistro setting dating back to 1876, this restaurant near the Drouot auction house in central Paris gets positive feedback from surveyors; regulars especially appreciate the "comfortable banquette in back" and the "lovely wine list."

Grenadin (Le) | 19 | 12 | 15 | fr399

44-46, rue de Naples, 8e (Villiers), 01 45 63 28 92

■ Respondents salute the "search for new flavors" evident in the Contemporary French cuisine of Patrick Cirotte, who dishes up the likes of melon and cucumber gazpacho and rack of lamb aux girolles in this space located between Villiers and the Parc Monceau; admirers call it "the best without pretension", even if it is a "little pricey."

Grenier de Notre Dame (Le) **S** ▽ | 15 | 16 | 18 | fr135

18, rue de la Bûcherie, 5e (St-Michel/Notre-Dame), 01 43 29 98 29

■ Aficionados of what's fresh and green call this "one of the best Vegetarians in Paris" and a good place to know about in the "touristy" area of Saint-Michel; what's more, it's "wonderfully friendly."

Grille (La)
▽ | 19 | 16 | 16 | fr245

80, rue du Fbg. Poissonnière, 10ᵉ (Poissonnière), 01 47 70 89 73
■ It's easy to spot the historic facade of this "very good" bistro in the 10th arrondissement where the wrought ironwork is key to the decor; respondents especially like its "excellent turbot in beurre blanc" sauce, "very good" value and owner (Geneviève Cullère) with "quite a personality."

Grille St-Honoré (A la)
14 | 9 | 13 | fr298

15, place du Marché St-Honoré, 1ᵉʳ (Pyramides/Tuileries), 01 42 61 00 93
■ A "well-run" "little jewel" on the edge of the new Saint-Honoré market serving "very good" French cuisine that successfully mixes "tradition and innovation"; some find the setting a little "dreary", but there's a charming terrace in summer and the "game in season is super."

Grizzli (Le)
15 | 11 | 13 | fr197

7, rue St-Martin, 4ᵉ (Châtelet/Hôtel-de-Ville), 01 48 87 77 56
■ Near the Pompidou Center, this "archetype of a Parisian bistro" boasts a pleasant terrace and is commended for its "good" service and food, not to mention its "moderate" prices; punsters say that in spite of the name it's a "gentle bear" and recommend it as a place "to try with good friends."

Guinguette de Neuilly (La) **S**
11 | 13 | 11 | fr234

12, bd. Georges Seurat, Neuilly-sur-Seine (Porte Maillot), 01 46 24 25 04
◪ "Dining outdoors in summer" on the edge of the Seine is the main appeal of this French on the Ile de la Jatte; the food "isn't brilliant", but the "advertising" execs and other "young, trendy" types who come here like its "warm", "friendly" ambiance, especially when paying "with a corporate credit card."

Guirlande de Julie (La) **S**
14 | 16 | 13 | fr277

25, place des Vosges, 3ᵉ (St-Paul), 01 48 87 94 07
■ Given "its location" under the historic arcades of the Place des Vosges and its bloodlines (it's under the aegis of Claude Terrail of La Tour d'Argent), this French is deemed a "very good value"; the "charm of the decor and of the food" complement each other say fans who find it "ideal in summer on the big terrace" and also satisfying in winter: "a good pot-au-feu – life could be worse."

GUY SAVOY
26 | 19 | 23 | fr695

18, rue Troyon, 17ᵉ (Charles de Gaulle-Etoile), 01 43 80 40 61
■ A "summit of nouvelle cuisine" exclaim admirers of Guy Savoy's flagship, located not far from the Etoile, where each meal is "a new voyage towards surprising flavors" concocted by a "first-class" chef; a few critics find it "overrated", and even some supporters are indifferent to the "seen-everywhere" decor, but for the majority it's a "marvel" and "one of Paris' greats."

Hammam Café ◗ⓈＳ

$\triangledown$ | 11 | 17 | 11 | fr198

4, rue des Rosiers, 4ᵉ (St-Paul), 01 42 78 04 45

■ For a "return to one's roots", regulars recommend this legendary and spectacular former bathhouse on the Rue des Rosiers, now a high-tech cafe serving North African and Central European fare in a "convivial" ambiance; it's also a "pleasant place to have a drink" and soak up the neighborhood atmosphere, with occasional entertainment as added enticement.

Hangar (Le) ◗Ⓔ⌦

18 | 13 | 15 | fr226

12, impasse Berthaud, 3ᵉ (Rambuteau), 01 42 74 55 44

■ "Off the beaten path" (hidden behind the Pompidou Center on a crooked street) but "worth the effort to find", since this French is filled with "pretty women, appealing wines" and, most of all, "culinary discoveries" thanks to a half-inventive, half-familiar menu marked by "nice little touches"; the nearby area may be trendy but the ambiance is "tranquil" and "unpretentious."

Hédiard

15 | 14 | 14 | fr283

21, place de la Madeleine, 8ᵉ (Madeleine), 01 43 12 88 99

■ On the second floor of the famed gourmet store on the Place de la Madeleine, this French "exudes class, even in the lunch-hour crush"; it offers "original combinations of flavors" (though some dishes can be "a bit heavy") in a "surprising", rather modern setting; a few say it's "likable for lunch, dull for dinner", but valet parking is a plus.

Hippopotamus

9 | 7 | 10 | fr170

29, rue Berger, 1ᵉʳ (Halles), 01 45 08 00 29
1, bd. Capucines, 2ᵉ (Opéra), 01 47 42 75 70
1, bd. Beaumarchais, 4ᵉ (Bastille), 01 44 61 90 40
9, rue Lagrange, 5ᵉ (Maubert), 01 43 54 13 99
119, bd. Montparnasse, 6ᵉ (Vavin), 01 43 20 37 04
5, bd. Batignolles, 8ᵉ (Place de Clichy), 01 43 87 85 15
6, av. Franklin Roosevelt, 8ᵉ (Franklin Roosevelt), 01 42 25 77 96
20, rue Quentin-Bauchart, 8ᵉ (George V), 01 47 20 30 14
42, av. Champs-Elysées, 8ᵉ (Franklin Roosevelt), 01 53 83 94 50
46, av. Wagram, 8ᵉ (Ternes), 01 46 22 13 96
8, bd. St-Denis, 10ᵉ (Strasbourg-St-Denis), 01 53 38 80 28
27, rue Dunkerque, 10ᵉ (Gare du Nord), 01 48 78 29 26
68, bd. Montparnasse, 14ᵉ (Montparnasse), 01 40 64 14 94
4, rue Louis Armand, 15ᵉ (Balard), 01 53 78 10 27
12, av. Maine, 15ᵉ (Montparnasse), 01 42 22 36 75
2, place de la Défense (La Grand Arche), 01 46 92 13 75

◪ Everyone has an opinion on this ubiquitous chain for carnivores: fans say it's "a sure bet" for a "good choice of meats" and "the best tartare in Paris", calling it "well run" and "perfect for kids", with "quick" service and "flexible hours"; critics retort: "industrial", "tacky", "enough to make you become a vegetarian", "no privacy possible"; on balance, it's affordable and "gives you what you ask of it", but it's wise to "avoid peak hours."

Hôtel du Nord ⑤

∇ | 8 | 12 | 9 | fr233 |

102, quai de Jemmapes, 10ᵉ (Jacques-Bonsergent), 01 40 40 78 78

◪ The main draws are "the name" and the atmosphere (the film of the same name by Marcel Carné was filmed here), since the traditional French fare served in this cafe/restaurant behind the canal Saint-Martin doesn't arouse much comment from surveyors; musical entertainment on some nights and the terrace in summer are pluses.

Huîtrier (L') ⑤

| 16 | 9 | 13 | fr246 |

16, rue Saussier Leroy, 17ᵉ (Ternes), 01 40 54 83 44

■ "Go to gorge on oysters" exhort regulars of this seafooder behind the Place des Ternes; if some say the wood-walled setting "lacks warmth", the "freshness" of the "good shellfish" and other aquatic fare more than makes up for it; what's more, prices are "reasonable."

Hulotte (La)

| – | – | – | M |

29, rue Dauphine, 6ᵉ (Odéon/Pont Neuf), 01 46 33 75 92

"Time flies, La Hulotte remains", tucked into the Rue Dauphine behind Odéon; this "delightful" French, "simple and classic", delivers food deserving of the same praise (andouillette, filet of lamb in tarragon sauce, chocolate mousse) and offers "very good value as well as ambiance."

I Golosi ◑

| 17 | 10 | 14 | fr224 |

6, rue de la Grange Batelière, 9ᵉ (Richelieu-Drouot/Rue Montmartre), 01 48 24 18 63

■ "A young Italian full of talent" behind the Grands Boulevards and the Drouot auction house that "constantly renews its cuisine" and offers a "picture-perfect welcome"; the two-floor setting isn't to everyone's liking ("original" vs. "a notch below"), but the place "deserves to be known" for its "refined" food (including some of "the best risotto in Paris") and "good" Italian wines.

Il Barone ◑⑤

| 16 | 9 | 14 | fr211 |

5, rue Léopold Robert, 14ᵉ (Raspail/Vavin), 01 43 20 87 14

■ This "quality" Italian in a quiet corner of the 14th earns praise for its "good choice of pasta, varied antipasto" and "charming and roguish (sometimes too much so) waiters", which might explain the sometimes "slow pace" of service; it's "one of the last Italians that still serves sabayon" and regulars advise "always choose the back room."

Il Carpaccio ⑤

| 15 | 15 | 15 | fr467 |

Hôtel Royal-Monceau, 37, av. Hoche, 8ᵉ (Charles de Gaulle-Etoile), 01 42 99 98 90

■ In the posh Royal-Monceau hotel is what some call "the best Italian in Paris"; the food is deemed "excellent" and if the "prices are too high", you're paying for a "rare" experience: "Italy in Paris."

Il Cortile
14 | 15 | 13 | fr288

*Hôtel Castille, 37, rue Cambon, 1er (Concorde/Madeleine),
01 44 58 45 67*

◪ Endowed with a "sumptuous" patio in the Hôtel Castille
between the Concorde and the Madeleine, this Italian
gets mixed reviews; some applaud a "good sampling of
Italian food", while others find it a "touch pretentious"; but it
was recently revamped by Alain Ducasse, and the whole
package is "good" enough to have earned a Michelin star.

Iles Marquises (Aux)
16 | 12 | 13 | fr314

15, rue de la Gaîté, 14e (Montparnasse-Bienvenue), 01 43 20 93 58

◪ The original decor complete with marine frescoes may
not be "on a par with the food (copious) and the reception
(charming)", but the "excellent fish is worth the visit" to
this place "full of character" "sandwiched between the
theaters and sex shops" of old Montparnasse; still, some
complain that prices are "too high for the quality."

Iles Philippines (Aux) ◑
▽ 14 | 11 | 15 | fr216

9, rue de Pontoise, 5e (Maubert-Mutualité), 01 43 29 39 00

◼ Near the quais on a little street in the 5th, this Filipino
pleases those who know it with its "exquisite flavors",
enhanced by colorful decor that makes for a "calm,
refreshing" ambiance, especially in summer.

Il Ristorante
16 | 14 | 14 | fr288

22, rue Fourcroy, 17e (Courcelles/Ternes), 01 47 63 34 00

◪ "Here's a real Italian" say admirers of this ristorante in
a posh residential street behind the Parc Monceau; some
find it "uneven" but dishes like the "Venetian-style calamari
are unique" and service is "simple, fast and friendly."

Il Vicolo ◑🅂
▽ 19 | 11 | 14 | fr226

*8, rue de Jouy, 4^e (Hôtel-de-Ville/Pont Marie/St-Paul),
01 42 78 38 86*

◼ "A young Italian chef" whips up "inventive" food that
draws a trendy crowd to this "very neat" setting in the
Marais; come summer it's "delightful in the garden" and in
any season the reception and service are "wonderful."

Impatient (L')
18 | 12 | 15 | fr220

14, passage Geffroy-Didelot, 17^e (Villiers), 01 43 87 28 10

◼ In a narrow passageway behind Villiers is a "pearl to
be discovered" for its "inventive, surprising" French food
and "cozy, intimate ambiance"; enthusiasts call it a "best
value" and say "it deserves to go places because the chef
likes what he does too much not to succeed."

Inagiku
– | – | – | M

14, rue de Pontoise, 5e (Maubert-Mutualité), 01 43 54 70 07

This Japanese restaurant on the slopes below the Panthéon
offers a classic selection of sushi and sashimi, but its
specialty is teppanyaki (food cooked on iron skillets) and
"when the chef works in front of you, it tastes even better."

Indiana Café ◗ ⑤
7 9 7 fr157

*72, bd. du Montparnasse, 14ᵉ (Montparnasse-Bienvenue),
01 43 35 02 34*

◪ Aficionados of Tex-Mex cuisine rate the version served at this Montparnasse eatery "mediocre" – ditto the "uneven" service that "needs work"; still, the atmosphere is "young" and "pleasant" (albeit "noisy and smoky") and it's handy before or after a "night at the movies" nearby.

Indra ◗
17 19 16 fr307

*10, rue du Commandant Rivière, 8ᵉ (St-Philippe-du-Roule),
01 43 59 46 40*

◼ Just behind Saint-Philippe-du-Roule is "a magic carpet that will transport you directly to India"; considered by many diners to be "the best Indian in Paris", it's appreciated for its "splendid" if slightly "cold" decor and "refined" cooking, even if prices are relatively high and service often "stuffy."

Isami ⑤
▽ 22 9 16 fr283

4, quai d'Orléans, 4ᵉ (Pont Marie), 01 40 46 06 97

◼ On the picturesque Ile Saint-Louis, this "excellent" Japanese is "simple and welcoming"; regulars say it's "currently one of the best sushi places around" and offers "good value for the money", so heed this tip from those in the know: "book ahead – it's very small."

Issé
22 12 14 fr355

*56, rue Ste-Anne, 2ᵉ (Palais-Royal/Quatre-Septembre),
01 42 96 67 76*

◼ One of the first Japanese restaurants to open around the Opéra has maintained its original chic in the face of a profusion of competitors; popular with many Japanese locals, including the designer Kenzo, it doesn't make much of an impression with its "banal" decor but leaves diners with a "good memory" of its food.

Jacky (Chez)
– – – M

109, rue du Dessous-des-Berges, 13ᵉ (Nationale), 01 45 83 71 55
There's some "very good cooking" to be had at this rustic auberge in the middle of Chinatown in the 13th; though few respondents commented, those who did appreciate the traditional French fare and "professional service."

JACQUES CAGNA
22 20 20 fr581

*14, rue des Grands-Augustins, 6ᵉ (Odéon/St-Michel),
01 43 26 49 39*

◼ This "temple of gastronomy" may have lost its second Michelin star, but that doesn't matter to enthusiastic surveyors who pronounce it practically "perfect" with "refined" French food and "marvelous decor" in a 17th-century house in Saint-Germain; while the prix fixe lunch menu is a deal, "good but expensive" remains the prevailing opinion.

Jacques Mélac
14 | 13 | 13 | fr180

42, rue Léon Frot, 11ᵉ (Charonne), 01 43 70 59 27

■ Near the Bastille, this "real neighborhood wine bar" offers "good value for the money" and a "really pleasant" ambiance; there's a large number of "well-chosen wines" to sample while enjoying the "rustic" French regional cooking and "listening to the owner's charming stories."

JAMIN
25 | 20 | 23 | fr665

32, rue de Longchamp, 16ᵉ (Trocadéro), 01 45 53 00 07

■ "The former temple of Robuchon is magnificently run by Benoît Guichard", whose French cuisine is the product of an "impeccable technique that is not without creativity"; "all is luxe, calme and volupté" at this dining room between Trocadéro and the Etoile catering to a cosseted clientele that doesn't seem to mind if the service is "slightly uptight" and prices are high.

Janou (Chez) ◖⑤≠
▽ 11 | 10 | 10 | fr194

2, rue Roger Verlomme, 3ᵉ (Chemin Vert), 01 42 72 28 41

■ Like "finding yourself in your grandmother's kitchen" is how surveyors describe this Provençal between the Place des Vosges and the Bastille; recently taken over by the trendy Costes brothers (and partners), it's become the summer hangout for stylish types from the Marais who come to relax on "the agreeable terrace in a small quiet street."

Jarasse
17 | 12 | 15 | fr387

4, av. de Madrid, Neuilly-sur-Seine (Pont de Neuilly), 01 46 24 07 56

■ In the heart of Neuilly, chef-owner Alain Hyvonnet offers a mostly fish and shellfish menu that's "on the pricey side" but served with "efficiency" in a slightly "old-fashioned" setting; most appreciate the "cushy atmosphere" and "good quality" of the ingredients whose "freshness is always a treat."

Jardin (Le) ⑤
20 | 21 | 19 | fr487

Hôtel Royal-Monceau, 37, av. Hoche, 8ᵉ (Charles de Gaulle-Etoile), 01 42 99 98 70

■ The "superb setting" of this glass-walled hotel restaurant near the Parc Monceau is equally apt for a "business lunch or an intimate dinner"; chef Bruno Cirino impresses most surveyors with his "extraordinary Provençale" cuisine, served in a "plush ambiance" at, alas, "very high prices."

Jardin des Cygnes (Le) ◖⑤
▽ 17 | 22 | 18 | fr466

Hôtel Prince de Galles, 33, av. George V, 8ᵉ (George V), 01 53 23 78 50

■ Off the "majestic lobby" of the recently renovated Prince de Galles hotel near the Champs-Elysées is this elegant French restaurant with a "sublime patio garden", offering the "inventive cooking" of Dominique Cécillon backed up by "very good" service; if the à la carte prices strike some as "excessive", the prix fixe tabs are more "modest."

Jardins de Bagatelle (Les) S   12 | 22 | 12 | fr336
Route de Sèvres à Neuilly, 16ᵉ (Pont de Neuilly), 01 40 67 98 29
■ "It's not easy to get to" this Classic French on the edge of the Bois de Boulogne, but all agree the setting and decor make it "worth the trip", especially in summer when you can "dine under the trees"; "too bad the food isn't at the same level" and is "a bit expensive" to boot, but it still makes for a "charming" outing; P.S. it's "recommended" you take a stroll in the rose gardens of the Bagatelle after lunch.

Jean (Chez) ☾   ▽ 15 | 9 | 12 | fr242
8, rue St-Lazare, 9ᵉ (Trinité), 01 48 78 62 73
■ "A real Parisian bistro" that recently moved to a slightly "out-of-the-way" location not far from the Gare Saint-Lazare; its '50s-vintage brasserie-style decor, "honest food" and "young ambiance" make it "a real treat."

Jenny (Chez) ☾S   13 | 16 | 13 | fr241
39, bd. du Temple, 3ᵉ (République), 01 42 74 75 75
■ "Alsace in Paris" sums up this "good value" near the Place de la République, where a "superb choucroute garnie" (various cuts of pork and sausage on a bed of sauerkraut) and other specialties of the region are served "in the grand tradition of Parisian brasseries" by "efficient" waitresses in Alsatian costume; admirers consider it "top flight in this category."

Je Thé...Me...   ▽ 17 | 17 | 15 | fr237
4, rue d'Alleray, 15ᵉ (Convention/Vaugirard), 01 48 42 48 30
■ With its "very original setting" in an old gourmet grocery store, this source of "grandmotherly" French bistro cooking in the 15th strikes surveyors as "ideal for lunch", especially since it's "efficient and not expensive"; the "friendly" owner is happy to chat with diners about the menu which is full of "good surprises", notably the "excellent desserts."

Joe Allen ☾S   9 | 12 | 10 | fr211
30, rue Pierre-Lescot, 1ᵉʳ (Etienne-Marcel), 01 42 36 70 13
☑ One of the first American restaurants to open in the heart of Les Halles is "aging well", according to partisans; it's appreciated first and foremost for its "casual", "lively" (hence "noisy") atmosphere, and while the food doesn't thrill everyone ("worst hamburger ever eaten"), others find it "always good" and practical since it's "open late."

Jo Goldenberg ☾S   10 | 10 | 9 | fr217
7, rue des Rosiers, 4ᵉ (St-Paul), 01 48 87 20 16
☑ This "institution" in the Marais is criticized by many as "living on its reputation", but defenders still enjoy its "traditional Jewish cooking" and say that even if it's something of an "assembly line" it provides a "convivial" "change of scenery"; there's also debate over the tab: "affordable" vs. "too high."

Joséphine
17 | **12** | **14** | fr367
117, rue du Cherche-Midi, 6ᵉ (Duroc), 01 45 48 52 40
■ Near Montparnasse is "an old bistro the way we like them", offering boeuf bourguignon and other traditional fare at reasonable prices from a menu that allows half portions of any dish; "everything's good – it's just too bad the decor is so sad."

JULES VERNE S
21 | **26** | **20** | fr625
Tour Eiffel, 2nd fl., 7ᵉ (Bir-Hakeim), 01 45 55 61 44
■ "Paris viewed from above" thrills diners at this elegant Contemporary French whose "unique setting" – the second platform of the Eiffel Tower – makes it "marvelous for a romantic dinner with the city lit up at your feet"; even if the scenery outshines the food (which some find "slightly impersonal"), most are more than satisfied by the "inventive, delicious cooking" of Alain Reix; just be sure to "reserve weeks in advance" and "ask for a table by the windows."

Julien ●S
14 | **21** | **13** | fr265
16, rue du Fbg. St-Denis, 10ᵉ (Strasbourg-St-Denis), 01 47 70 12 06
■ Part of the Flo chain, this big, "popular" brasserie near the old Saint-Denis gateway and the Grands Boulevards always amazes with its "magnificent decor", a "masterpiece of art nouveau" style; the "food's pretty good" but "prices are drifting higher" and the service, while "thoughtful", can be "overwhelmed" by the crowds.

Juvenile's
14 | **10** | **14** | fr197
47, rue de Richelieu, 1ᵉʳ (Palais-Royal), 01 42 97 46 49
■ Just a few steps from the Palais-Royal is "one of the best wine bars in Paris", run by a British duo; besides "very rare wines" at "good value" prices, it offers "simple but substantial" fare plus "delicious tapas" in an atmosphere that's always "convivial" thanks to "mischievous" Scotsman Tim Johnston, a co-owner.

Kambodgia
16 | **20** | **13** | fr295
15, rue de Bassano, 16ᵉ (George V), 01 47 23 31 80
■ For a "Zen" atmosphere far removed from the frenzy of the nearby Champs-Elysées, go down a few steps to this Asian that's "very originally decorated" with carved wood paneling ("a good setting for a romantic dinner"); there's "very good cooking" too, including a "magnificent seafood pot-au-feu", at "reasonable prices."

Khun Akorn S
– | **–** | **–** | M
8, av. de Taillebourg, 11ᵉ (Nation), 01 43 56 20 03
"The welcome is charming" from "waitresses in native costume" even if the decor's a bit "kitsch" at this well-liked traditional Thai in the Place de la Nation neighborhood; admirers appreciate its "delicious", "well-presented" food as well as the terrace in summer.

Kifuné
– – – M

44, rue St-Ferdinand, 17ᵉ (Argentine/Porte Maillot), 01 45 72 11 19
This little-known Japanese conveniently located near the
Porte Maillot specializes in sushi and sashimi; in spite of
its innocuous decor, fans recommend it for its "always
good" food and "a fig tart to die for."

Kim Anh S
▽ **21 12 17 fr303**

15, rue de L'Eglise, 15ᵉ (Charles-Michels), 01 45 79 40 96
◪ Though "minuscule" and "without much ambiance",
this Vietnamese serves "excellent food in a lost street in
the 15th arrondissement"; the menu is "unchanging but
very good" (the "charming" owner is happy to explain dishes
to novices), and though some find the prices "exorbitant",
others say you get "good value for the money."

Kinugawa
22 14 16 fr394

9, rue du Mont-Thabor, 1ᵉʳ (Tuileries), 01 42 60 65 07
4, rue St-Philippe-du-Roule, 8ᵉ (St-Philippe-du-Roule),
01 45 63 08 07
■ With branches near the Tuileries gardens and Saint-
Philippe-du-Roule, this "typical Japanese" with "minimal
decor" is judged "extraordinarily good but expensive";
especially appreciated are "the authentic kaiseki" and "raw
fish of indisputable freshness"; in sum, "a reliable good bet."

Kiosque (Le) ◐S
– – – M

1, place de Mexico, 16ᵉ (Trocadéro), 01 47 27 96 98
Journalism is the theme of this trendy new spot (run by –
what else? – an ex-journalist) pulling in the *jeunesse dorée*
of the 16th; the big news here: a regularly changing French
menu by chefs who are proposed by various regional
newspapers as best representing the cuisine of their area;
moderate prices are a plus.

Lac Hong
▽ **21 12 17 fr253**

67, rue Lauriston, 16ᵉ (Boissière/Victor Hugo), 01 47 55 87 17
■ Tucked away in a residential street in the 16th, this "cozy"
spot with "ultra-kitschy" decor earns high praise for its
"authentic Vietnamese cooking", including a "pho soup
that has nothing to do with what's served in Chinatown";
"discreet" service is a plus, but some complain that the
prices are "a little expensive."

Ladurée S
15 19 9 fr220

75, av. des Champs-Elysées, 8ᵉ (George V), 01 40 75 08 75 ◐
16, rue Royale, 8ᵉ (Concorde/Madeleine), 01 42 60 21 79
■ At its new Champs-Elysées branch, this "very stylish
tearoom" draws an ultra-"bourgeois clientele" that doesn't
mind "if the wait is sometimes discouraging" and service
"a bit slow", since the payoff is "superb macaroons" and
other "sublime desserts"; it's also "good for a ladies' lunch"
or brunch at "reasonable" prices, as is its big sister on the
Rue Royale with its timeless Belle Epoque setting.

Languedoc (Le) ⑤
▽ | 15 | 10 | 13 | fr180

64, bd. de Port-Royal, 5ᵉ (Les Gobelins/RER Port-Royal), 01 47 07 24 47

■ This "ordinary folks type of restaurant" with rustic decor near Val-de-Grâce specializes in "classics" from Southwestern France – the peppered filet mignon and the *boeuf miroton* are especially appreciated; "you can't ask for better", particularly for such "cheap prices."

Lapérouse
15 | 24 | 16 | fr447

51, quai des Grands-Augustins, 6ᵉ (St-Michel), 01 43 26 68 06

◪ An "old classic" on the quais in Saint-Michel that remains "one of the good bets in Paris" thanks largely to its "superb" decor and "pleasant little private salons"; it offers Classic French cuisine that some judge "very good" and full of "unexpected flavors", but which critics say "isn't up to its former distinction"; valet parking is a "plus", and there's a lower-priced cafe upstairs.

LASSERRE
22 | 25 | 23 | fr744

17, av. Franklin Roosevelt, 8ᵉ (Franklin Roosevelt), 01 43 59 53 43

■ Something of "a cult" to devotees, this Classic French "institution" offers "great luxury in a superb setting" near the Champs-Elysées; if it leaves a few voters cold ("heavy food"), most praise its "very classy cooking", service that "works like a Swiss watch" and "magic" retractable roof in summer, regretting only "that prices don't allow us to go more often."

LAURENT
22 | 24 | 23 | fr688

41, av. Gabriel, 8ᵉ (Champs-Elysées-Clémenceau), 01 42 25 00 39

■ "Very chic, very good and very expensive" sums up this "grand" Classic French where "the pleasure is intense from start to finish"; a "very attractive clientele" comes here to enjoy such "elegant" fare as "the best lobster with truffles", served amidst "sumptuous decor in the splendid gardens of Marigny"; an "exceptional terrace" makes it especially "wonderful in summer."

LEDOYEN
22 | 23 | 21 | fr630

1, av. Dutuit, 8ᵉ (Champs-Elysées-Clémenceau), 01 53 05 10 01

■ "A great classic" with "superb decor" by Jacques Grange and an "exceptional" location in a Napoléon III pavilion in the gardens at the *rond point* of the Champs-Elysées; directed by Ghislaine Arabian, the kitchen turns out "refined", "inventive" French fare that can most affordably be enjoyed via the "excellent prix fixe lunch menu", making this one of "the best" for "a power lunch" or for "telling your mother-in-law you're getting a divorce."

Lescure
15 13 17 fr189

7, rue de Mondovi, 1ᵉʳ (Concorde), 01 42 60 18 91

■ Hidden in a tiny street near the Place de la Concorde, this "rustic bistro's" "menu hasn't changed in 50 years, but it doesn't matter because the ambiance is marvelous, the food honest" and "you can't beat the prices"; though rather crowded, the "clientele of regulars" and "tourists" gives it a "convivial" feel, as do the "funny waiters."

Lina's
11 10 8 fr97

4, rue Cambon, 1ᵉʳ (Concorde), 01 40 15 94 95
7, av. de l'Opéra, 1ᵉʳ (Pyramides), 01 47 03 30 29
UGC Forum des Halles, 1ᵉʳ (Les Halles), 01 42 21 36 64
50, rue Etienne-Marcel, 2ᵉ (Etienne-Marcel/Sentier), 01 42 21 16 14
22, rue des Saints-Pères, 6ᵉ (St-Germain), 01 40 20 42 78
27, rue St-Sulpice, 6ᵉ (Odéon/St-Sulpice), 01 43 29 14 14
105, rue du Fbg. St-Honoré, 8ᵉ (Miromesnil), 01 42 56 42 57
8, rue Marbeuf, 8ᵉ (Alma-Marceau), 01 47 23 92 33
Galeries Lafayette, 9ᵉ (Chaussée-d'Antin), 01 42 82 87 44
30, bd. des Italiens, 9ᵉ (Opéra), 01 42 46 02 06 **S**
Bercy/Palais Omnisports, 12ᵉ (Bercy), 01 43 40 42 42
23, av. de Wagram, 17ᵉ (Charles de Gaulle-Etoile/Ternes), 01 45 74 76 76
156, av. Charles de Gaulle, Neuilly-sur-Seine (Pont de Neuilly), 01 47 45 60 60
CNIT Parvis La Défense (La Défense), 01 46 92 28 47 **S**

■ "Delicious sandwiches" are served in a "hip, stylish ambiance" at this popular chain of American-style sandwich shops that's deemed "pleasant, fast and practical", but also a bit "pricey" for what it is, with service that can be "overwhelmed" at noon; the original branch near the Place des Victoires is "a perfect time-out during a day of shopping"; P.S. check out the tasty brownies ("best in Paris").

Livio (Chez) **S**
12 11 12 fr220

6, rue de Longchamp, Neuilly-sur-Seine (Pont de Neuilly), 01 46 24 81 32

◪ Neuilly's "Italian standby" offers what fans call "the best pizzas in Paris" and is "ideal for a simple dinner with friends" or "the family on weekends" since "prices are reasonable" and the trattoria-style decor "pleasant"; regulars report a "very friendly" welcome, but dissenters find the atmosphere a bit "snobby" and label the food "overrated."

Lous Landès
19 14 17 fr416

157, av. du Maine, 14ᵉ (Mouton-Duvernet), 01 45 43 08 04

■ Not far from Denfert-Rochereau and off the beaten tourist track is this source of "grand gastronomic cooking from the Southwest" of France, offering "copious" portions and "excellent" cassoulet and foie gras; expect attentive service and "an outstanding welcome" by "the chef and his wife who receive you as if you were visiting their home."

Lozère (La)
▽ | 16 | 9 | 14 | fr194

4, rue Hautefeuille, 6ᵉ (St-Michel), 01 43 54 26 64

■ Surveyors are grateful to find "real food in the jungle of fast-food places" around the fountain of Saint-Michel in the Latin Quarter; it's a good place to "help you through a wintery day" while enjoying fare from the namesake region in central France that's "up to standard and inexpensive."

LUCAS CARTON
26 | 25 | 24 | fr812

9, place de la Madeleine, 8ᵉ (Madeleine), 01 42 65 22 90

■ "Tops in all ways" say acolytes of this "high temple of gastronomy" with "spectacular decor" (art nouveau wood carvings and paneling by Majorelle) on the Place de la Madeleine; it may be "incredibly expensive", but most gladly pay for the "exceptional" French fare of Alain Senderens (assisted by Frédéric Robert) and "impeccable" (a few say "a bit too present") service; "the lunch menu is a celebration for the taste buds" and it's lovely for "grand occasions."

Luna (La)
19 | 11 | 13 | fr370

69, rue du Rocher, 8ᵉ (St-Lazare/Villiers), 01 42 93 77 61

■ "Excellent fish" is the lure at this "rare jewel" between the Parc Monceau and the Gare Saint-Lazare; the decor may be "ordinary", but the "refined" cooking makes it a "place to go with confidence" for piscatory pleasures plus a "fabulous baba au rhum" and potato puree that's "worth the trip."

Ma Bourgogne
14 | 11 | 12 | fr279

133, bd. Haussmann, 8ᵉ (Miromesnil), 01 45 63 50 61

■ Dubbed "the pope of Beaujolais" by one admirer, this wine bistro near Saint-Augustin in the 8th serves "good quality brasserie-style food" with a Burgundy accent accompanied by "excellent wines at good prices"; "classic" and "unpretentious", it's especially touted "for lunch."

Macéo
▽ | 17 | 16 | 15 | fr292

15, rue des Petits-Champs, 1ᵉʳ (Bourse/Palais-Royal), 01 42 96 98 89

■ Near the Palais-Royal and the Place des Victoires, this trendy bistro is the newest venture from Willi's Wine Bar owner Mark Williamson (in association with Steven Spurrier); in the old Mercure Galant space, it's larger and more elegant than nearby Willi's, offering cooking deemed "a good deal", plus "attentive service" and "nice wines."

Magnolias (Les)
– | – | – | E

48, av. de Bry, Le Perreux-sur-Marne (RER Nogent), 01 48 72 47 43

There's no question that this suburban Classic French is "far away", on the banks of the Marne river in Le Perreux; but once there the setting is "beautiful", complete with a handsomely paneled dining room, and there's "excellent fish" among other offerings from a traditional menu; just be forewarned that the à la carte prices are lofty.

Maison (La) ◗⑤ ▽ 11 15 10 fr221
*1, rue de la Bûcherie, 5ᵉ (Maubert-Mutualité/St-Michel),
01 43 29 73 57*
▣ Overlooking a tree-filled square across the Seine from
Notre Dame in the Latin Quarter, this stylish French run by
Claude Aurensan (ex Palace nightclub) draws "a varied
crowd" that usually includes a few famous faces; some
rate the food "good", others find it uninspiring, ditto
service that's often "long and overwhelmed", but regulars
like "the original decor and pretty terrace in summer."

MAISON BLANCHE 20 23 18 fr540
15, av. Montaigne, 8ᵉ (Alma-Marceau), 01 47 23 55 99
▣ "New York in Paris": this "chic in-spot" atop the Théâtre
des Champs-Elysées on the elegant Avenue Montaigne
draws a starry clientele to its "modern" dining room with
a "panoramic" view; though some find the minimalist
decor a bit "cold" and the ambiance "pretentious", the
"imaginative" French-Asian fare is generally judged
"good" if "expensive"; "recommended for business
lunches", though the crowd's more glamorous at night.

Maison d'Alsace (La) ◗⑤ 14 13 13 fr286
*39, av. des Champs-Elysées, 8ᵉ (Franklin Roosevelt),
01 53 93 97 00*
▣ "Ideal at 3 AM when you must have onion soup", oysters
or "other Alsatian delights" like choucroute garnie say
night-owl fans of this round-the-clock brasserie with an
"appealing setting"; dissenters claim it's "a bit of a factory"
with "ordinary" food and variable service, but to partisans
"it's the best value on the Champs-Elysées."

Maison de l'Amérique Latine (La) 15 23 15 fr342
*217, bd. St-Germain, 7ᵉ (Rue du Bac/Solférino),
01 45 49 33 23*
▣ "Best in summer" when you can dine in the "enchanting
garden" of this handsome old townhouse, now a South
American cultural center, on the Left Bank near the
Assemblée Nationale ("you'll often spot politicians"); in
spite of the name, the food is traditional French, and while
some judge it "middling" and "expensive", the setting
makes it a "charming oasis."

Maison du Caviar (La) ◗⑤ 17 13 16 fr412
21, rue Quentin-Bauchart, 8ᵉ (George V), 01 47 23 53 43
▣ Partisans say this "calm" and "cozy" caviar specialist
serves "the ne plus ultra of the little black grains" as well
as "wonderfully fresh salmon" and "excellent omelets";
Parisians especially like to come to this "ultra-chic" "classic
with professional service" "before or after a show" on the
Champs-Elysées; no surprise that it's "pricey."

Maison du Valais (La) ◑   13 | 15 | 13 | fr273
20, rue Royale, 8ᵉ (Concorde/Madeleine), 01 42 60 22 72
■ "A charming little Swiss chalet" on the Rue Royale filled with the pungent aromas of "good raclette [melted cheese on boiled potatoes], fondues and other excellent Alpine specialties"; some find it a bit "expensive", but it's an "amusing" change of pace – after a meal here "you'll want to head for the mountains."

Maison Prunier   20 | 22 | 19 | fr559
16, av. Victor Hugo, 16ᵉ (Charles de Gaulle-Etoile), 01 44 17 35 85
☑ The art deco decor of this venerable fish specialist near the Arc de Triomphe is "elegant" and "superb", and many find the seafood "excellent and very refined" since it reopened under the management of Taillevent's J.C. Vrinat; still, a majority feels "it's much too expensive" and some find service "insolent" and "slow"; tip: it's "very pleasant to eat at the bar."

Maître Paul (Chez) ⑤   16 | 11 | 16 | fr288
12, rue Monsieur le Prince, 6ᵉ (Odéon), 01 43 54 74 59
■ Specializing in the rustic cooking of the Jura and Franche-Comté regions near the Swiss border, this venerable spot not far from the Luxembourg gardens "has all the virtues of the provinces" – "excellent" food, friendly service, "somber but decent decor" and "reasonable" prices; in sum, "a very good little place."

Mandragore (La) ⑤   – | – | – | M
74, rue Botzaris, 19ᵉ (Botzaris), 01 42 39 86 18
"A great little address in a slightly forsaken neighborhood" near the romantic Buttes-Chaumont park in eastern Paris; it offers tasty bistro fare, good service and a young, relaxed ambiance, with the big plus of very reasonable prices.

Manoir Detourbe (Le)   18 | 15 | 17 | fr408
6, rue Pierre Demours, 17ᵉ (Charles de Gaulle-Etoile/Ternes), 01 45 72 25 25
☑ Young star chef Philippe Detourbe recently acquired this old classic with "kitschy but amusing decor" in the 17th arrondissement and is "trying to relaunch it"; the "welcome is excellent" and the French food, which some previously found "mediocre", has been much improved so now "one goes with pleasure."

Mansouria ◑⑤   20 | 17 | 13 | fr247
11, rue Faidherbe, 11ᵉ (Faidherbe-Chaligny), 01 43 71 00 16
■ This "very authentic Moroccan" with pretty *Arabian Nights* decor between Bastille and the Place de la Nation in eastern Paris serves what admirers consider "the best couscous and b'steeya in Paris", which is why the size of the check is "justified"; be advised: "you have to book since it's always full."

Manufacture (La) S
16 | 16 | 14 | fr272

20, Esplanade de la Manufacture, Issy-les-Moulineaux (Corentin-Celton), 01 40 93 08 98

■ The neighborhood may be "without interest", but the "innovative" Contemporary French cooking "makes the trip worthwhile" to this "trendy", "airy" restaurant in a redone tobacco factory; with a "well broken-in prix fixe formula", it's "not too expensive" and the terrace is appealing.

Marais-Cage
19 | 15 | 17 | fr237

8, rue de Beauce, 3e (Filles-du-Calvaire/République), 01 48 87 31 20

■ Fans of Caribbean fare tout this "excellent" address in the "very pleasant" Marais area; the decor may be slightly "faded" and prices "a little high", but the "inventive cooking" based on "high-quality" ingredients compensates.

Marcande (Le)
17 | 15 | 15 | fr402

52, rue de Miromesnil, 8e (Miromesnil), 01 42 65 19 14

■ "Great for lunch" in a businessy part of the 8th say admirers of the Classic French cooking in this comfortable dining room with patio seating in summer; it pleases a largely professional clientele even if some find it "a bit expensive."

Marcel (Chez)
▽ 14 | 10 | 13 | fr187

7, rue Stanislas, 6e (Vavin), 01 45 48 29 94

■ In a residential part of Montparnasse, this "neighborhood bistro" is an "engaging" place with "owners who really commit themselves" to serving "good food" at reasonable prices; too bad about the "indifferent decor."

Marcello S
– | – | – | M

105, rue de Prony, 17e (Pereire), 01 44 40 05 88

This relaxed Italian off the Place Pereire draws the same kind of local crowd as did Périsphère, its predecessor; the menu is modestly priced and the setting comfortable, with attractive modern decor; brunch has an Italian accent too.

MARÉE (LA)
23 | 15 | 20 | fr588

1, rue Daru, 8e (Ternes), 01 43 80 20 00

■ "Classic" is a word often used to describe this "excellent fish restaurant" with a "royal wine cellar" next to the Salle Pleyel concert hall in the 8th arrondissement; while critics say that means cooking "without originality", the majority appreciates its "high quality" even if the "narrow" quarters "inhibit intimacy" and prices are "very steep."

Mariage Frères S
15 | 18 | 14 | fr188

30-32, rue du Bourg-Tibourg, 4e (Hôtel-de-Ville), 01 42 72 28 11
13, rue des Grands-Augustins, 6e (St-Michel), 01 40 51 82 50
260, rue du Fbg. St-Honoré, 8e (Ternes), 01 46 22 18 54

■ "A must for tea lovers", this Marais tearoom/shop offers over 350 types ("taste a new one each visit"); with "pretty colonial decor" and "delicious pastries", it's "ideal for a refined lunch" or brunch even if service can be "irregular."

Marianne (Chez) ◗⑤

12 | 11 | 8 | fr153

2, rue des Hospitalières-St-Gervais, 4ᵉ (St-Paul), 01 42 72 18 86

■ In the heart of the Marais, this popular little place serves "Central European cooking in a warm ambiance" with the "best poppy-seed cake in Paris"; it's judged a "good value" even if service is lacking, there's "too many people" and "you often have to wait" for a table – it's best to "book ahead and show up on time."

Marie et Fils

13 | 13 | 11 | fr260

34, rue Mazarine, 6ᵉ (Odéon), 01 43 26 69 49

■ Even if some say the kitchen "has its ups and downs", most consider this to be "a pleasant neighborhood restaurant" in Saint-Germain-des-Prés with a "trendy", "appealing" atmosphere and a "good, light prix fixe menu at noon"; "too many tourists" and "arrogant" service draw a few grumbles, however.

Marie Louise

17 | 7 | 15 | fr250

52, rue Championnet, 18ᵉ (Porte de Clignancourt), 01 46 06 86 55

■ "A testament to the atmosphere of old Paris" in a small street near the Porte de Clignancourt, this bistro prepares "good traditional French" fare with "excellent" ingredients; the service is "amiable" and prices aren't too high.

Marines (Les)

16 | 13 | 14 | fr320

27, av. Niel, 17ᵉ (Pereire/Ternes), 01 47 63 04 24

■ Overlooking the Place Pereire in the 17th arrondissement is what locals call "a good neighborhood fish house with reasonable prices" and pleasant service; but while most approve of the "excellent" cooking, some say "a little originality" wouldn't hurt and find the decor "too bourgeois to be of any interest."

Marius

17 | 11 | 14 | fr339

82, bd. Murat, 16ᵉ (Porte de St-Cloud), 01 46 51 67 80

■ "Excellent quality fish" is the bait that lures diners to this seafooder in a somewhat off the beaten track part of the 16th arrondissement; even if "prices have been going up" recently, it remains a "convivial" place offering a "personal" welcome and the convenience of valet parking.

Marius (Chez)

19 | 16 | 15 | fr338

5, rue de Bourgogne, 7ᵉ (Assemblée Nationale/Invalides), 01 45 51 79 42

☑ Next to the beautiful square in front of the Palais-Bourbon in the 7th arrondissement and steps from the Assemblée Nationale (thus popular with deputies), this veteran serving assiduously Classic French cooking in a dressy setting gets a split vote; some call it "worthy of praise" for its "very fine" cooking and "pleasant" welcome, while others shrug "banal and expensive."

Marius et Janette ●⬤Ⓢ
19 | 16 | 15 | fr445

4, av. George V, 8ᵉ (Alma-Marceau), 01 47 23 84 36

▨ Opinions are mixed on this seafooder "with a grand reputation" near the Pont de l'Alma; while fans applaud "superb" dishes featuring "very fresh fish cooked simply", others say it's "sometimes disappointing" and "not what it was"; likewise, the marine decor strikes some as "amusing", others as "trite", but on one point all agree: it's "very pricey" – "you eat the most expensive sole in France here."

Marlotte (La)
15 | 13 | 16 | fr288

55, rue du Cherche-Midi, 6ᵉ (Sèvres-Babylone), 01 45 48 86 79

■ Not far from the Bon Marché department store on the Left Bank is this "simple but very good" source of traditional French fare; though a few find the food "heavy", admirers say the "welcoming service", "upmarket" atmosphere and "wonderful owner" mean "one is never disappointed."

Maroussia
– | – | – | M

9, rue de L'Eperon, 6ᵉ (Odéon), 01 43 54 87 50

Unlike other Russian restaurants in Paris, this Latin Quarter venue with homey, rustic decor is not a wallet-buster; it offers standards like blinis with smoked salmon, and if some say the atmosphere's "a little sad", that may be what "makes it really Russian."

Marronniers d'Auteuil (Les)
▽ 12 | 9 | 12 | fr208

75, rue d'Auteuil, 16ᵉ (Michel-Ange Auteuil), 01 46 51 28 43

■ Though they're obviously indifferent to the decor, habitués like this "very nice neighborhood" place in Auteuil with "an owner who's passionate about his métier"; it serves "real" French "home cooking", the "welcome is very warm" and the ambiance "agreable"; moderate prices don't hurt either.

Marty Ⓢ
15 | 15 | 16 | fr262

20, av. des Gobelins, 5ᵉ (Les Gobelins), 01 43 31 39 51

■ A "very good Parisian brasserie" in the Gobelins district of the 5th arrondissement that's "always full" thanks to cooking that enthusiasts call "delicious", backed up by "very good" service; this veteran is actually two-in-one, since the brasserie (upstairs) has "much lower prices" than the main restaurant below.

Mathusalem (Le)
16 | 12 | 17 | fr169

5 bis, bd. Exelmans, 16ᵉ (Exelmans), 01 42 88 10 73

■ This "typical little French restaurant" in the heart of the 16th arrondissement is considered "a great buy" for "good traditional cooking plus several original dishes like grilled Camembert with sour cherries"; it draws lots of regulars who appreciate its pleasant, relaxed atmosphere and "smiling service."

101

Maupertu

▽ 18 | 12 | 20 | fr262

*94, bd. de La Tour-Maubourg, 7ᵉ (La Tour-Maubourg),
01 45 51 37 96*

■ At this "lovely, small place with a view of the Invalides" in the 7th, surveyors enjoy "rustic" French cooking in "an originally decorated dining room"; "the hostess is charming, service is perfect and the prices are very reasonable" croon contented clients; there's a pretty terrace too.

Mauzac (Le)

– | – | – | I

7, rue de l'Abbé-de-l'Epée, 5ᵉ (Luxembourg), 01 46 33 75 22

Run by "a pleasant and passionate owner", this wine bar next to the Luxembourg Gardens allows diners to "discover unusual wines while eating good, simple" French food at easy-to-swallow prices; the decor may be nothing special but there's a "nice terrace in summer."

Mavrommatis S

19 | 13 | 16 | fr245

42, rue Daubenton, 5ᵉ (Censier-Daubenton), 01 43 31 17 17

■ Deep in the 5th arrondissement, "one of the best Greeks in Paris" serves "excellent traditional food" with "really nice" service to match; patrons also appreciate the comfortable dining room with sophisticated decor that's leagues away from the faux ruins motifs found elsewhere.

MAXIM'S

15 | 25 | 20 | fr672

3, rue Royale, 8ᵉ (Concorde/Madeleine), 01 42 65 27 94

☑ Surveyors disagree on this legendary art nouveau "monument" near the Place de la Concorde; owned by Pierre Cardin, it still enchants admirers who say that even if the French food "isn't the best, the setting is sumptuous" and service "very good", hence it "shouldn't be missed"; but critics blast the "kept-woman decor and uninteresting fare", labeling it a "rip-off", to which fans retort "this is Maxim's and you don't come here to count."

Méditerranée (La) ◐ S

14 | 15 | 14 | fr346

2, place de l'Odéon, 6ᵉ (Odéon), 01 43 26 02 30

☑ There's a "beautiful view of the Odéon theater" and "it's always a pleasure to see the Cocteau-designed menu" at this Left Bank fish house; but while partisans rate the food "excellent" if "a little expensive", others feel it's "not what it used to be" and find the "atmosphere a bit stiff."

MEURICE (LE) S

20 | 25 | 23 | fr587

*Hôtel Meurice, 228, rue de Rivoli, 1ᵉʳ (Concorde/Tuileries),
01 44 58 10 50*

■ Across from the Tuileries gardens, this lavishly decorated restaurant, once a Salvador Dalí favorite , is "a classic of great quality" with "very good" French cuisine, "high-level service" and an "aristocratic" setting that "transports you to another dimension" – in sum, "all the comfort of a grand hotel at relatively reasonable prices"; it's best loved for its "sumptuous lunch menu" or a "celebratory dinner."

Michel (Chez) ◐
`19` `9` `14` `fr251`

*10, rue de Belzunce, 10ᵉ (Gare du Nord/Poissonnière),
01 44 53 06 20*

■ Young chef Thierry Breton runs this Contemporary French bistro, offering "absolutely delicious", innovative cooking with a focus on specialties from Brittany; the price of his prix fixe menu is "extraordinary" given such "good and very original" fare, so who cares if there's "no decor" and the location near the Gare de Nord lacks charm; P.S. the "lobster menu is a real treat in season."

Michel Courtalhac
▽ `20` `11` `18` `fr262`

47, rue de Bourgogne, 7ᵉ (Invalides/Varenne), 01 45 55 15 35

■ With "all the charm of a little Parisian restaurant", this oasis near the Assemblée Nationale boasts an "imaginative" chef-owner, Michel Courtalhac, whose "short menu" offers "dishes of remarkable freshness" inspired by daily market visits; "fair prices" add to the satisfaction.

MICHEL ROSTANG
`25` `19` `23` `fr648`

20, rue Rennequin, 17ᵉ (Ternes), 01 47 63 40 77

■ Since the consensus on Michel Rostang's French cuisine is "exceptional", it hardly matters if some quibble that it's "too chichi" and "warrants more original decor" than the traditional look of this 17th arrondissement dining room; high prices also cause "indigestion", but for the majority this is "one of the tops", a "warm" place with "good service" and "remarkable" food that inspires such paeans as "you must eat the pressed duck to understand life."

Mille Colonnes (Les) ⑤
`–` `–` `–` `M`

Hôtel Mercure, Forum Val de Loire, 20 bis, rue de la Gaîté, 14ᵉ (Edgar-Quinet/Gaîté), 01 40 47 08 34

Even if it's "poorly located" in a Hôtel Mercure behind the Montparnasse train station, this French has a "pretty" interior patio and is handy for business travelers.

Milonga (La) ◐⑤
`–` `–` `–` `M`

18, rue Guisarde, 6ᵉ (Mabillon/St-Germain-des-Prés), 01 43 29 52 18

A very basic but "nice" Argentinean in the middle of the liveliest bar district in Saint-Germain-des-Prés; it caters to carnivores with "authentic dishes" like empanadas, blood sausage and a mixed grill, and there's tango and milonga music to melt a gaucho's heart Friday and Saturday nights.

Mirama ⑤
▽ `20` `3` `10` `fr136`

17, rue St-Jacques, 5ᵉ (Maubert-Mutualité/St-Michel), 01 43 54 71 77

■ The steamy windows, bare-bones decor and less-than-stellar service of this popular Latin Quarter Chinese near Saint-Julien-le-Pauvre church are forgiven because the cooking is "delicious and authentic", not to mention cheap; don't miss the "fabulous soup with shrimp ravioli."

Miravile
17 | 13 | 14 | fr401

72, quai de l'Hôtel-de-Ville, 4ᵉ (Hôtel-de-Ville/Pont Marie), 01 42 74 72 22

☑ Given the superb Seine-side view of Notre-Dame and the Ile Saint-Louis, all agree the "setting is very pleasant", but opinions on the French food are less uniform: "high quality", "intelligent" vs. "uneven", "very expensive" with "service that's too slow"; the recent arrival of chef David Féau, former second at Guy Savoy, may set things simmering again.

Moissonnier S
16 | 10 | 15 | fr295

28, rue des Fossés-St-Bernard, 5ᵉ (Cardinal Lemoine/Jussieu), 01 43 29 87 65

■ Admirers urge "hurry here before it disappears" since so many "pleasant", "old-fashioned" bistros like this one in the Jussieu district of the 5th arrondissement have closed shop; come with a "solid appetite", as it offers "copious" portions of traditional Lyonnaise cuisine, including a famed assortment of cold hors d'oeuvres; some feel it's time to "spruce up the decor" though.

Monde des Chimères (Le)
▽ 16 | 13 | 14 | fr262

69, rue St-Louis-en-l'Ile, 4ᵉ (Pont Marie), 01 43 54 45 27

■ A homey place in the middle of the Ile Saint-Louis where the "good" French cooking of Cécile Ibane attracts island-dwellers as well as tourists; both appreciate the "vegetables and preserves straight from her garden", even if prices can seem a bit high.

Moniage Guillaume
▽ 16 | 14 | 13 | fr349

88, rue de la Tombe Issoire, 14ᵉ (Alésia), 01 43 22 96 15

■ Considered "very classic" and "very good", this little auberge is "worth the trip" to the Alésia quarter of the 14th for food that produces "excellent memories", especially the fish and bouillabaisse; like many Paris seafood specialists, though, it's also seen as "very expensive."

Monsieur Lapin ●◗S
17 | 15 | 17 | fr282

11, rue Raymond Losserand, 14ᵉ (Gaîté/Pernety), 01 43 20 21 39

■ There's "rabbit, of course, but also other succulent fare" at this "good and welcoming little" French behind the cemetery in Montparnasse; regulars recommend that you "eat in the alcove", a cozy niche in the homey dining room.

Montalembert (Le) S
11 | 18 | 14 | fr312

Hôtel Montalembert, 3, rue de Montalembert, 7ᵉ (Rue du Bac), 01 45 49 68 03

☑ Book editors, art and antique dealers and politicians come to "lunch stylishly and well" in the minimalist contemporary decor of this ground-floor space in a chic hotel off the Rue du Bac in the 7th; the "designer" French food is "successful enough" and it's a "haven of peace in the neighborhood."

Montparnasse 25
20 | 15 | 18 | fr519

Hôtel Méridien-Montparnasse, 19, rue du Commandant
René Mouchotte, 14ᵉ (Gaîté/Montparnasse-Bienvenue),
01 44 36 44 25

☑ Jean-Yves Guého put this French in the Hôtel Méridien-Montparnasse on the map before recently leaving for Nantes; those who found his food "excellent" hope new chef Christophe Moine (ex Meurice and Maxim's) does as well, but what diners really focus on here is the "heavenly" cheese tray with some "165 varieties according to season" served by a maître fromager; a few feel the "'20s-style decor" is "cold", though good service helps compensate.

Monttessuy (Le)
▽ 13 | 10 | 10 | fr248

4, rue de Monttessuy, 7ᵉ (Alma-Marceau), 01 45 55 01 90

■ The Eiffel Tower, beautifully lit at night, looms over the little street in the 7th arrondissement that's home to this "real Lyonnais"; if some describe it as "classic, with nothing distinctive" and find "service a bit distant", it's still "very satisfying for its price level."

MOROT-GAUDRY
20 | 19 | 19 | fr461

8, rue de la Cavalerie, 15ᵉ (La Motte-Picquet Grenelle),
01 45 67 06 85

☑ "The elevator ride up is always amazing" and the "Eiffel Tower view is splendid" from this French set atop a building in the 15th; but while most call it "elegant and affordable" with "refined" food and "an unforgettable tasting menu", a few find its "reputation exaggerated", terming it "pretentious and expensive" and citing "little effort to please customers."

Moulin à Vent "Chez Henri" (Au)
19 | 13 | 16 | fr331

20, rue des Fossés-St-Bernard, 5ᵉ (Jussieu), 01 43 54 99 37

■ "For those who really like to eat French style", this Latin Quarter bistro serves "excellent traditional cooking" with "some of the best meat in Paris" in a "noisy but nice" atmosphere; the tables may be "too tightly spaced" but it offers "good value for the money."

Moulin à Vins (Le) ◐
▽ 12 | 11 | 14 | fr201

6, rue Burq, 18ᵉ (Abbesses/Blanche), 01 42 52 81 27

■ Recommended for Montmartre buffs, this "very good little wine bar" run by "an absolutely charming female owner" offers "good" bistro cooking and "very good wines" in "an among-friends type atmosphere"; "on Saturday nights an accordionist livens up the room with songs of Montmartre."

Muniche (Le) ◐⑤
11 | 12 | 11 | fr267

7, rue St-Benoît, 6ᵉ (St-Germain-des-Prés), 01 42 61 12 70

☑ Though it's hard to beat the location (around the corner from the Café de Flore "in the heart of Saint-Germain"), this "traditional brasserie" is knocked by critics for having "no originality" in its cuisine or decor; still, others say it will do "in a pinch" and it's "a landmark for oysters at midnight."

Muses (Les)
18 | 15 | 18 | fr380

Hôtel Scribe, 1, rue Scribe, 9ᵉ (Opéra), 01 44 71 24 26

■ In an "agreeable, restful" setting in the Hôtel Scribe near the Opéra, surveyors find "well-executed" "classic" French cuisine complemented by "a good wine list"; business types and others appreciate the "excellent service" and "good value" prix fixe menus, but as some note, "you have to like basement dining rooms."

Napoléon Chaix
13 | 11 | 14 | fr348

46, rue Balard, 15ᵉ (Balard/Javel), 01 45 54 09 00

■ "If owner André Pousse is around, there's a show" on top of the "refined French cooking", "very warm decor and excellent choice of wines" at this outpost in a slightly lost corner of the 15th; it's "good, classic and expensive", but "who could ask for more from a Parisian bistro?"

Natacha ◑
10 | 11 | 11 | fr237

17 bis, rue Campagne-Première, 14ᵉ (Raspail), 01 43 20 79 27

☑ A long-running Montparnasse hit with "fashionable" Paris night people and paparazzi stalking stars, this "trendy" (some say "very snobby") little Eclectic earns unimpressive food ratings but "happily, one doesn't really come here to eat" – it's a "place to be seen", with a "dining room in the cellar" that's ideal "for bachelor parties or student soirees."

Navarin (Le) Ⓢ
– | – | – | I

3, av. Philippe-Auguste, 11ᵉ (Nation), 01 43 67 17 49

"Good to know about" if looking for "reasonable prices and a calm setting" near the Place de la Nation; a team of pros who trained in some very grand kitchens (Gérard Besson's and Joël Robuchon's among them) serves "fine" French classics like smoked salmon, foie gras and roast lamb at this "pleasant little address"; respondents especially appreciate the "fast, friendly" service and "good value."

Nénesse (Chez)
▽ 17 | 8 | 10 | fr195

17, rue de Saintonge, 3ᵉ (Filles-du-Calvaire), 01 42 78 46 49

■ This "surprising" little "neighborhood bistro" in a quiet corner of the Marais changed hands in January '98, but regulars hope it continues to serve "refined" French fare that "really stands out from the ordinary" – "everything is fresh", even if the "service can be rather overwhelmed" and some find the decor "sad."

New Nioullaville ◑Ⓢ
13 | 10 | 10 | fr158

32-34, rue de l'Orillon, 11ᵉ (Belleville), 01 40 21 96 18

☑ "Eastern exoticism and a parade of dim sum carts" are to be found in this enormous Chinese-Asian in Belleville; fans find it "kitschy and fun" and insist "you eat well here for little money", while critics claim quality has dropped "since it reopened" (after a remodeling) and label it "a little factory-like."

Ngo (Chez) ◑⑤   18 | 16 | 13 | fr264
70, rue de Longchamp, 16ᵉ (Trocadéro), 01 47 04 53 20
■ "One of the best Chinese restaurants in Paris" say admirers of this "pretty" place on a quiet street near the Trocadéro; though some find service "uneven", the "excellent value" keeps most diners happy, and those seeking "tranquil" dining appreciate the "little private rooms with tables for four."

Nikita ◑   – | – | – | E
6, rue Faustin-Hélie, 16ᵉ (La Muette/Trocadéro), 01 45 04 04 33
For a real Russian repast, this place deep in the 16th arrondissement is recommended for its "excellent cooking, decor and good atmosphere", with the added attraction of live Russian music.

Noces de Jeannette (Les) ⑤   ▽ 13 | 14 | 12 | fr229
14, rue Favart, 2ᵉ (Richelieu-Drouot), 01 42 96 36 89
■ "A typically Parisian bistro – the kind you see in the movies" sums up the ambiance at this little spot near the Salle Favart concert hall; surveyors say the food is "honest" and service can be "excellent"; it's also equipped for groups.

Noura ◑⑤   15 | 11 | 13 | fr235
121, bd. Montparnasse, 6ᵉ (Vavin), 01 43 20 19 19
Pavillon Noura ◑⑤
21, av. Marceau, 16ᵉ (Alma-Marceau), 01 47 20 33 33
■ "Beirut in Paris" say habitués who come to these siblings "for quality Lebanese cooking", whether in the "very chic" Avenue Marceau branch or Montparnasse offshoot with its "large flowered patio"; the food is "pricey and spicy", and if the "waiters are sometimes unpleasant", the "setting is comfortable" and "the ingredients are fresh"; there's "interesting takeaway" too.

Nouveau Village Tao Tao ◑⑤   15 | 12 | 11 | fr189
159, bd. Vincent Auriol, 13ᵉ (Nationale), 01 45 86 40 08
■ This Chinese in the heart of Paris' Chinatown in the 13th arrondissement earns praise for its "very good cooking including steamed dumplings" and an "exceptional Peking duck"; but service can be "a little slow" and some say that "even for this type of place, it feels a little bit like a factory."

O à la Bouche (L')   ▽ 21 | 10 | 16 | fr217
157, bd. du Montparnasse, 6ᵉ (Raspail/Vavin), 01 43 26 26 53
■ In Montparnasse, a talented young chef has been packing them into this converted cafe with a "short" but reasonably priced French menu; it's "calm" and "pleasant" with cooking deemed "remarkably creative" and "good for the palate and the wallet", though some warn "it's always full and prices are creeping up."

Obélisque (L') ⑤
18 18 19 fr384

Hôtel de Crillon, 4, rue Boissy-d'Anglas, 8ᵉ (Concorde), 01 44 71 15 15

☑ Some diners say "the little brother of the excellent Les Ambassadeurs restaurant" at the Hôtel Crillon on the Place de la Concorde is "even better" than its sibling, while others judge that chef "Dominique Bouchet hasn't yet reached the top"; but either way, it offers "class at gentle prices", and if the "decor's a bit cold" the welcome is "warm."

Oeillade (L')
16 10 13 fr253

10, rue St-Simon, 7ᵉ (Rue du Bac/Solférino), 01 42 22 01 60

■ "This quality bourgeois address with a plush atmosphere" offers some of the "best value" in the 7th, just off the Boulevard Saint-Germain, with a lunch prix fixe that's a "good buy"; locals head here for classics like stuffed tomatoes, skate in caper sauce and other "well-considered" French fare that's "nicely served" by a "generous" staff.

Oenothèque (L')
15 11 13 fr326

20, rue St-Lazare, 9ᵉ (Notre-Dame-de-Lorette), 01 48 78 08 76

■ "An exciting spot at which to discuss the relationship between food and wine" in an "attractive" setting near the Gare Saint-Lazare with wine racks lining the walls; besides "a beautiful wine list", it offers French fare that most judge "good quality", and if the check is "expensive", "the idea of having top wines by the glass is very seductive."

Oie Cendrée (L')
▽ 20 16 18 fr206

51, rue Labrouste, 15ᵉ (Plaisance), 01 45 31 91 91

■ For "a satisfying intimate experience", surveyors tout this quiet nook in the 15th where the "dedicated owner serves Southwestern French specialties" in "a warm ambiance" with "charming decor"; "good value" is the icing on the cake.

Olivades (Les)
19 12 14 fr259

41, av. de Ségur, 7ᵉ (Ecole Militaire/Ségur), 01 47 83 70 09

■ Thanks to talented Flora Mikula, who trained at L'Arpège before setting out on her own to cook food recalling her Avignon childhood, this place "merits being better known" and "is worth the detour" to a residential part of the 7th; the "minuscule" room "feels like Provence and one can almost hear the cicadas" while savoring food "full of sunshine", served by "friendly" staff at "not too expensive" prices.

Omar (Chez) ◑⑤
14 10 12 fr170

47, rue de Bretagne, 3ᵉ (Arts-et-Métiers/Temple), 01 42 72 36 26

■ Just north of the Marais in the 3rd, this pretty old bistro reincarnated as a popular North African serves "terrific couscous" in a lively setting presided over by genial Algerian owner Omar, who's friendly with some top designers and artists (hence the "switched-on atmosphere"); "fast", "friendly" service and "low prices" add to the good spirits.

Opium Café ◖S
11 | 19 | 10 | fr214

5, rue Elzevir, 3ᵉ (St-Paul), 01 40 29 93 40

■ This "very cool" "mix of a bar and restaurant" in a former public bathhouse in the middle of the Marais "serves late" and has "a warm, very gay", "loungy" atmosphere; some find the French fare "innovative", others say "too expensive."

ORANGERIE (L') ◖S
17 | 22 | 19 | fr429

28, rue St-Louis-en-l'Ile, 4ᵉ (Pont Marie), 01 46 33 93 98

■ "To get away from it all on the Ile Saint-Louis", "*le tout Paris*" heads to Jean-Claude Brialy's "gorgeous" little Classic French filled with "magnificent floral arrangements" that make it "one of the most romantic places" in town; comments on the food run from "you always dine well" to "leaves no lasting memories", but its prix fixe menu includes wine, mineral water and coffee and service is "excellent."

Orient-Extrême
17 | 9 | 10 | fr289

4, rue Bernard Palissy, 6ᵉ (St-Germain-des-Prés), 01 45 48 92 27

■ Falling under the heading of "trendy intelligentsia" spots, this Japanese in Saint-Germain-des-Prés has a "modern" wood-paneled dining room plus a sushi bar with stools; the food is "very good", but it's "not being given away", and some say service improves "once they know you."

Osaka S
▽ 15 | 7 | 9 | fr278

163, rue St-Honoré, 1ᵉʳ (Louvre-Rivoli/Palais-Royal), 01 42 60 66 01

■ "Conveniently located" just behind the Palais-Royal, this Japanese is rated "rather average" by some, "excellent" by others; either way, it's highly recommended that you "sit at the counter", since the dining room decor leaves much to be desired.

Os à Moelle (L') ◖
20 | 10 | 14 | fr242

3, rue Vasco-de-Gama, 15ᵉ (Lourmel), 01 45 57 27 27

■ "A real find" that's "worth the trip to the 15th" for "excellent", "original" French food at fair prices enhanced by "good wines and a good welcome"; Parisians have fallen big for its prix fixe formula (a single five-course menu served daily), so even if "diners are on top of each other" and "they should improve the decor", many consider it "the quintessence of a really nice bistro."

Osteria (L')
▽ 19 | 6 | 10 | fr217

10, rue de Sévigné, 4ᵉ (St-Paul), 01 42 71 37 08

■ Habitués of this very clubby railroad car of an Italian in the Marais heap praise on the "very fine cuisine prepared by Toni", a native of Venice; it may be "too noisy but service is friendly", and since it's "often full it's wise to book ahead" if you want a table in "this little room where you eat good pasta at fair prices."

Ostréade (L') S
13 | 12 | 10 | fr228
11, bd. de Vaugirard, 15ᵉ (Montparnasse-Bienvenue), 01 43 21 87 41

■ Part of the complex that includes the ultramodern Montparnasse train station, this is, not surprisingly, "a good choice if waiting for a train", especially since it serves "very original fish dishes in a contemporary setting"; while perhaps not worth going out of your way for, it's better than run-of-the-mill station fare, though it's recommended more for lunch as some feel "it lacks charm for dinner."

Oulette (L')
17 | 13 | 18 | fr319
15, place Lachambeaudie, 12ᵉ (Dugommier), 01 40 02 02 12

■ Ever since he moved to the "out of the way" Bercy quarter several years ago, talented chef Marcel Baudis has slightly fallen off the map (though he still directs the Baracane in the Marais), but fans say his "excellent Southwestern French" fare is "worth the trip" to this roomy, "modern" (some say "impersonal") space; a few find prices "high", but others insist you get good "value."

Oum el Banine
19 | 11 | 15 | fr272
16 bis, rue Dufrenoy, 16ᵉ (Rue de la Pompe), 01 45 04 91 22

■ Admirers find all "the charm and gastronomy" of Morocco at this eatery in the middle of the 16th; partisans claim it serves "without a doubt the best couscous in Paris", even if the decor's simple and the check "a little overpriced."

Pactole (Au)
15 | 12 | 15 | fr347
44, bd. St-Germain, 5ᵉ (Maubert-Mutualité), 01 46 33 31 31

■ At the easternmost end of the Boulevard Saint-Germain is what supporters call "a serious restaurant that deserves compliments", even if it's so discreet that it's little-known among surveyors; it offers "an attractive menu" of typical dressed-up French dishes in "an agreeable setting", but some feel it "should pay attention to the service."

Paolo Petrini S
19 | 10 | 15 | fr361
6, rue du Débarcadère, 17ᵉ (Argentine/Porte Maillot), 01 45 74 25 95

■ The strong points of this "excellent Italian" just behind the Porte Maillot are "the refinement of the cooking and the wines" – it's "exceptional during the fall mushroom season" for the likes of porcini soup and does "spectacular" things with white truffles (as in risotto); many consider it one of the best highbrow Italians in town, but even fans find the decor "sad" and say "it's too expensive."

Papillote (La)
– | – | – | I
22, rue Desnouettes, 15ᵉ (Convention), 01 48 56 66 26

Proof that "you shouldn't trust the decor" say admirers of this little bistro in the 15th arrondissement; the setting may be "without interest", but the French cooking is judged "excellent" and a "good value."

Paprika (Le)
– | – | – | M

28, av. Trudaine, 9ᵉ (Anvers/Notre-Dame-de-Lorette), 01 44 63 02 91

One of the rare Hungarians in Paris, serving classic Magyar dishes in a calm corner of the 9th arrondissement with a tranquil terrace in summer; the few surveyors who know it say the female chef-owner is "talented, the host solicitous and the musicians play as if possessed."

Parc aux Cerfs (Le) S
16 | 13 | 14 | fr227

50, rue Vavin, 6ᵉ (Vavin), 01 43 54 87 83

■ Offering "an art gallery atmosphere" in an arty quarter of Montparnasse, this bistro is run by "a dynamic team" that serves "smartly updated, hearty regional [Lyons] dishes at reasonable prices"; more good news: "the welcome and service are very warm" and "there's a little outside terrace in good weather."

Paris (Le)
▽ 19 | 20 | 19 | fr484

Hôtel Lutétia, 45, bd. Raspail, 6ᵉ (Sèvres-Babylone), 01 49 54 46 90

■ With its "grand traditional setting" in the celebrated Hôtel Lutétia near the Bon Marché department store and "'30s-style" deco decor by designer Sonia Rykiel, this intimate Classic French provides a stately backdrop for food that most rate "excellent"; fans say it's "worth a detour" even if prices are on the high side and the ambiance strikes some as rather "somber."

Passy Mandarin S
16 | 12 | 13 | fr262

6, rue d'Antin, 2ᵉ (Opéra), 01 42 61 25 52 ◗
6, rue Bois le Vent, 16ᵉ (La Muette), 01 42 88 12 18

■ "A really excellent Chinese" with "chic decor" in the 16th arrondissement (there's also a younger sibling near the Opéra in the center of town); surveyors applaud "good" Peking duck and the "best spring rolls in Paris", but grumble that "it's a little expensive."

Paul Chêne
19 | 11 | 16 | fr410

123, rue Lauriston, 16ᵉ (Trocadéro/Victor Hugo), 01 47 27 63 17

■ "Very good traditional" French food served in a "very old-fashioned" setting with "well-worn banquettes" draws a following of regulars to this veteran in a quiet street between the Place Victor Hugo and the Trocadéro in the 16th; the ambiance strikes some as "a bit starchy", but "the owner's warm welcome and his truffles" help make it "a sure bet."

Paul (Chez) ◗S
15 | 13 | 12 | fr197

13, rue Charonne, 11ᵉ (Bastille), 01 47 00 34 57

■ "Always packed" (hence you must "always book ahead"), this "lively" bistro near the Bastille is a "favorite" for its "consistently good cooking" and "really good value"; it's "not very comfortable" and "often smoky" and "noisy" but that doesn't bother the trendy young things who come to let their hair down in its "very warm atmosphere."

Pauline (Chez)
20 | 16 | 17 | fr410

5, rue Villédo, 1ᵉʳ (Palais-Royal/Pyramides),
01 42 96 20 70

☑ Near the Palais-Royal, this "typically Parisian bistro" serves "good traditional" fare in a slightly "overwhelming" decor of mirrors, wood paneling and red banquettes; fans find it "comfortable" with food that's "full of flavor", advising "don't miss it when game's in season"; but to critics it's "a disappointing old classic" that's "declined a lot in quality" while "prices have become excessive."

Paul Minchelli
22 | 16 | 17 | fr582

54, bd. de La Tour-Maubourg, 7ᵉ (La Tour-Maubourg),
01 47 05 89 86

☑ While most commend this seafooder near the Invalides for its "excellent, ultrafresh fish with original seasonings", not everyone enjoys Paul's sense of humor, like listing a tin of sardines at an exorbitant price on his "off-the-wall" menu; with "cozy" if "not very cheerful" decor by Slavik, it's the "rendezvous for 'did you see me' TV/show biz types", hence some brand it "for snobs", and others say that while "the quality is very good, prices have become unjustifiable."

Pavillon des Princes ⧈
15 | 13 | 15 | fr345

69, av. de la Porte d'Auteuil, 16ᵉ (Porte d'Auteuil),
01 47 43 15 15

■ In a "slightly out of the way" area near the Porte d'Auteuil, this dressy, "refined" French with "attentive service" offers an appealing prix fixe menu featuring luxurious dishes like a sauté of lobster and langoustines with baby leeks; some find the decor "superb", others say "too classic", but you can "forget about it by looking at what's on your plate" and it's lovely "to dine on the terrace at affordable prices."

Pavillon Montsouris ⧈
16 | 22 | 16 | fr367

20, rue Gazan, 14ᵉ (Cité-Universitaire), 01 45 88 38 52

■ This Belle Epoque pavilion where Mata Hari once practiced her intrigues wins high praise for its "superb decor" and "exceptional setting", which is "especially pleasant on summer nights" when one can sit outside in the gardens of the Parc Montsouris in the 14th; "it's expensive but worth it" for "good, inventive" French cooking from a prix fixe menu; "the valet parking is very practical" too.

Pavillon Panama ⧈
11 | 20 | 11 | fr264

Port de Javel-Haut, 15ᵉ (Javel/RER C), 01 44 37 10 21

■ Ideal when you "want to eat riverside in the middle of Paris" say surveyors about this barge moored in the Seine at the Port de Javel in the 15th; it "needs to make an effort" with the French food and service, but it's pleasant "for business meals" or just to "feel away from it all."

Pavillon Puebla
16 | 19 | 15 | fr369

*Parc des Buttes-Chaumont, 19ᵉ (Buttes-Chaumont/Pyrénées),
01 42 08 92 62*

◪ Set amidst the "greenery" of the Parc des Buttes-Chaumont is a "haven of peace in the middle of Paris, especially on the terrace"; most say it offers "refined" Franco-Catalan cuisine with an "interesting" prix fixe menu, but a few complain of "insipid cooking" and poor service.

Pento (Chez)
▽ 18 | 15 | 16 | fr185

*9, rue Cujas, 5ᵉ (Cluny-La Sorbonne/RER Luxembourg),
01 43 26 81 54*

■ This "little restaurant behind the Sorbonne" dishes up "good, traditional" bistro fare "in a slightly narrow space"; surveyors find it "original and pleasant", especially "at lunch", and appreciate its "varied" menu and "reasonable prices" that draw a young crowd including many students.

Père Claude (Le) ◖⧁
13 | 9 | 12 | fr245

51, av. La Motte-Picquet, 15ᵉ (Motte-Picquet), 01 47 34 03 05

◪ To admirers, this "nice little bistro" run by Claude Perraudin near the Ecole Militaire offers "good value for the money plus a lot of atmosphere", even if the "decor is indifferent"; on the other hand, dissenters find it "overrated", with "ordinary food for high prices", but they're outvoted.

Pergolèse (Le)
18 | 15 | 17 | fr426

*40, rue Pergolèse, 16ᵉ (Porte Dauphine/Porte Maillot),
01 45 00 21 40*

■ This French in the 16th between the Porte Maillot and the Porte Dauphine is "worth recommending" according to supporters who say "you feel deliciously well" here thanks to its "reasonably comfortable setting, good, inventive cuisine and warm welcome", even if "service is slow" and the check high; popular with business diners at noon, it draws well-heeled neighbors at night.

Perraudin ⊭
13 | 11 | 14 | fr158

157, rue St-Jacques, 5ᵉ (RER Luxembourg), 01 46 33 15 75

■ "For those who remain eternal penniless students in the Latin Quarter", regardless of age, this bistro almost in the shadows of the Panthéon offers "authentic French fare" that's "not at all expensive" in a setting that's "crowded" but "deliciously old-fashioned"; "warm service" is a plus.

Perron (Le) ◖⧁
▽ 16 | 10 | 15 | fr219

6, rue Perronet, 7ᵉ (St-Germain-des-Prés), 01 45 44 71 51

■ "At last, a good Italian that doesn't serve pizza" say some who appreciate this cozy spot with '70s "retro decor" in a little street near the Ecole de Médecine in the 7th; pizza-phobic or not, most diners laud its "authentic" fare, served by the "charming" owner at relatively affordable prices.

Petit Colombier (Le)

20 | 15 | 18 | fr402

42, rue des Acacias, 17ᵉ (Argentine/Charles de Gaulle-Etoile), 01 43 80 28 54

■ Designed to resemble a rustic auberge, this Regional French near the Etoile is an "enjoyable escape" for a well-dressed affluent crowd that comes to savor its "good classic cooking" and service; it's called a "very good value for high-quality game and truffle dishes", though otherwise some find it "a bit expensive."

Petite Auberge (La)

15 | 12 | 13 | fr270

38, rue Laugier, 17ᵉ (Pereire/Ternes), 01 47 63 85 51

■ "A quality restaurant that's worth discovering" say admirers of this Regional French in the 17th between the Place Pereire and Ternes; the Burgundy-style food is "ordinary but good, and the rustic setting makes the place appealing" in the eyes of some; "pleasant" service and "reasonable" prices are pluses.

Petite Bretonnière (La)

▽ 17 | 11 | 17 | fr353

2, rue de Cadix, 15ᵉ (Porte de Versailles), 01 48 28 34 39

■ "The new chef isn't as good as his predecessor but is still a fine cook" opine regulars of this French restaurant near the Porte de Versailles; even if the dollhouse-like decor doesn't win high ratings, it's "a place to discover" for "excellent" food including "good fish" like cod in hazelnut oil with a honeyed onion puree, served by a professional staff at rather lofty prices.

Petite Chaise (A La) 🅂

11 | 13 | 12 | fr211

36, rue de Grenelle, 7ᵉ (Sèvres-Babylone), 01 42 22 13 35

☑ Dating to 1680, this is one of "the oldest restaurants in Paris" so it's only appropriate that it serves Classic French cuisine "from the good old times" in a "traditional" setting; a few critics claim it's "living on its reputation" and "attracts too many tourists" due to its Saint-Germain location, but prices remain "very moderate."

Petite Cour (La) 🌑🅂

15 | 15 | 12 | fr280

8, rue Mabillon, 6ᵉ (Mabillon), 01 43 26 52 26

■ It may be in a "touristy" area near the Place Saint-Sulpice, but this is considered a "classy little restaurant that's worth a trip" for "good if slightly expensive" French fare served in a "pleasant setting", especially in summer when one can dine on the terrace and in the garden.

Petites Sorcières (Les)

15 | 10 | 13 | fr220

12, rue Liancourt, 14ᵉ (Denfert-Rochereau), 01 43 21 95 68

☑ While supporters call this little family-style French near the Place Denfert-Rochereau "very, very good from all points of view", with a "charming welcome" and affordable prices, some snipe that "portions are stingy and the food sometimes dull", adding that the reception can also be a bit cold.

Petite Tour (La)
17 | **12** | **15** | fr**400**

11, rue de la Tour, 16ᵉ (Passy), 01 45 20 09 31

■ Surveyors find "excellent cooking in an old-fashioned setting" at this pleasant little French in Passy, praising its "incomparable turbot", "attractive wines" and "good prix fixe menu"; the "plush" "family-style" atmosphere attracts "BCBG [bourgeois]" types who don't seem to mind if it's easy to run up a big tab here.

Petit Gavroche (Le) ●
▬ | ▬ | ▬ | ▬

15, rue Ste-Croix-la-Bretonnerie, 4ᵉ (Hôtel-de-Ville), 01 48 87 74 26

A young, pennywise crowd finds its way to this bistro behind the Hôtel-de-Ville to enjoy "tasty food at easy prices" served in a "pretty, Parisian-style" setting with an "easygoing" feel.

Petit Keller (Le) ●
▬ | ▬ | ▬ | ▬

13, rue Keller, 11ᵉ (Bastille), 01 47 00 12 97

While popular with young trendies who like to hang out in the lively Bastille district and its many art galleries, this "good neighborhood" French is also a "family-style restaurant par excellence"; unbeatable prices are a big part of the appeal.

Petit Laurent (Le)
▽ **18** | **14** | **17** | fr**385**

38, rue de Varenne, 7ᵉ (Rue du Bac), 01 45 48 79 64

■ "Sophisticated, calm and refined" is how surveyors describe this Classic French in a part of the 7th that's dense with ministries and embassies; even if "the ownership changes regularly, it remains really good", offering reinvented classics like quail stuffed with foie gras and John Dory in anchovy butter in a "warm", intimate room done in tones of pale blue and yellow.

Petit Lutétia (Au) ⑤
14 | **13** | **14** | fr**234**

107, rue de Sèvres, 6ᵉ (Vaneau), 01 45 48 33 53

■ The fly-in-amber, circa 1900 charm of this "solidly traditional bourgeois brasserie" not far from the Bon Marché department store and Rue de Sèvres shops is complemented by classic fare (oysters, steaks, etc.) that's deemed an "excellent value"; given its "typically Parisian decor" and "friendly service", it's considered a "good place to recommend to out-of-towners."

Petit Mâchon (Le)
14 | **9** | **11** | fr**210**

123, rue de la Convention, 15ᵉ (Boucicaut), 01 45 54 08 62

■ Respondents who've ventured to this "simple" little bistro in a slightly out of the way corner of the 15th arrondissement say it serves "good", "solid Lyonnaise food" that's "not too expensive" in a "really pleasant and warm atmosphere"; perhaps it's "nothing to talk about", but it's "not disappointing" either.

Petit Marguery (Le)   20 | 15 | 17 | fr308
9, bd. de Port-Royal, 13ᵉ (Les Gobelins), 01 43 31 58 59
■ A "total delight" of a bistro in the Gobelins district run by the Cousin brothers, who are hailed as "fine, friendly restaurateurs"; perhaps "the decor doesn't please everyone", "it's a little expensive and service can be overwhelmed", but "the welcome is excellent" and so is the food – it's especially "interesting in game season" and there's a "Grand Marnier soufflé that's worth the trip."

Petit Navire (Le)   16 | 13 | 17 | fr252
14, rue des Fossés-St-Bernard, 5ᵉ (Jussieu), 01 43 54 22 52
■ "For over 30 years" this seafooder has represented "tradition and excellence" in the Jussieu district of the 5th arrondissement; it serves "authentic cooking from Sète" (a Mediterranean port with an important fishing fleet) in a "family-style" atmosphere with nautical decor and "good service" led by a "smiling" hostess-owner; prices are relatively modest compared to other Paris fish houses.

Petit Niçois (Le)   18 | 8 | 13 | fr231
10, rue Amélie, 7ᵉ (La Tour-Maubourg), 01 45 51 83 65
■ This "solid", "no-frills" seafood specialist in a residential part of the 7th is noted by surveyors for its "very good bouillabaisse" and the "consistency" and "freshness" of its Provençal-accented offerings; the setting may be "simple" but it offers "extremely fine value for the money."

Petit Plat (Le)   ▽ 17 | 11 | 14 | fr253
49, av. Emile Zola, 15ᵉ (Charles-Michels), 01 45 78 24 20
■ "Very good value" is a recurring compliment for this little French in a slightly remote residential part of the 15th; the food is judged "excellent" and the welcome is "pleasant" in this small, vaguely deco dining room with a decidedly easygoing ambiance; note that some complain of "poor ventilation" and no real nonsmoking area; N.B. the gently priced wine list is the work of Henri Gault of Gault et Millau, whose daughter is one of the owners.

Petit Poucet (Le) ◗🅂   12 | 16 | 12 | fr248
4, rd-pt Claude Monet, Levallois (Porte de Levallois), 01 47 38 61 85
■ You "feel miles away from the city" at this "pretty" place perched on the edge of the Seine on the Ile de la Jatte ("ask for a table overlooking the river"); the atmosphere is "trendy and friendly", and if the French food "isn't transcendent", most find it "varied and original", as well as "reasonable"; popular with "advertising types" at noon, it pulls a stylish young crowd at night.

Petit Prince de Paris (Le) ◖🅂 $\boxed{14}$ $\boxed{13}$ $\boxed{15}$ $\boxed{\text{fr199}}$

12, rue de Lanneau, 5ᵉ (Maubert-Mutualité), 01 43 54 77 26

■ Surveyors happily "let themselves be tamed" by this polite, "very gay and cosmopolitan" French on the slopes of the Panthéon; a "fine value", it offers "good, simple food" in a "pretty" ochre-toned setting with a wine list that's "well chosen, even if there are no remarkable bottles"; "the preferences of the clientele are quite open so it's not for the narrow-minded", but on the other hand "it's the perfect gay restaurant to dine at with your mother."

Petit Rétro (Le) $\boxed{13}$ $\boxed{11}$ $\boxed{12}$ $\boxed{\text{fr237}}$

5, rue Mesnil, 16ᵉ (Victor Hugo), 01 44 05 06 05

■ "A good little neighborhood place" in a very bourgeois part of town just steps from the Place Victor Hugo; the bistro cooking, which runs to steaks and a fish or two, is solid, tasty and "reasonably priced", served in a simple but pleasant setting with art nouveau tiles and a zinc bar; it's "great for a light lunch" even if "you're sort of on top of each other."

Petit Riche (Au) ◖ $\boxed{14}$ $\boxed{17}$ $\boxed{14}$ $\boxed{\text{fr282}}$

25, rue Le Peletier, 9ᵉ (Le Peletier/Richelieu-Drouot), 01 47 70 68 68

◪ The "elegant salons are perfect for a business meal" at this handsome Regional French in the 9th featuring "unique decor" that evokes the Paris of Balzac and Flaubert with original gas lamps (now electric), wood paneling and etched glass; the kitchen serves dishes from the Loire Valley, but some find the quality "uneven" and cynics note "tradition has its price" – "here everything is rich: the cooking, the clients and the bill."

Petit Robert (Le) ◖🚭 $\boxed{-}$ $\boxed{-}$ $\boxed{-}$ $\boxed{\text{ }|\text{ }}$

10, rue Cauchois, 18ᵉ (Blanche), 01 46 06 04 46

A reasonably priced little Basque in Montmarte that's appreciated by the few surveyors who know it for its "frequently changing prix fixe menu" and "highly convivial" atmosphere enhanced by occasional cabaret acts and the banter of owner Henri Fischer.

Petit St-Benoît (Le) 🚭 $\boxed{10}$ $\boxed{10}$ $\boxed{9}$ $\boxed{\text{fr169}}$

4, rue St-Benoît, 6ᵉ (St-Germain-des-Prés), 01 42 60 27 92

■ This "institution" just down the street from the Café de Flore in Saint-Germain is very "likable and cheap", even if the bistro cooking "leaves something to be desired"; fans like its old Paris touches ("there's even a napkin rack") and find the waitresses "down to earth" and "charming", if sometimes "tired from the hectic pace."

Petit Victor Hugo (Le) ◗

11 | 11 | 11 | fr239

143, av. Victor Hugo, 16ᵉ (Rue de la Pompe/Victor Hugo),
01 45 53 02 68

◪ Critics dismiss this "very 16th arrondissement" brasserie as "uninteresting", citing "an unfriendly welcome" and "declining quality"; but they're outnumbered by defenders who insist "it's pleasant and reasonably priced", serving "nicely cooked traditional dishes" including a popular Camembert omelet; "late hours are a plus."

Petit Zinc (Le) ◗ⓢ

13 | 15 | 13 | fr283

11, rue St-Benoît, 6ᵉ (St-Germain-des-Prés), 01 42 61 20 60

◪ Everyone likes the "pretty setting" of this 1930s vintage bistro with lovely ceramics and wood paneling in the heart of Saint-Germain, but opinions on the food are mixed: "good cooking" vs. "a shadow of itself", "a factory"; still, it attracts a "clientele of regulars and tourists" even if it's a bit "expensive for what it serves."

Pétrus ⓢ

19 | 16 | 16 | fr454

12, place du Maréchal Juin, 17ᵉ (Pereire/Levallois), 01 43 80 15 95

■ This plush traditional fish house in the 17th is mostly well regarded; regulars love the "excellent sea bass cooked in a salt crust" and also cite the shellfish and "best potato puree in Paris"; "too expensive" is the other resounding verdict, but most feel the quality merits the stiff tab.

Pharamond

15 | 19 | 14 | fr334

24, rue de la Grande-Truanderie, 1ᵉʳ (Etienne-Marcel),
01 42 33 06 72

◪ The "superb decor" (art nouveau wall tiles and winding wooden stairway to the second floor) continues to charm at this venerable spot in Les Halles; once a favorite of the late president François Mitterrand, it's "slipping" according to some, but admirers still extol their *tripes à la mode de Caen* (cooked in cider) and other Norman specialties.

PHILIPPE DETOURBE

22 | 14 | 18 | fr295

8, rue Nicolas Charlet, 15ᵉ (Pasteur), 01 42 19 08 59

■ Most Parisians judge the prix fixe menu offered by this rising young chef to be "excellent for the price", lauding his "succulent, imaginative" bistro cooking featuring "original combinations of flavors and textures"; however, a few lament "bird-sized" portions and the "expensive" wine list, and everyone wishes it were easier to get a reservation.

Pichet (Le) ◗ⓢ

17 | 11 | 15 | fr353

68, rue Pierre Charron, 8ᵉ (Franklin Roosevelt), 01 43 59 50 34

■ This brasserie with a stylish crowd just off the Champs-Elysées wins high praise for its "always remarkably fresh" fish and shellfish; political bigwigs, racing-car drivers and media types give it a buzz, but some say it's "too showy" and "you have to fight the celebs to get a table"; many also find it "a little too expensive", with "uninteresting" decor.

Pied de Chameau (Au) ●◗⑤   14 | 20 | 12 | fr211
20, rue Quincampoix, 4ᵉ (Hôtel-de-Ville), 01 42 78 35 00
■ "Plunge into a Moroccan atmosphere" at this intimate
Marais restaurant that's "made a big effort with the decor";
most applaud the "excellent Moroccan cooking", such as
a tagine of preserved duck with dates, but some find the
service "impersonal" and prices "a little high."

Pied de Cochon (Au) ●◗⑤   13 | 14 | 12 | fr265
*6, rue Coquillière, 1ᵉʳ (Châtelet-Les Halles/Louvre Rivoli),
01 40 13 77 00*
☑ While fans say this long-running, 24-hour brasserie in Les
Halles serves "the best pigs' feet in Paris", foes call it a
"tourist trap" that's "living on its reputation"; still, most enjoy
eyeing the late-night crowd and "pretty decor", and though
the famous onion soup can now be "watery and tepid",
it's ok for oysters and a steak "after a night on the town."

Pied de Fouet (Au) ⌀   13 | 11 | 12 | fr204
45, rue de Babylone, 7ᵉ (Vaneau), 01 47 05 12 27
■ Once frequented by Cocteau, this "minuscule" "mythical
place" in a chic 7th arrondissement neighborhood serves
"excellent family-style French cuisine" – "why go home
when you can come here for home cooking?", and at such
"good-value prices" that it's "ideal for a meal with friends
who are broke"; regulars get a coveted space in the old-
fashioned napkin rack, creating a certain "snobbery."

"Pierre" à la Fontaine Gaillon ●◗⑤ 17 | 16 | 16 | fr344
1, place Gaillon, 2ᵉ (Opéra), 01 47 42 63 22
■ The "marvelous terrace" and "pleasant rooms on the
first floor" make this "classic" near the Opéra "ideal for a
business lunch"; the traditional French cooking also wins
approval ("good memories of the grilled salmon"), as does
the "excellent service."

Pierre au Palais Royal ●   17 | 11 | 15 | fr329
10, rue Richelieu, 1ᵉʳ (Palais-Royal), 01 42 96 09 17
☑ Though some say "the Dez family is difficult to replace",
most feel that the arrival of Jean-Paul Arabian (husband of
Ledoyen's Ghislaine Arabian) has sparked a "renaissance"
at this French next to the Palais-Royal; the new regime
has freshened the decor with low lighting and flowers,
creating a stylish setting for fare made with "excellent"
ingredients and a more contemporary touch; "good
value" is the majority verdict.

Pierre (Chez)   ▽ 15 | 10 | 15 | fr254
117, rue de Vaugirard, 15ᵉ (Falguière), 01 47 34 96 12
■ Regulars of this homey bistro near the Montparnasse
Tower love its "extremely honest, quality" cooking, "good
little wines" and "excellent game in season", calling it a
"good classic address" "for when you can't afford Drouant."

PIERRE GAGNAIRE 🅂   26 | 20 | 21 | fr740

Hôtel Balzac, 6, rue Balzac, 8ᵉ (George V), 01 44 35 18 25

■ The latest contender in the world of French haute cuisine, Pierre Gagnaire, formerly of Saint-Etienne and now in the Hôtel Balzac, wins accolades as "one of the great chefs of our time" and "a genuis at associating different tastes"; it's his "superb imagination" that most impresses, so even if some find his cooking "too intellectual" and the modern setting less than inspiring, it's deemed "an extraordinary experience" – but it's "too bad he has so few good wines."

Pierre Vedel   18 | 12 | 15 | fr310

19, rue Duranton, 15ᵉ (Boucicaut), 01 45 58 43 17

■ Regulars revere the eponymous chef-owner at this bistro deep in the 15th, praising his "generous, good quality food" along with the "excellent value" and service; "superb tête de veau" and "good bourride" are favorites from the mix of French classics and dishes of Sète on the Mediterranean.

Pile ou Face   19 | 13 | 17 | fr387

52 bis, rue Notre-Dame-des-Victoires, 2ᵉ (Bourse), 01 42 33 64 33

◩ A change of owners at this intimate eatery near the stock exchange lowered its value for some ("less good since it changed hands", "lots of cinema, mediocre food"), but as solid ratings attest, most are still bullish on its "good cuisine and wines", "cozy", "elegant" decor and staff "that works hard to please"; the free-range poultry gets high marks: "one of my best memories – the perfect pigeon."

Pinocchio   ▽ 15 | 11 | 15 | fr241

124, av. du Maine, 14ᵉ (Gaîté), 01 43 21 26 10

■ "This restaurant doesn't lie" say admirers of its "good traditional Italian cooking"; it's a standby for many of its 14th district neighbors, and while the decor doesn't earn high marks, diners like "listening to the owner speak Sicilian dialect" and enjoy the small front terrace in summer.

Plancha (La) ◗⇱   ▽ 21 | 17 | 15 | fr175

34, rue Keller, 11ᵉ (Bastille), 01 48 05 20 30

■ Fans say "the only real tapas in Paris" are found near the Bastille at this tiny Basque where "the ambiance is warm but informal, so not to everyone's taste"; while most rate the fare "very good", not all are charmed by the owner's patter.

Planet Hollywood ◗🅂   6 | 15 | 8 | fr189

76-78, av. des Champs-Elysées, 8ᵉ (Franklin Roosevelt/George V), 01 53 83 78 27

◩ This is one planet most Parisians would rather not visit: "once is more than enough", "put in orbit as far away as possible"; the Champs-Elysées outpost of this movie-themed chain has "amusing" decor, and it's "one of the only places in Paris to find Gerard Départdieu's Chateau Tigné wine", but the American-style menu is a box office flop: "overpriced" "fast food", "gastronomes, stay away."

Polidor ◑⑤≠ 11 14 13 fr162
41, rue Monsieur le Prince, 6ᵉ (Luxembourg/Odéon),
01 43 26 95 34
☑ "Classic cooking for students" in the Latin Quarter is
dished up at this "simple, efficient" old bistro with elbow-
to-elbow seating (so "businessmen abstain"); partisans
call it a "timeless institution" for low-cost, grandmotherly
French fare, but a few critics claim it's become a "tourist
trap", asking "what have our handsome students become?"

Poquelin (Le) 17 14 17 fr328
17, rue Molière, 1ᵉʳ (Palais-Royal), 01 42 96 22 19
■ "An intelligent kitchen" "without pretensions" and
offering "very good value" draws a loyal crowd to this bistro
midway between the Palais-Royal and the Opéra; grilled
salmon in parsley cream and roast lamb with thyme are
typical of the "honest" cooking here.

Port Alma 19 14 17 fr417
10, av. de New York, 16ᵉ (Alma-Marceau), 01 47 23 75 11
☑ With its "excellent seafood", "very friendly welcome"
and fine view of the Eiffel Tower, this Seine-side fish
house provides most surveyors with an agreeable night
out; but a few nitpickers note it's "a litte expensive" and
find the atmosphere "a bit sad" and "not much fun."

Port du Salut (Le) ⑤ ▽ 13 12 13 fr172
163 bis, rue St-Jacques, 5ᵉ (Luxembourg), 01 46 33 63 21
☑ This classic Latin Quarter budget address and its old-
fashioned bistro fare draw mixed reviews: "pleasant" for
some, touristy for others; still, the young regulars who come
for sturdy fare in this former cabaret with a cozy basement
dining room give it a lively atmosphere.

Porte Océane (La) ⑤ ▽ 14 11 11 fr253
11, bd. Vaugirard, 15ᵉ (Montparnasse-Bienvenue),
01 43 21 78 28
☑ Adjacent to the Montparnasse train station, this fish
house has sought to reinvent the grand tradition of train
station dining in Paris, with mixed results: cynics say it
allows you "to leave Paris without regrets", but supporters
find it "a pleasant place to eat before a train" with "good
seafood"; some feel the decor could use a boost, though.

Poste (La) ◑⑤ 10 19 10 fr246
22, rue de Douai, 9ᵉ (Blanche/Place de Clichy),
01 45 26 50 00
☑ While everyone loves the lush decor of this 19th-century
townhouse on the edge of Pigalle, the Asian-Eclectic food
needs "to be improved", ditto the "poor welcome"; frequent
changes of management and chef have blurred the
reputation of this place, though that doesn't necessarily
discourage "fashion victims" who come to "show off."

Poule au Pot (La) ◐ S ▽ 17 | 17 | 16 | fr211

9, rue Vauvilliers, 1er (Les Halles/Louvre-Rivoli), 01 42 36 32 96

■ The "warm welcome" at this "pleasant", "typically Parisian" old bistro open all night in Les Halles is almost as much of a draw as the food; poule au pot and calf's kidneys are specialties on a menu judged to offer "good value."

Pré Carré (Le) ◐ 17 | 12 | 17 | fr326

Hôtel Splendid-Etoile, 3, av. Carnot, 17e (Charles de Gaulle-Etoile), 01 46 22 57 35

◪ While some enjoy the "calm" atmosphere at this elegant French with black lacquered walls near the Arc de Triomphe, others find it "a little somber"; as for the traditional food, most rate it "good", though it doesn't always leave a lasting impression: "can't remember what I ate."

PRÉ CATELAN (LE) S 21 | 25 | 20 | fr576

Bois de Boulogne, route de Suresnes, 16e (Porte Dauphine), 01 44 14 41 14

■ There's a "marvelous" sunset view in summer, which is the preferred season for this "splendidly decorated" French with a "delightful terrace" in the Bois de Boulogne; if the traditional food does't provoke the same ecstasies as the setting, most find it "very honorable" and "sophisticated", though some regret "stingy portions", high prices and desserts that can be "disappointing."

Président (Le) ◐ S 12 | 15 | 8 | fr186

120, rue du Fbg. du Temple, 11e (Belleville), 01 47 00 17 18

◪ This "gigantic", "noisy" Chinese in Belleville is perfect "for a dinner for 130" or just "with a group of friends"; the decor (with a monumental stairway and a cupola) is "worth a detour" and they serve late, so it doesn't matter if there's debate over the food: "authentic", "best dim sum and Peking duck" vs. "mediocre", "no surprise to the taste buds."

PRESSOIR (AU) 23 | 17 | 20 | fr436

257, av. Daumesnil, 12e (Michel-Bizot), 01 43 44 38 21

■ In spite of its "slightly remote" location in the 12th arrondissement, this traditional French pulls crowds due to its "excellent cooking" (including "very delicate dishes like a millefeuille of truffles") and "exceptional wine list"; the "charming welcome", "pretty decor" and "generous portions" add to the pleasure.

Procope (Le) ◐ S 11 | 19 | 12 | fr279

13, rue de l'Ancienne-Comédie, 6e (Odéon), 01 40 46 79 00

◪ "Benjamin Franklin would have appreciated it more than we do" is one judgment on this historic 17th-century cafe-turned-restaurant near the Odéon; critics hope he and Voltaire "ate better" than modern-day diners who mostly find the French fare "run-of-the-mill" and "disappointing"; but the "pretty decor" is a consolation at what some call a "sad exploitation of a fine history."

P'tit Troquet (Le)   ▽ 23 | 19 | 25 | fr283
28, rue de L'Exposition, 7ᵉ (Ecole Militaire),
01 47 05 80 39

■ "A little pearl where the menu changes every day, but the welcome is always friendly" say fans of this bistro near the Ecole Militaire; "the chef learned his trade with some of the greats" and works with "ingredients fresh from the market", turning out "good food" that's nicely served in a cozy room with '20s decor; "since it's small", you're advised to "book in advance."

Quai Ouest ◐Ⓢ   11 | 17 | 10 | fr249
1200, quai Marcel Dassault, St-Cloud (Pont de St-Cloud),
01 46 02 35 54

☑ "Popular with advertising and show biz types" and "a stylish young crowd", this Saint-Cloud French is "great in summer" when the "wonderful terrace" and Seine-side location make "you believe you're in San Francisco or Cape Town"; some find the trendy food "good", others label it "cafeteria" grade, but all enjoy the "great atmosphere."

404 (Le) ◐Ⓢ   18 | 23 | 13 | fr227
69, rue des Gravilliers, 3ᵉ (Arts-et-Métiers),
01 42 74 57 81

■ Expected to reopen at press time, this "stylish" spot owned by Smaïn, the popular French comedian, is known for its "excellent North African" fare served in an ambiance that recalls "the Casbah in Algiers."

Quercy (Le)   – | – | – | M
36, rue Condorcet, 9ᵉ (Anvers), 01 48 78 30 61

This old-fashioned Southwestern French bistro is buried away in the 9th arrondissement but the "cooking merits the trip" since it's "honest and good", "the cassoulet is the lightest in town" and prices are "good value"; too bad about the "rather sad" decor.

Quincy (Le) ⋈   20 | 15 | 20 | fr323
28, av. Ledru-Rollin, 12ᵉ (Gare de Lyon/Quai de la Rapée),
01 46 28 46 76

■ Devotees are "happy to be alive" after a meal at this "charming place" not far from the Bastille and the Gare de Lyon; with an "outgoing owner" and "copious portions" of "rustic", "succulent regional French" food, it's "always a pleasure", even if it can be "a bit expensive."

Ravi   ▽ 20 | 18 | 14 | fr315
50, rue de Verneuil, 7ᵉ (Rue du Bac), 01 42 61 17 28

■ "One of the best and most expensive Indian" restaurants in Paris, this "minuscule" Left Bank nook with "artistic decor" near the Musée d'Orsay is "warm and exceptionally good"; just don't be in a rush: "a meal here can take hours."

Récamier (Le)
19 | 16 | 16 | fr428

4, rue Récamier, 7ᵉ (Sèvres-Babylone), 01 45 48 86 58

■ The decor "needs to be refreshed" at this "intellectual", "elitist" Left Bank classic frequented by editors, "the whole Assemblée Nationale" and "rightist, but never leftist, politicians", yet everyone loves its "refinement" and "very pleasant" terrace; the "classic" Burgundian fare is a "sure bet" if "sometimes heavy", and the wine list is "exceptional."

Rech
16 | 12 | 14 | fr305

62, av. des Ternes, 17ᵉ (Charles de Gaulle-Etoile/Ternes), 01 45 72 29 47

■ Despite the "sad decor", "a slightly old-fashioned clientele" remains loyal to this bourgeois classic in the 17th arrondissement; they delight in its "good shellfish" and "delicious fish" (carnivores are catered to as well, but fish is the specialty) along with the Camembert served whole and "famous" giant éclair.

Réconfort (Le)
▽ 15 | 19 | 12 | fr220

37, rue de Poitou, 3ᵉ (St-Sébastien-Froissart), 01 42 76 06 36

■ Tucked away in the Marais, this stylish bistro with "superb decor" (flower-print fabrics and large round tables) is a hit with the fashion crowd; the food's "original" too and service is "attentive" – all in all, a "good value."

Régalade (La) ◑
21 | 11 | 14 | fr274

49, av. Jean Moulin, 14ᵉ (Alésia), 01 45 45 68 58

■ Vexing though it may be to reserve three weeks in advance at this "noisy" bistro in a remote corner of the 14th, the contemporary cooking of Yves Camdeborde ("the best young chef in Paris") is "excellent" and an "exceptionally good value"; the main complaint: "it's too successful", which may explain gripes about "mediocre" service and "too closely spaced" tables.

RÉGENCE (LE) ⑤
23 | 24 | 23 | fr688

Hôtel Plaza-Athénée, 25, av. Montaigne, 8ᵉ (Alma-Marceau/Franklin Roosevelt), 01 53 67 65 00

■ The "elegant" dining room at the Hôtel Plaza-Athénée serves "excellent" traditional French food and has "all the class expected of a grand hotel"; "here all is luxury, and real luxury has its price" observes one regular; in good weather, the floral bower of an interior courtyard is the place to be.

Relais d'Auteuil
20 | 15 | 19 | fr430

31, bd. Murat, 16ᵉ (Michel-Ange-Molitor/Porte d'Auteuil), 01 46 51 09 54

■ This "luxury bistro" deep in the 16th arrondissement wins raves for its "impeccable cuisine", "excellent welcome" and "efficient service"; frequented by a well-heeled clientele, the small beige-toned room can get a bit "noisy at noon" and the bill can be "expensive", but most consider it well worth it.

Relais de Sèvres (Le)   ▽ | 19 | 16 | 19 | fr496
*Sofitel-Porte de Sèvres, 8-12, rue Louis Armand, 15ᵉ
(Balard), 01 40 60 33 66*
■ "A lot of class" say admirers of this Contemporary French in the Sofitel hotel on the edge of Paris in the 15th; lamb sautéed with baby artichokes is typical of the "good cooking" and it's a handy option if you're attending a trade show at the nearby exhibition halls.

Relais de Venise (Le) ◑Ｓ   18 | 11 | 15 | fr200
271, bd. Pereire, 17ᵉ (Porte Maillot), 01 45 74 27 97
■ At the Porte Maillot, this steakhouse with a "well-merited reputation" has offered "the same formula for 20 years – delicious steaks with frites" and "the quality's always constant"; the prix fixe meal starts with a green salad and ends with "excellent desserts", making it a real "deal", but no reserving vexes many and nonsmokers wish they were given more breathing room.

Relais du Parc (Le) Ｓ   18 | 18 | 16 | fr396
*Le Parc Westin Demeure Hôtel, 55-57, av. Raymond
Poincaré, 16ᵉ (Trocadéro/Victor Hugo), 01 44 05 66 10*
☑ Alain Ducasse, whose eponymous restaurant is next door, directs the kitchen of this handsome restaurant surrounding a "dreamy" courtyard in the Parc Westin Demeure Hôtel; while many praise its "good, inventive" cooking, others feel "the details need attention" and wonder about the extent of Ducasse's involvement at this "purported annex"; the recent introduction of a new round-the-world menu may augur well for the future.

Relais Louis XIII   21 | 20 | 20 | fr456
*8, rue des Grands-Augustins, 6ᵉ (Odéon/St-Michel),
01 43 26 75 96*
■ Chef Manuel Martinez has staged an impressive comeback in taking over the kitchen at this venerable Left Bank address after his nine-year stint at La Tour d'Argent; "Martinez is on the right track" say admirers of his "excellent cooking" that represents "very good value" in this price range; "pretty decor" with "nice paintings and marble" makes a meal here like "eating in a museum."

Relais Plaza (Le) ◑Ｓ   16 | 18 | 19 | fr399
*Hôtel Plaza-Athénée, 21, av. Montaigne, 8ᵉ
(Alma-Marceau/Franklin Roosevelt), 01 53 67 64 00*
☑ The "superb oceanliner decor" at this "very chic" art deco dining room in the Hôtel Plaza-Athénée and the "surprising" human scenery ("at last, some elegant women") are more of a draw than the French food, which is labeled circa "1960" by critics who complain that "the necktie requirement is more important than what's on your plate"; you can get a "good club sandwich" though.

Réminet 🅂   – | – | – | M
3, rue des Grands Degrés, 5ᵉ (Maubert-Mutualité), 01 44 07 04 24
Parisians are starting to discover this tiny Latin Quarter
bistro where a young chef "seduces with the quality and
originality of his cooking", which has "a lot of flavor"; though
the dining room is likened to a "hallway", the "friendly
service and welcome" of the chef's wife compensate.

Rendez-vous des   11 | 8 | 13 | fr162
Camionneurs (Au) 🍴
34, rue des Plantes, 14ᵉ (Alésia/Plaisance), 01 45 40 43 36
■ This "tiny spot with a hard-working couple dishing up
good simple food" is a popular traditional French budget
address just behind Montparnasse; if looking for a gourmet
feed, go elsewhere, but "to eat on the cheap it's fun."

Rendez-vous des Chauffeurs (Au) 🅂   – | – | – | M
11, rue des Portes-Blanches, 18ᵉ (Marcadet-Poissonniers),
01 42 64 04 17
A rendezvous for serious bargain hunters, since it's buried
away in the remotest reaches of the 18th arrondissement;
fans say it offers "low-cost pleasure" with French food
"like Grandma's" served in a setting "like home"; the three-
course prix fixe, including some harmless red wine, is a deal.

René (Chez)   16 | 12 | 16 | fr260
14, bd. St-Germain, 5ᵉ (Maubert-Mutualité), 01 43 54 30 23
☑ It's "the perfect bistro" for many, but some note that
this sepia-toned spot in the Latin Quarter "has its ups
and downs"; "real Burgundian cooking like coq au vin
and boeuf bourguignon" and "superb charcuterie" served
with "the best Beaujolais" keep admirers loyal, even though
prices are creeping up.

Repaire de Cartouche (Le)   19 | 12 | 13 | fr250
99, rue Amelot, 11ᵉ (St-Sébastien-Froissart), 01 47 00 25 86
■ Young chef Rodolphe Paquin, who won a big following
at Le Saint Amarante with his bold, earthy take on French
regional home cooking, has been a hit since he took over
this split-level bistro not far from the Bastille: "outstanding",
"excellent since the change in ownership" are typical
accolades for this talent to watch.

Réservoir (Le) ◐   11 | 20 | 10 | fr242
16, rue de la Forge-Royale, 11ᵉ (Ledru-Rolllin),
01 43 56 39 60
☑ This trendy nightspot near the Bastille pleases with its
"surprising decor" in a "dark old warehouse", but most
come more for the "cool scene" than to eat – the traditional
French food "is dull" "but the place rocks"; amateurish
service leads to complaints of "waiting much too long."

Restaurant (Le) ●   ▽ 18 | 11 | 11 | fr230
32, rue Véron, 18ᵉ (Abbesses/Blanche), 01 42 23 06 22
☑ Yves Peladeau wins good marks for spicy Contemporary French cooking at this often "full and noisy" Montmartre venue with "colonial" decor and a "show-biz clientele"; but one thing customers might hope for is improved service.

Restaurant A ●●⑤   ▽ 18 | 6 | 19 | fr243
5, rue de Poissy, 5ᵉ (Maubert-Mutualité), 01 46 33 85 54
■ The fashion and media crowd has moved on from this Latin Quarter Chinese popular in the '80s, but it still fascinates with its "art of making human and animal figures in rice paste" and "carving ice and vegetables" "with exceptional talent"; however, some fear that the kitchen "confuses cooking with sculpting."

Restaurant de la Tour   ▽ 16 | 10 | 13 | fr268
6, rue Desaix, 15ᵉ (Dupleix), 01 43 06 04 24
■ This bistro near the Champ-de-Mars is the stronghold of Roger Conticini; while his two sons cook innovative dishes at La Table d'Anvers, the kitchen here is traditional with Southwestern French and Provençale food; "follow Papa Conticini's advice" when you order from the "good value" menu and don't miss the "excellent wines."

RESTAURANT D'ERIC FRÉCHON   23 | 11 | 17 | fr285
10, rue du Général Brunet, 19ᵉ (Botzaris/Danube), 01 40 40 03 30
■ Young chef Eric Fréchon's "divinely inventive and refined" contemporary bistro cuisine, noted as being an "excellent value for the money", has Parisians happily making the pilgrimage to this remote corner of the 19th arrondissement; "efficient, discreet service" also wins praise, but some find the ambiance "too bistro for food of this class."

Restaurant des Beaux Arts ⑤   9 | 11 | 9 | fr167
11, rue Bonaparte, 6ᵉ (St-Germain-des-Prés), 01 43 26 92 64
☑ Given its "bohemian charm with paper tablecloths" and "relaxed" atmosphere, many surveyors are forgiving of the "sad" French cooking at this classic student's bistro in Saint-Germain; it's "ok for el cheapo" eats "when you're broke" or "want to hang around backpackers."

Restaurant des Chauffeurs ⑤   10 | 6 | 12 | fr152
8, chaussée-de-la-Muette, 16ᵉ (La Muette), 01 42 88 50 05
■ This "good old neighborhood standby" near La Muette is "a working-class island" in the ritzy 16th and one of the district's "best bargains" according to those who love its "blue-collar diner atmosphere" and "unpretentious" daily specials; "fast" and "practical" sums it up.

Restaurant du Marché
19 | 11 | 15 | fr319

59, rue de Dantzig, 15ᵉ (Porte de Versailles), 01 48 28 31 55
■ "Very good Southwestern French cooking" including "one of the best cassoulets in Paris" draws mature well-heeled bon vivants to this spot near the Porte de Versailles; the "provincial decor" is a fine backdrop for the likes of "great foie gras" and "an Armagnac from your birth year", but "indecent" prices lead some to call it "overestimated."

Restaurant du Musée d'Orsay S
10 | 22 | 11 | fr250

1, rue de Bellechasse, 7ᵉ (Solférino), 01 45 49 47 03
◩ With its parquet floors, ormolu and painted ceilings, the "superb decor" of the dining room at the Musée d'Orsay rates higher than the "not very good" French fare; while strident critics call it a veritable "cafeteria of frozen foods", most find it "acceptable for a museum meal."

Restaurant du Palais Royal
18 | 20 | 14 | fr260

110, Galerie-de-Valois, 1ᵉʳ (Bourse), 01 40 20 00 27
■ "The best time is when you can sit in the gardens", and the gardens of the Palais-Royal are surely some of the world's most beautiful, framed by this 17th-century landmark's grand architecture; happily, the "excellent" French food with modern touches holds its own, and diners also enjoy the "relaxed atmosphere" and "friendly" service.

Restaurant Opéra
20 | 21 | 20 | fr405

Grand Hôtel, 5, place de l'Opéra, 9ᵉ (Auber/Opéra), 01 40 07 30 10
■ The "very prestigious" restaurant of the Grand Hôtel has the same resplendent Napoleon III decor as the neighboring Opéra Garnier and serves "extremely good classical" French fare, with seafood that's "especially well done"; devotees say this is what happens "when a hotel director decides to go after stars, with decor that lends itself to this quest – everything becomes an enchantment."

Restaurant Toutoune S
15 | 12 | 14 | fr237

5, rue de Pontoise, 5ᵉ (Maubert-Mutualité), 01 43 26 56 81
◩ Though some say this venerable Latin Quarter bistro "isn't what it used to be", its "good, old-fashioned" French cooking still has fans; the "family-style" fare may be "without surprises", but it's a "pleasant" place with "nice atmosphere" and "good value for money."

Ribe (Chez)
11 | 10 | 12 | fr231

15, av. de Suffren, 7ᵉ (Bir-Hakeim/RER Champ-de-Mars), 01 45 66 53 79
◩ The neo–Belle Epoque decor and proximity to the Eiffel Tower and Hilton hotel have "overwhelmed" this bistro with tourists, which may be why some locals pronounce it "without interest and banal"; while critics find the traditional French cooking "disappointing", others insist that its prix fixe menus offer "excellent value" for the money.

River Café ◐ S
13 | 19 | 12 | fr256

146, quai de Stalingrad, Issy-les-Moulineaux (RER Issy Plaine), 01 40 93 50 20

☑ Most surveyors enjoy the "pleasant waterside setting" of this "trendy", "chic" magnet for "the advertising crowd" and "celebs" set on a barge in the suburb of Issy-les-Moulineaux, even if views on the French food run the gamut from "good" to "inadequate."

Romantica (La)
19 | 15 | 15 | fr359

73, bd. Jean Jaurès, Clichy (Mairie-de-Clichy), 01 47 37 29 71

■ Initiates of this "slightly secret address" in Clichy laud its "excellent Italian cooking", calling owner Claudio "a real magician" – "the linguine in cream sauce flambéed with cognac in a hollowed-out whole Parmesan is worth the trip"; the "spacious terrace evokes vacation" and the wines are "good" too; but some say "for pasta, it's too expensive."

Rond de Serviette (Le)
15 | 11 | 15 | fr241

97, rue du Cherche-Midi, 6ᵉ (Vaneau), 01 45 44 01 02

■ The "cozy decor" and "warm welcome" at this Left Bank bistro not far from the Bon Marché department store make it a perfect "neighborhood restaurant" and "a find" for first-timers; "they make a real effort" with the traditional bistro cooking here, turning out "good" dishes with "delicate flavors" served by an "efficient" staff.

Rosimar
▽ 14 | 8 | 18 | fr229

26, rue Poussin, 16ᵉ (Michel-Ange Auteuil/Porte d'Auteuil), 01 45 27 74 91

☑ "Unfortunately, there's very little Latin charm" say those unimpressed by the mirrored decor at this Catalan "off the beaten track" deep in the 16th arrondissement; but "a business clientele" enjoys its "carefully prepared Spanish cuisine" that sometimes includes "very good fish."

Rôtisserie d'Armaillé
16 | 13 | 14 | fr272

6, rue d'Armaillé, 17ᵉ (Charles de Gaulle-Etoile), 01 42 27 19 20

■ One of three rotisseries run by chef Jacques Cagna, this "very professional" place not far from the Etoile wins praise for its "good value" and "great prix fixe menus"; "generous" portions are also appreciated at what some deem "the most successful of all Cagna's restaurants."

Rôtisserie d'en Face
17 | 14 | 15 | fr281

2, rue Christine, 6ᵉ (Odéon/St-Michel), 01 43 26 40 98

☑ "Super roast chicken" and meats, "good desserts" and "good value" please many at the original Jacques Cagna rotisserie on the Left Bank just across the sreet from his eponymous restaurant; it's often "crowded" though, and cynics snipe "Cagna must be making a fortune"; service ranges from "attentive" to "erratic" to "rude."

Rôtisserie du Beaujolais 🅂   15 | 10 | 13 | fr259

19, quai de la Tournelle, 5ᵉ (Jussieu), 01 43 54 17 47

■ The "wonderful spit-roasted meats" and "irresistible mashed potatoes" are crowd-pleasers at this Seine-side Left Bank rotisserie owned by Claude Terrail of La Tour d'Argent; but that pedigree leads some to say "it should be better in view of its ownership" and to query: "paper tablecloths at an annex of La Tour d'Argent?"

Rôtisserie Monsigny ●🅂   15 | 11 | 14 | fr264

1, rue Monsigny, 2ᵉ (Quatre-Septembre), 01 42 96 16 61

■ "A warm welcome" and "good, clean, healthy" food make this Jacques Cagna rotisserie near the stock exchange ideal "for a business lunch" or "agreeable after the theater."

Ruc Univers ●🅂   11 | 9 | 11 | fr264

159, rue St-Honoré, 1ᵉʳ (Louvre-Rivoli), 01 42 60 97 54

◩ The post-*Survey* takeover by the Costes brothers of this strategically located brasserie just steps from the Palais-Royal and the Louvre is probably a good development, given comments such as "very average"; there's new modern decor with low lighting and a simple, stylish menu running to grills and salads.

Saint Amarante (Le)   ▽ 21 | 7 | 14 | fr228

4, rue Biscornet, 12ᵉ (Bastille), 01 43 43 00 08

■ Even if the "nonexistent" decor is "cold", the welcome is "warm" at this popular bistro near the Opéra Bastille; admirers call it a "good neighborhood" place offering "very original" food that's "excellent for the money" and say "the recent change of chefs has been a success."

Saint Amour (Le)   14 | 7 | 14 | fr328

8, rue de Port-Mahon, 2ᵉ (Opéra), 01 47 42 63 82

◩ While the "solid Lyonnaise cooking" of this "good bourgeois" restaurant near the Opéra appeals to most surveyors, many say "the decor really needs to be freshened up"; "friendly service" helps compensate.

Saint Pourçain (Le)   – | – | – | I

234, rue du Fbg. St-Antoine, 12ᵉ (Nation), 01 43 70 83 22

"Pretty good" "rustic" cooking from the Auvergne is the draw at this "tiny" bistro between the Bastille and Nation in the 12th arrondissement; some find it "a bit expensive for what it is" but appreciate the "very cordial" atmosphere.

Saint Vincent (Le)   ▽ 17 | 13 | 15 | fr242

26, rue de la Croix-Nivert, 15ᵉ (Cambronne), 01 47 34 14 94

■ This "chic and welcoming" little Lyonnais bistro just behind the Ecole Militaire in the 15th arrondissement is well regarded by surveyors who give it solid scores and encouraging comments: "excellent", "a relatively modest place to achieve this degree of perfection."

Salle à Manger (La) 🆂   16 | 20 | 17 | fr415
Hôtel Raphaël, 17, av. Kléber, 16ᵉ (Kléber), 01 44 28 00 17
☑ The "cozy" dining room of the elegant Hôtel Raphaël near the Arc de Triomphe offers "classy" French cooking and "good quality service", though thrill-seekers find its tranquility "boring"; it's worth noting for what some call "the best breakfast in Paris with excellent pastries."

San Valero   15 | 11 | 14 | fr299
209 ter, av. Charles de Gaulle, Neuilly-sur-Seine (Pont de Neuilly), 01 46 24 07 87
■ According to admirers, there's no need to head south of the Pyrénées when this "excellent address for Spanish cuisine" is to be found in Neuilly; though the decor strikes some as "sad", the "original, very good" food makes it "one of the best Spanish restaurants in Paris"; there's a first-rate wine list too.

Sarladais (Le)   15 | 12 | 14 | fr333
2, rue de Vienne, 8ᵉ (St-Augustin/St-Lazare), 01 45 22 23 62
■ Just behind the Gare Saint-Lazare, this bistro serving "good Southwestern French cooking" attracts a "business clientele" that appreciates its "agreeable atmosphere" and "friendly owners"; while a meal here creates pleasant "memories" for many, a few doubters say "there are better Southwestern places in Paris."

Saudade   17 | 14 | 18 | fr296
34, rue des Bourdonnais, 1ᵉʳ (Châtelet-Les Halles), 01 42 36 03 65
■ "The best Portuguese in Paris" say surveyors of this Les Halles eatery offering "a huge choice of cod dishes" and "fabulous Ports" in a "typically Portuguese setting" featuring "painted tiles"; it's "tranquil", "original" and "very comfortable" with a "slightly chic" clientele.

Saveurs (Les)   ▽ 18 | 14 | 14 | fr328
Sofitel Maison des Centraliens, 8, rue Jean-Goujon, 8ᵉ (Champs-Elysées-Clémenceau), 01 40 74 64 94
■ While some find "good quality" French cooking at this restaurant set in a 19th-century townhouse, part of the Sofitel hotel complex near the Champs-Elysées, others judge the value only "medium" and the service "uneven"; an "excellent cigar cave" is a plus, and "for a family reunion" or other event there are a number of private rooms, ancient and modern, for rent.

Savy (Chez)   15 | 11 | 16 | fr274
23, rue Bayard, 8ᵉ (Franklin Roosevelt), 01 47 23 46 98
☑ Banquettes with old-fashioned brass rails add to the charm of this "bistro the way we love them" in the 8th arrondissement near the famous shopping street of Avenue Montaigne; "rare in this quarter", it serves "honest regional cooking" from the Auvergne (calf's liver with pureed peas, for example) that "warms the heart."

Sawadee
16 | 7 | 12 | fr226

53, av. Emile Zola, 15ᵉ (Charles-Michels), 01 45 77 68 90

■ "One of the best Thai restaurants in Paris" has a "constant and precise" kitchen that turns out dishes "full of flavor"; "the decor needs to be redone" say many "but it's so good and reasonably priced" that people go anyway; "the best table's next to the aquarium."

Scheffer (Le)
14 | 9 | 12 | fr228

22, rue Scheffer, 16ᵉ (Trocadéro), 01 47 27 81 11

■ A "neighborhood bistro" in the 16th arrondissement serving "good-quality homestyle" fare such as "well-prepared marrow bones and steak tartare", i.e. "real" food made "with fresh ingredients"; the cooking, along with the "convivial" ambiance and "good value", have made it very popular, hence "too noisy", "too smoky" and "you have to reserve."

Sébillon Neuilly ◑Ⓢ
14 | 12 | 14 | fr278

20, av. Charles de Gaulle, Neuilly-sur-Seine (Porte Maillot), 01 46 24 71 31

Sébillon Elysées ◑Ⓢ
66, rue Pierre Charron, 8ᵉ (Franklin Roosevelt), 01 43 59 28 15

☒ Roast lamb with flageolets is the dish on which the renown of this sprawling old Neuilly brasserie is based, but while loyalists say it's still "so tender" and "the best in Paris", critics insist it's "tired" and claim "those who knew this place 20 years ago can't help but be disappointed"; the 8th arrondissement branch is newer.

Senteurs de Provence (Aux)
▽ 19 | 13 | 16 | fr279

295, rue Lecourbe, 15ᵉ (Lourmel), 01 45 57 11 98

☒ Some of "the best bouillabaisse" in Paris is part of the attraction at this stylish Provençal in the 15th; "since we love fish, we love this restaurant" say admirers of its "good quality" and "calm" atmosphere; a few detractors feel it's "slipping", however.

Shozan
17 | 18 | 13 | fr349

11, rue de la Trémoille, 8ᵉ (Alma-Marceau), 01 47 23 37 32

■ "French-Japanese cuisine at a very high level" is the draw at this 8th arrondissement hybrid; offering a "refined" "East-West synthesis" with "new, iconoclastic dishes" in a "sublime" setting, it's popular even if some find it "rather pricey."

6 Bosquet (Le)
18 | 12 | 16 | fr257

6, av. Bosquet, 7ᵉ (Alma-Marceau), 01 45 56 97 26

■ An "imaginative" young chef and his "lovely wife" have created this bistro in the space formerly occupied by Le Duquesnoy in the 7th arrondissement; most enjoy its "relaxing" atmosphere and say its "good-quality" fare offers "fine value for the money."

Sologne (La)
16 | 11 | 16 | fr281
164, av. Daumesnil, 12ᵉ (Daumesnil), 01 43 07 68 97
■ Deep in the heart of the 12th arrondissement, this "good little restaurant" is famous for its "excellent game" and "serious provincial cooking"; if it "lacks originality", most don't mind.

Sormani
21 | 16 | 18 | fr459
4, rue du Général Lanrezac, 17ᵉ (Charles de Gaulle-Etoile), 01 43 80 13 91
■ "Excellent Italian cooking that's refined and authentic" is the overwhelming consensus on this fashionable venue composed of several "elegant" small rooms in the 17th arrondissement not far from the Arc de Triomphe; it earns raves for the likes of "fantastic risotto" and "very good ravioli with truffles", but even fans find it "too expensive."

Soufflé (Le)
16 | 10 | 15 | fr259
36, rue du Mont-Thabor, 1ᵉʳ (Concorde), 01 42 60 27 19
■ "As its name indicates", this small spot near the Place de la Concorde specializes in soufflés, which most find "an amusing concept" even if it draws "many tourists"; tables may be "tightly spaced" and it's a bit "noisy" but the "very good cheese and chocolate soufflés" ensure that it doesn't fall flat.

Soupière (La)
16 | 10 | 15 | fr286
154, av. de Wagram, 17ᵉ (Wagram), 01 46 22 80 10
■ A "creative little" bistro in the 17th arrondissement that's a must "for mushroom lovers", since the chef prepares them imaginatively, but it's also pleasant for anyone thanks to a "variety of tasty dishes" enhanced by a "friendly welcome."

Sousceyrac (A)
21 | 13 | 15 | fr332
35, rue Faidherbe, 11ᵉ (Charonne), 01 43 71 65 30
■ "One of the best classic Southwestern French tables in Paris", this pleasantly old-fashioned place with decor that hasn't been touched in years serves "excellent", "hearty" dishes like hare à la royale ("a must!"), macaroni gratin with truffles, game and cassoulet; "a warm welcome" and "excellent wines" make it well worth a trip deep into the 11th, but be sure to bring "a big appetite."

Spicy Restaurant ◖Ⓢ
- | - | - | I
8, av. Franklin Roosevelt, 8ᵉ (Franklin Roosevelt/St-Philippe-du-Roule), 01 56 59 62 59
Launched by the creators of the Hippopotamus and L'Appart' concepts, this new in-spot near the *rond-point* of the Champs-Elysées offers French rotisserie fare, but the real spice comes more from the attractive staff and modern decor (bricks, tiles, unfinished woods) than from the food; both the prix fixe and à la carte fare is reasonably priced.

Square Trousseau (Le) ●⑤   16 | 15 | 14 | fr231
1, rue Antoine Vollon, 12ᵉ (Bastille/Ledru-Rollin),
01 43 43 06 00
☑ Decorated in turn-of-the-century style with "red banquettes and plaster moldings", this "pretty" Bastille bistro is "a pleasant neighborhood spot" that attracts a "trendy young clientele", but some find service "mediocre."

Stella Maris   – | – | – | E
4, rue Arsène Houssaye, 8ᵉ (Charles de Gaulle-Etoile),
01 42 89 16 22
Japanese chef Taderu Yoshino has set up shop in the former premises of Vancouver, just steps from the Arc de Triomphe; though pricey, it offers the delicate French cooking of one of chef Joël Robuchon's most meticulous students, served in a minimalist mezzanine dining room where the wrought-iron deco frame of the big front window constitutes most of the decor.

Stresa (Le)   18 | 12 | 14 | fr371
7, rue Chambiges, 8ᵉ (Alma-Marceau), 01 47 23 51 62
☑ This Italian near the Avenue Montaigne fashion houses in the 8th arrondissement offers great "people-watching" since it attracts "TV and cinema stars", though some find the celebrity scene "pretentious" and "snobby"; the food is "good and simple" but be advised "prices have been lifted as high as the faces of the clientele."

Studio (The) ◖⑤   8 | 16 | 10 | fr175
41, rue du Temple, 4ᵉ (Hôtel-de-Ville), 01 42 74 10 38
■ Set in a courtyard with a "great" summer terrace where you can "watch the dancers in the neighboring dance schools", this Marais Tex-Mex is "pleasant" even if the food is "not very good"; fine margaritas make it easier to appreciate the "superb ambiance."

Sud (Le) ◖   15 | 21 | 14 | fr264
91, bd. Gouvion-St-Cyr, 17ᵉ (Porte Maillot), 01 45 74 02 77
☑ You can "hear the cicadas singing" at this Provençal in the 17th arrondissement with "well-considered, successful decor" complete with Souleiado fabrics – and even if the chirping is "canned", it makes you "forget the gray weather"; some rate the cooking "good", especially the bourride and baked sea bass, others find it "mediocre" and "not up to the decor."

Suntory ⑤   21 | 15 | 17 | fr423
13, rue Lincoln, 8ᵉ (George V), 01 42 25 40 27
■ Just off the Champs-Elysées, what some call "the best Japanese in Paris" is "a pleasure every time" – "the chefs give a real show" while preparing "excellent sushi" in a "haven of serenity"; in sum, "everything's perfect, but it's a bit too expensive."

Table d'Anvers (La) ☽
22 | 12 | 17 | fr458

2, place d'Anvers, 9ᵉ (Anvers), 01 48 78 35 21

■ The "originality" of the Conticini brothers' French standout in Montmartre inspires ecstasies from admirers who call it "a perfect two-star restaurant" with "one of the most creative kitchens in Paris today" and "desserts to die for"; but service that's "not up to the cooking" and decor that's "without interest" detract from the experience for some.

Table de Babette (La) ⑤
▽ 13 | 14 | 11 | fr307

(fka Villa Créole)

1, allée de Longchamp, 16ᵉ (Porte Maillot), 01 45 00 35 73

■ "Exoticism without leaving Paris" can be found at this French West Indian near the Porte Maillot with a "very pleasant ambiance" and food that's "excellent if you like the cooking of the islands – spicy blood sausage, chicken fritters" and the like; some feel service could be improved.

Table de Pierre (La)
19 | 14 | 15 | fr310

116, bd. Pereire, 17ᵉ (Pereire), 01 43 80 88 68

■ "Excellent Basque cooking" draws diners to the outer reaches of the 17th arrondissement, where they find a "warm welcome" and "an attractive, young crowd in a restaurant with atmosphere"; a few find the service "stuffy."

Table du Marché (La) ⑤
14 | 11 | 13 | fr324

14, rue de Marignan, 8ᵉ (Franklin Roosevelt), 01 40 76 34 44

■ "A wet firecracker" is one description of this trendy bistro off the Champs-Elysées run by media-oriented Saint-Tropez chef Christophe Leroy; as for the food, some find it "good", others say "pricey" and "pretentious."

TAILLEVENT
28 | 25 | 27 | fr818

15, rue Lamennais, 8ᵉ (George V), 01 44 95 15 01

■ "An institution always at the summit" of Paris dining, this truly "grand" Classic French is, "in a word, fantastic"; rated No. 1 for Food, Service and Popularity, it's "the ne plus ultra of gastronomy" and almost "exasperating in its permanent perfection", with "service as exceptional as the cooking" of Philippe Legendre, a "clubby" setting near the Etoile and a "superior wine cellar" that's "one of the best for its prices"; you may have to "get yourself invited by an Arab prince" to afford it, but "who cares about the cost?" – it's "the best."

Taïra
20 | 8 | 15 | fr346

10, rue des Acacias, 17ᵉ (Argentine), 01 47 66 74 14

■ "An original experience of creative cooking" and "a fish restaurant for those who don't like fish" are among the flattering assessments of this Franco-Japanese in the 17th arrondissement; there's not much decor but the chef's East-meets-West approach mixes "quality and imagination" and yields some "unequaled" treatments of aquatic fare.

Taka
`- - - I`

1, rue Véron, 18ᵉ (Abbesses), 01 42 23 74 16
"Perched on the slopes of Montmartre just above Pigalle",
this "little" Japanese offers "authentic cooking" and
pleasant service in a "calm" atmosphere; the trendy, arty
crowd doesn't mind the "simple, somber" decor.

Tan Dinh ✍
`20 12 17 fr380`

60, rue de Verneuil, 7ᵉ (Rue du Bac/Solférino), 01 45 44 04 84
■ "Superb Vietnamese cooking and a remarkable wine
cellar" make this "discreet, comfortable" place near the
Musée d'Orsay on the Left Bank "always a pleasure", even if
it is "a bit pricey"; the "ravioli of smoked goose is a must"
at this "well-run", "refined" home of "exotic flavors."

Tante Louise (Chez)
`17 12 15 fr333`

41, rue Boissy-d'Anglas, 8ᵉ (Concorde/Madeleine),
01 42 65 06 85
▨ "Traditional" and "classic" are the recurring adjectives
for this old-fashioned French midway between the Place de
la Concorde and the Madeleine; while much recommended
for business lunches, it's "a little sad at night"; N.B. changes
are in store: Bernard Loiseau (of La Côte d'Or in Saulieu)
has reportedly bought this place and plans to turn it into a
showcase for the food of Burgundy.

Taroudant II (Le) ◖🅂
`▽ 16 13 13 fr198`

8, rue Aristide Briant, 18ᵉ (Abbesses/Blanche), 01 42 64 95 81
■ "A very pleasant neighborhood Moroccan" not far from
the Place de Clichy with "respectable cooking and delicious
pastries made by the owner's wife"; "ceramics and
mosaics" set the scene for "magic tagines" and other
"authentic family" fare served at reasonable prices.

Taverne Kronenbourg ◖🅂
`10 12 11 fr228`

24, bd. des Italiens, 9ᵉ (Opéra/Richelieu-Drouot), 01 55 33 10 00
▨ This "big Alsatian machine" in the heart of town near the
Opéra is considered a "well-oiled", "classic" brasserie
by fans of its choucroute and shellfish; dissenters find it
"mediocre" with "negligent service" and say it's best "if
you like noise"; either way, late hours make it "practical."

Télégraphe (Le) ◖🅂
`- - - M`

41, rue de Lille, 7ᵉ (Rue du Bac), 01 42 92 03 04
Just reopening at press time after having fallen out of
favor and closing last year, this stylish spot behind the
Musée d'Orsay occupies a Belle Epoque townhouse
newly redecorated by François-Joseph Graf, known for
his stunning decor at L'Ambroisie; now run by the team
that's also behind La Véranda and Chiberta, it offers a
menu ranging from classic bistro to contemporary fare
and boasts a gorgeous garden which, alas, is open only
for lunch in good weather.

Temps des Cerises (Le)

14 | 11 | 14 | fr168

18, rue de la Butte-aux-Cailles, 13ᵉ (Place d'Italie),
01 45 89 69 48

⬛ Founded as a "worker's cooperative" during the '60s, this bistro in the 13th pleases partisans with its "good value for the money", "very cordial atmosphere" and "authentic decor"; a few critics find it "dull", but they're a minority.

Terminus Nord ●⧄

14 | 16 | 14 | fr242

23, rue de Dunkerque, 10ᵉ (Gare du Nord), 01 42 85 05 15

⬛ Across the street from the Gare du Nord, this "classically Parisian" brasserie is part of the Flo group, which means "speedy service, a lovely setting" and cooking that most rate "good" if "limited"; some call it "best in the group", others say "not bad but noisy" – either way it's fine for oysters or a bite before or after the train.

Terroir (Le)

▽ 16 | 6 | 14 | fr264

11, bd. Arago, 13ᵉ (Les Gobelins), 01 47 07 36 99

⬛ "At last, a real bistro" with a "warm welcome", "good, abundant homestyle cooking" and an "ambiance recalling the old Les Halles market of Paris"; set in the 13th near the Place d'Italie, it's recommended for a feed that's "serious and solid, with everything needed to satisfy those who are really hungry."

Thanksgiving ⧄

13 | 9 | 13 | fr168

20, rue St-Paul, 4ᵉ (St-Paul), 01 42 77 68 28

⬛ "Perfect for cheesecake or bagels when you're missing New York", this grocery in the Marais offers "American products for cooking plus take-away dishes" and also has "a few tables upstairs" where it serves "meals that are typically other-side-of-the-Atlantic"; partisans consider it "the American restaurant to recommend."

Thoumieux ●⧄

12 | 11 | 12 | fr224

79, rue St-Dominique, 7ᵉ (Invalides/La Tour-Maubourg),
01 47 05 49 75

⬛ This "good old classic", a "real traditional brasserie" in the 7th arrondissement, is liked for its solid "value", even if some label it a "Big Bertha for tourists"; expect "good cassoulet" and other "traditional Southwestern French cuisine" from a "kitchen without pretensions" (to cynics that means "overrated").

Timgad (Le) ⧄

18 | 18 | 16 | fr352

21, rue Brunel, 17ᵉ (Argentine), 01 45 74 23 70

⬛ "Very good couscous in a very pretty setting" with stucco-work and fountains makes this "perfect when you want to take a trip to Morocco" without leaving the 17th arrondissement; "the best b'steeya" and "excellent *mechoui* (whole sheep barbecue)" have fans too, though some find prices a bit high.

Timonerie (La)
20 | 13 | 15 | fr458

35, quai de la Tournelle, 5ᵉ (Maubert-Mutualité), 01 43 25 44 42
■ Chef Philippe de Givenchy leaves no one indifferent at his "austere" little French on the Seine in the Latin Quarter: "very original and surprising cooking", "excellent", a "great but too-little-known chef" who "doesn't want for originality" sums up one side, while others say "inconsistent", "paying too much for the chef's ego."

Tong Yen ◗⑤
16 | 10 | 14 | fr349

1 bis, rue Jean Mermoz, 8ᵉ (Franklin Roosevelt), 01 42 25 04 23
■ The "great welcome" from owner Thérèse ("the soul of the place") and an "elegant clientele" sprinkled with "jet-setters" have won this Chinese off the Champs-Elysées a loyal following; most find the food "delicious and refined" but the decor is very "'80s" and one tall customer claims "the ceiling crushes you – don't come if you're over 1.75 meters."

Tonnelle Saintongeaise (La)
15 | 15 | 15 | fr288

32, bd. Vital-Bouhot, Neuilly-sur-Seine (Pont de Levallois), 01 46 24 43 15
■ A well-received steak tartare and "warm", intimate wood-paneled decor are two reasons why this French Regionalist on the Ile de la Jatte in Neuilly has its fans; its "good value" is also appreciated, but some apparently find service slow: "the cooking is perhaps done in Sarlat and then sent to Paris on the back of a mule."

Tonton Yang (Chez)
– | – | – | I

11, rue Biot, 17ᵉ (Place de Clichy), 01 45 22 36 75
This "excellent Chinese" near the Place de Clichy is deemed a fine example of "Chinese gastronomy" by regulars, who appreciate the cooking as well as the "friendly" service.

Toque (La)
▽ 15 | 7 | 14 | fr301

16, rue de Tocqueville, 17ᵉ (Villiers), 01 42 27 97 75
■ Considered a "great value" for what it is, this intimate Classic French in the 17th arrondissement pleases habitués; though the "traditional cuisine refuses all innovations" and some find the "tables too close together", it's called "an honest neighborhood restaurant" with a "calm" atmosphere and "attentive" service.

Totem (Le) ◗⑤
– | – | – | M

17, place du Trocadéro, 16ᵉ (Trocadéro), 01 47 27 28 29
Taking its name from the striking totem poles in the Musée de l'Homme, in which it's located, this stylish place draws a sophisticated young crowd with a well-executed menu of French classic and contemporary dishes enhanced by a splendid view of the Eiffel Tower across the Seine; it's a good bet for a chicly romantic, affordably priced meal.

Toupary (Le) ◗ | 11 | 24 | 12 | fr276
2, quai du Louvre, 1er (Pont Neuf), 01 40 41 29 29

☑ "You must go for the view, but you can't eat it", which poses a problem since many find the French fare "weak" at this stylish perch atop the Samaritaine department store overlooking the Seine in the heart of the city; still, with that "superb" view and modern decor by the "talented" Hilton McConnico, it's "the poor man's Tour d'Argent", so get a "table by the window" and enjoy.

TOUR D'ARGENT (LA) 🅂 | 22 | 28 | 23 | fr817
15-17, quai de la Tournelle, 5e (Cardinal Lemoine/Maubert-Mutualité/Pont Marie), 01 43 54 23 31

☑ Visit this "myth" "at least once in your life" for the "marvelous view of Notre Dame", which "gives the duck its wings back" (and "get there early enough not to miss sunset"); while the famed duck (each is numbered) is "exceptional" and owner Claude Terrail is "a presence", many feel the "grand, traditional" French fare is "good without being better" and service is "refined" but too "fancy shmancy"; still, with an "incredible wine list" and one of the *Survey*'s top decor ratings, it's more than "ok", especially "if someone else pays."

TRAIN BLEU (LE) 🅂 | 14 | 26 | 14 | fr337
Gare de Lyon, 12e (Gare de Lyon), 01 43 43 09 06

☑ "The gorgeous setting makes you forget the uneven" brasserie fare at this landmark inside the Gare de Lyon with decor that captures "1900 in all its splendor"; most agree "it's more of a historic than gastronomic monument" and critics say if "it doesn't catch up with the era of the TGV [high-speed train] it'll get canceled"; N.B. new management hopes to get the kitchen back on track.

Trentaquattro ◗🅂 | 13 | 9 | 10 | fr289
34, rue de Bourgogne, 7e (Assemblée Nationale/Varenne), 01 45 55 80 75

☑ Not far from the Assemblée Nationale, this Italian is appreciated for its "good cooking" even if some remark you can "eat like this in Italy for less" money; regulars say it's "better in the evening" when the ambiance is "romantic."

TROIS MARCHES (LES) 🅂 | 24 | 23 | 21 | fr644
1, bd. de la Reine, Versailles, 01 39 50 13 21

☑ The "sumptuous decor" and "extremely pleasant setting" of chef Gérard Vié's French restaurant at the Hôtel Trianon in Versailles are most "sublime" on a summer's night "when they serve on the terrace"; most find the food "excellent" with special praise for "the best cheese tray in France", but a few call it "overrated" with "stiff" service.

Trou Gascon (Au) ◗ 　　21 | 15 | 17 | fr420
40, rue Taine, 12ᵉ (Daumesnil), 01 43 44 34 26
■ Enthusiasts think the "excellent" Southwestern French fare at Alain Dutournier's original venue in the 12th "is better than at his other restaurant" (Le Carré des Feuillants) – "I've never eaten a cassoulet as good as it was voluminous" says one contented diner; "the best menu of Armagnac ever seen" and the "Belle Epoque decor" are also attractions.

Troyon (Le) 　　▽ 20 | 14 | 19 | fr318
4, rue Troyon, 17ᵉ (Charles de Gaulle-Etoile), 01 40 68 99 40
■ "Fine, inventive cooking" and the "adorable welcome and service" at this "charming" little French near the Arc de Triomphe make young chef Jean-Marc Notelet a rising star; along with attractive, dressy decor, it offers "good value."

Truffe Noire (La) 　　19 | 11 | 15 | fr398
2, place Parmentier, Neuilly-sur-Seine (Porte Maillot), 01 46 24 94 14
■ "A sure value" in Neuilly, this "classic" serves "very French" cooking and is "solid in all respects"; "pleasant and quiet", it's "useful for business lunches with people based in La Defense" and a fine "place to celebrate your successes."

Truffière (La) 🯅 　　17 | 16 | 14 | fr282
4, rue Blainville, 5ᵉ (Place Monge), 01 46 33 29 82
■ Located in a "pretty arched cellar", this Latin Quarter bistro provides "good cooking", "efficient service" and "value for the money", but some say "it's gone down since a change of owners" last year; tip: "have your after-dinner drink in front of the fireplace."

Tsé-Yang ◗🯅 　　18 | 19 | 17 | fr346
25, av. Pierre 1ᵉʳ de Serbie, 16ᵉ (Alma-Marceau/Iéna), 01 47 20 70 22
■ "A sure value on the Hong Kong stock exchange" with "businessmen from around the world working on contracts worth millions in low voices", the 16th arrondissement branch of this Chinese restaurant group has "delicious" food and "spectacular" decor, but some say it "isn't as good as the one in New York."

Tsukizi 🯅 　　▽ 21 | 7 | 14 | fr289
2 bis, rue des Ciseaux, 6ᵉ (Mabillon/St-Germain-des-Prés), 01 43 54 65 19
■ This "tiny" Japanese in Saint-Germain has "a very good sushi bar" that some call the "best in Paris"; another good sign: "three-quarters of the clientele is Japanese."

Ty Coz 　　15 | 10 | 12 | fr314
35, rue St-Georges, 9ᵉ (St-Georges), 01 48 78 42 95
☑ "Long live Brittany" cheer fans of the "good fish at reasonable prices" served at this Breton in the 9th, even if some say it could use "ozone to pep up the ambiance"; "good Muscadet and Gros Plant" wines are a plus.

Vagenende ◐🅂 ⸨ 11 ⸩ ⸨ 19 ⸩ ⸨ 12 ⸩ fr279

142, bd. St-Germain, 6ᵉ (Mabillon/Odéon), 01 43 26 68 18

☑ This Belle Epoque brasserie in Saint-Germain with its "historic, discreet and elegant" turn-of-the-century setting is "for the pleasure of the eyes" since some feel "the contents don't live up to the container"; the term "tourist trap" is also tossed about.

Val d'Isère (Le) ◐🅂 ⸨ 12 ⸩ ⸨ 11 ⸩ ⸨ 14 ⸩ fr258

2, rue de Berri, 8ᵉ (George V), 01 43 59 12 66

☑ "The decor hasn't changed in 50 years" at this "cozy" "Alpine-style" spot off the Champs-Elysées; "decent" French food, "good fondue" and an oyster bar attract a loyal "post-theater or -cinema" crowd, even if it is too "noisy" and "smoky."

Vaudeville (Le) ◐🅂 ⸨ 12 ⸩ ⸨ 14 ⸩ ⸨ 13 ⸩ fr266

29, rue Vivienne, 2ᵉ (Bourse), 01 40 20 04 62

☑ This "pretty", "classic", "solid" art deco brasserie facing the stock exchange is part of the Flo group and appreciated for its "rapid service", "good shellfish platters" and "good enough cooking" (a few brand it "industrial strength"); "tables are too closely spaced" and "it's noisy", but that equals "lively" for some.

Venantius 🅂 ▽ ⸨ 18 ⸩ ⸨ 19 ⸩ ⸨ 19 ⸩ fr458

Hôtel Ambassador, 16, bd. Haussmann, 9ᵉ (Chaussée-d'Antin/ Opéra/Richelieu-Drouot), 01 44 83 40 58

■ The "refined and tranquil" setting of this "classic", "serious", "luxurious" French in the Hôtel Ambassador near Galeries Lafayette in the 9th arrondissement makes it perfect "for business meals without suprises"; "marvelous fish", "excellent desserts" and "good wines" are singled out for praise, but it's "a bit expensive."

Vendanges (Les) ▽ ⸨ 15 ⸩ ⸨ 12 ⸩ ⸨ 12 ⸩ fr264

40, rue Friant, 14ᵉ (Porte d'Orléans), 01 45 39 59 98

■ This little bistro near the Porte d'Orléans in the 14th arrondissement is a place "where the quality and quantity go together well"; the food's "very good" and the "wine cellar's decent" but some feel "service could be improved."

Véranda (La) ⸨ – ⸩ ⸨ – ⸩ ⸨ – ⸩ M

40, av. George V, 8ᵉ (George V), 01 53 57 49 49

In the space near the Champs-Elysées that formerly housed the trendy Spanish, La Dorada, comes a trendy Italian with just as much ambition, drawing business lunchers by day and beautiful people at night to its big, circular dining room with a central cupola that opens in summer; the menu is moderately priced, the staff is attractive and there's dancing at night (if you can get past the doorman at the velvet rope out front).

Verre Bouteille (Le) ◗ S
11 | 10 | 12 | fr189

85, av. des Ternes, 17ᵉ (Porte Maillot), 01 45 74 01 02

◪ "Steak tartare and a bottle of Brouilly" are the ticket at this "agreeable" 17th arrondissement wine bar/bistro with "decent" prices and convenient late hours, but it's "nothing special" and it can be "difficult to book a table."

Viaduc Café (Le) ◗ S
11 | 18 | 12 | fr193

43, av. Daumesnil, 12ᵉ (Bastille/Gare de Lyon), 01 44 74 70 70

◪ A "pleasant neighborhood" place "with a fashionable clientele" (some say "too fashionable"), this French near the Bastille has "pretty decor" and an unusual setting in the arches of an old viaduct; some say "the food could be improved" (critics contend "the microwave oven doesn't work properly"), but late hours are a plus.

Vieille (Chez la)
19 | 9 | 12 | fr355

37, rue de l'Arbre Sec, 1ᵉʳ (Louvre-Rivoli), 01 42 60 15 78

◼ "The old woman isn't there anymore, but she left behind her cooking, which is based on tradition, love and generosity" says one fan of this tiny bistro near Les Halles where Adrienne Biasin, the original "vieille", won a reputation for her authentic French home cooking; the food is still "very good" and "copious", even if the decor won't win any awards.

Vieux Bistro (Le) S
19 | 12 | 14 | fr302

14, rue du Cloître-Notre-Dame, 4ᵉ (Cité/RER St-Michel), 01 43 54 18 95

◼ "One of the last real bistros" is across the street from Notre Dame and serves "real meals like you eat in the country" with cooking "of quality" in a "traditional" setting; "plan a siesta afterwards" since the food's "a bit heavy."

Vieux Métiers de France (Les)
14 | 15 | 14 | fr367

13, bd. Auguste Blanqui, 13ᵉ (Place d'Italie), 01 45 88 90 03

◪ The "pretty", "rustic" medieval-themed decor at this traditional French in the 13th makes an "attractive setting" for "attractive cooking", which is enhanced by "good service and a nice wine list"; "very pleasant" sums it up.

Village d'Ung et Li Lam ◗ S
▽ 16 | 17 | 16 | fr233

10, rue Jean Mermoz, 8ᵉ (St-Philippe-du-Roule), 01 42 25 99 79

◼ The decor at this Chinese-Thai off the Champs-Elysées is "amusingly kitsch" and "charming", and both parts of the menu have fans: "very good Thai food" and "one of the best Chinese restaurants in Paris"; note, too, that it's perhaps "ideal for seducing the woman of your life."

Villaret (Le) ◗
19 | 11 | 14 | fr246

13, rue Ternaux, 11ᵉ (Parmentier), 01 43 57 89 76

◼ This "ideal bistro" deep in the 11th arrondissement is an "authentic place that you want to keep to yourself"; expect "excellent, original cooking" from a "menu that changes every night" plus "good wines", all at "good value prices."

Villa Vinci
16 | 13 | 15 | fr341

23, rue Paul Valéry, 16ᵉ (Boissière/Victor Hugo), 01 45 01 68 18

■ "A good neighborhood Italian" not far from the Arc de Triomphe; the "welcoming owner" and "honest" cooking make it "completely recommendable" even if some find it a little "too expensive for what it is."

Vincent (Chez)
18 | 9 | 14 | fr239

5, rue du Tunnel, 19ᵉ (Botzaris/Buttes-Chaumont), 01 42 02 22 45

■ "Magnificent antipasti" get a meal off to a good start at this "superb" Italian in the remote reaches of the 19th; "mini-pizzas to die for" and an "unpretentious" setting with "authentic" "trattoria atmosphere" help make it "one of the best Italians" in Paris for admirers.

Vin et Marée S
16 | 10 | 15 | fr238

108, av. du Maine, 14ᵉ (Gaîté), 01 43 20 29 50 ◐
2, rue Daunier, 16ᵉ (Porte St-Cloud), 01 46 47 91 39

■ "Good fresh fish cooked well at affordable prices" reels diners into these "convivial" seafooders in Montparnasse and the 16th arrondissement; "they make a real effort with the quality" and you're advised to "save room" for the "delicious baba au rhum for two"; note: "for fish lovers only, since there's no meat on the menu."

Vin sur Vin
17 | 12 | 17 | fr374

20, rue de Monttessuy, 7ᵉ (Pont de l'Alma), 01 47 05 14 20

■ "Have you ever heard a man talk about wine as if he were talking about the woman he loves?" – Patrice Vidal, the "very nice" owner of this little wine bistro near the Eiffel Tower, is an "artist" when it comes to discussing his "fantastic selection of wines"; there's "very good food" too, though some find it a bit "expensive."

VIOLON D'INGRES (LE)
25 | 17 | 20 | fr429

135, rue St-Dominique, 7ᵉ (Ecole Militaire), 01 45 55 15 05

■ Christian Constant (ex Crillon hotel) "is at the summit of his art and offers remarkable value for the money" at his "cozy" 7th arrondissement contemporary bistro with service "befitting a grand restaurant"; "an attractive clientele including Belmondo and his family" comes to enjoy "top quality and creativity" at this "lovely" new success.

Virgin Café S
10 | 11 | 8 | fr172

Virgin Megastore, 52-60, av. Champs-Elysées, 8ᵉ (Franklin Roosevelt), 01 42 89 46 81

◪ This "very noisy" cafe in the Virgin Megastore on the Champs-Elysées is part of a Paris trend toward in-store dining; it's "useful before or after a movie" and "ideal for teen birthday parties" even if service can be lacking and the French food, from a menu devised but not cooked by Olympe (one of the city's better-known female chefs), can be "simple and good" or "mediocre."

Vishnou
17 | 19 | 14 | fr267

13, rue du Commandant Mouchotte, 14ᵉ (Gaîté/Montparnasse), 01 45 38 92 93

■ Just across the street from the Tour Montparnasse, this "refined" northern Indian has a "very pretty dining room" and food of "constant quality", though some say it's too "adapted to European palates" and find the bill a bit "heavy."

Vivario
▽ 14 | 8 | 11 | fr304

6, rue Cochin, 5ᵉ (Maubert-Mutualité), 01 43 25 08 19

■ The Latin Quarter space that's home to "one of the rare Corsican restaurants in Paris" is "a little narrow", but it has a "bistro ambiance" and serves some "good dishes" from "a kitchen that works with products *d'origine controlé*" (an official guarantee of quality and authenticity) – "not too common."

VIVAROIS (LE) ●
23 | 14 | 19 | fr628

192, av. Victor Hugo, 16ᵉ (Rue de la Pompe), 01 45 04 04 31

☑ The "worn-out", "cold" "'60s decor" pleases few at this venerable French in the 16th arrondissement, but surveyors call Claude Peyrot "an exceptional chef who's unfairly little known"; his cooking is "sometimes dazzling", as in "an unforgettable saddle of rabbit", but to a minority it's "irregular" and "too expensive."

Voltaire (Le)
19 | 17 | 17 | fr375

27, quai Voltaire, 7ᵉ (Rue du Bac), 01 42 61 17 49

■ This bistro in what was once Voltaire's home on the banks of the Seine in St-Germain is "very good, very chic and very expensive"; it draws an "attractive and loyal clientele" (including lots of "loud" Americans) with its "excellent" food and "warm, intimate" ambiance; in sum, a good place "for understanding the Left Bank."

Vong (Chez) ●
17 | 17 | 16 | fr363

27, rue de Colisée, 8ᵉ (Franklin Roosevelt), 01 43 59 77 12

☑ Though "it's one of the best Chinese restaurants in Paris", some feel this 8th arrondissement spot with "very refined decor" "needs to make serious efforts to return to the level it was at several years ago"; still, even if its Les Halles sibling gets higher ratings, for most it remains an enjoyable "trip to an imaginary China."

Vong (Chez) ●
18 | 19 | 15 | fr332

10, rue de la Grande-Truanderie, 1ᵉʳ (Les Halles), 01 40 26 09 36

☑ "Do what the Chinese do – go in a group of 10 and order lots of food and you'll feel you're in a gourmet paradise" at this Chinese in Les Halles that's "refined and original as much for the food as for the decor"; while its sibling in the 8th arrondissement pulls a business crowd, this place is "the trendiest Chinese in Paris" and "filled with stars at night."

Wally Le Saharien
18 **13** **14** fr307

36, rue Rodier, 9ᵉ (Anvers), 01 42 85 51 90

■ The "excellent couscous" served at this 9th district venue inspires admirers to declare it "the must of North African cooking"; the kitchen "is authentic without concessions", desserts are "good", the owner "likable" and the setting "warm", but some find it a bit "pricey."

Wepler ◐S
12 **11** **12** fr266

14, place de Clichy, 18ᵉ (Place de Clichy), 01 45 22 53 24

☑ "It's a pleasure to be able to eat shellfish at any hour of the day" at this "traditional" Place de Clichy brasserie where some come "out of admiration for Marcel Proust", a one-time client; but doubters fear that this "sure value" is "slipping" and report that "the more complicated dishes are the most variable."

Willi's Wine Bar
15 **12** **14** fr257

13, rue des Petits-Champs, 1ᵉʳ (Palais-Royal/Bourse), 01 42 61 05 09

■ What many call "the best wine bar in Paris", near the Place des Victoires in the 1st arrondissement, is a "relaxed" place run by Englishman Mark Williamson where "the food accompanies the wine rather than the other way around"; it "makes one believe the English actually know how to cook", and is a veritable "temple of Côtes du Rhône" with "a very good list of Bordeaux" too.

Woolloomooloo ◐S
12 **13** **12** fr228

36, bd. Henri IV, 4ᵉ (Bastille), 01 42 72 32 11

☑ Near the Bastille, "the only Australian restaurant in Paris" is "original" and the place "to eat kangaroo", but some dishes leave critics grumbling "was it ostrich or rubber? – our jaws are still wondering"; service is "smiling" if sometimes "disinterested", and there's "an excellent list of Australian wines."

Yit Foong
– **–** **–** **l**

32, rue Frémicourt, 15ᵉ (Cambronne), 01 45 67 36 99

"One of the rare Malaysian restaurants in Paris", set in an arched-ceiling cellar near the Place Cambronne; the few surveyors who know it give it favorable reviews: "original and good", "really nice welcome and service."

Yugaraj S
19 **13** **15** fr288

14, rue Dauphine, 6ᵉ (Odéon/Pont Neuf), 01 43 26 44 91

☑ The decor may be a bit "sad" and the bill a bit "high", but many say this Saint-Germain Indian is "the best in Paris", offering "remarkably subtle", "refined" cooking and "pleasant" service; still, a critic sighs "since the French don't accept spicy food, they'll never know real Indian cooking."

Yvan ◗
16 | 16 | 15 | fr334
1 bis, rue Jean Mermoz, 8ᵉ (Franklin Roosevelt), 01 43 59 18 40
▣ "I'm the only person he doesn't kiss" one respondent says of Yvan, chef-owner of this 8th arrondissement place "that's been fashionable for many years"; the French food is "very good" and "the prix fixe menus are of a high level and affordable for all", plus there's a "great cheese tray" and "very pretty" decor, albeit with "maybe too many real – or fake – flowers."

Yvan, Petit (Le) ◗
14 | 12 | 13 | fr233
1 bis, rue Jean Mermoz, 8ᵉ (Franklin Roosevelt), 01 42 89 49 65
▪ Not far from the *rond point* on the Champs-Elysées, this bistro "clone" of Yvan earns a "bravo for the quality and prices", but it "really is little" – "you're squeezed in like sardines" in a "very noisy" space; the menu (prix fixe only) is "reasonable and classic" and the atmosphere is lively, with "Michou [famed Paris nightclub owner] and Yvan often putting on a show."

Yvan sur Seine ◗ Ⓢ
13 | 15 | 13 | fr227
26, quai du Louvre, 1ᵉʳ (Louvre-Rivoli), 01 42 36 49 52
▣ A "trendy" satellite of Yvan, this "small, narrow" bistro on the Seine in the 1st arrondissement has "yachting decor" that creates a "relaxed", "festive", "gay" atmosphere, but the food, while "honest", can be "mediocre."

Yves Quintard
▽ 20 | 10 | 16 | fr306
99, rue Blomet, 15ᵉ (Vaugirard), 01 42 50 22 27
▪ "Very fine" French cooking that's "frank and refined at the same time" plus a "super welcome" and "good value for the money" characterize this little restaurant in the 15th arrondissement; "there's not a cloud on the horizon" even if the decor's "a little scratched."

Zebra Square ◗ Ⓢ
11 | 15 | 10 | fr263
3, place Clément Ader, 16ᵉ (Mirabeau), 01 44 14 91 91
▣ "Another fashionable place that takes itself seriously" with a "hyper-trendy" crowd, "young, relaxed ambiance" and "New York–style" decor "that's very zebra"; next to the Maison de la Radio in the 16th arrondissement, it offers "neo-modern" French fare (including a collection of tartares) that critics call "unreliable" (ditto the service), but those here to "see and be seen" may not notice.

Zéphyr (Le)
– | – | – | M
1, rue du Jourdain, 20ᵉ (Jourdain), 01 46 36 65 81
The 1930 vintage decor of this brasserie in the 20th "creates an ambiance that's rare in Paris" and the cooking is "without frills but delicious"; it's the kind of place that might "have you taste wines for free just for the fun of discussing them", perhaps on the tree-shaded terrace during the summer.

Zeyer ●⑤

62, rue d'Alésia, 14ᵉ (Alésia), 01 45 40 43 88

▢ This "mythic art deco restaurant" in the Alésia quarter of Montparnasse is appreciated by some as a "brasserie without pretensions offering very good value"; a few feel it's "slipping", though, and so is "for dining late in Alésia, that's all."

Zygomates (Les)

7, rue de Capri, 12ᵉ (Daumesnil/Michel-Bizot), 01 40 19 93 04

▉ The *zygomates*, or muscles used to smile, get a workout at this tiny Daumesnil French in a former butcher shop; it's "a pleasant neighborhood place" with "very good food", "a nice welcome and service" and relatively "low prices", though some find the decor "austere."

Indexes to Restaurants

Special Features and Appeals

TYPES OF CUISINE

Algerian
Omar
Wally Le Saharien

American
Barfly
Café Bennett
Chicago Meatpackers
Chicago Pizza Pie Factory
Joe Allen
Lina's
Planet Hollywood
Thanksgiving

Asian
Buddha Bar
Poste

Australian
Woolloomooloo

Belgian
Bouillon Racine
Graindorge

British
Bertie's

Cambodian
Coin des Gourmets
Kambodgia
New Nioullaville

Caribbean
Coco d'Isles
Flamboyant
Marais-Cage
Table de Babette

Caviar
Caviar Kaspia
Cochon d'Or
Comptoir du Saumon Fumé
Daru
Dominique
Maison du Caviar
Maison Prunier
Nikita

Central European
Goldenberg Wagram
Hammam Café
Jo Goldenberg
Marianne
Paprika

Chinese: All Regions
China Town Belleville
Diep
Foc-Ly
Gastronomie Quach
New Nioullaville
Nouveau Village Tao Tao
Restaurant A
Tong Yen
Village d'Ung et Li Lam
Vong
Yit Foong

Chinese: Cantonese/Mandarin
Champs-Elysées Mandarin
China Club
Chinatown Olympiades
Grand Chinois
Mirama
Ngo
Passy Mandarin
Président

Chinese: Dim Sum
Champs-Elysées Mandarin
China Club
China Town Belleville
New Nioullaville
Ngo
Nouveau Village Tao Tao
Restaurant A
Tong Yen
Vong
Yit Foong

Chinese: Regional
Canard Laqué Pékinois
Chen (Shanghai)
Tonton Yang (Szechuan)
Tsé-Yang (Pekinoise)

Cuban
Casa del Habano

Eclectic/International
Ailleurs
Barfly
Café du Passage
Café Marly
Coffee Parisien
Colette
Cosi

Costes
Cou de la Girafe
Deux Abeilles
Flèche d'Or Café
Fumoir
Juvenile's
Natacha
Poste
Rest. de la Tour

Ethiopian
Entoto

Filipino
Iles Philippines

French: Bistro (Contemporary)
Absinthe
Anacréon
Avant Goût
Bistro 121
Bistro d'Hubert
Bistrot de l'Etoile Lauriston
Bistrot de l'Etoile Niel
Bistrot de l'Etoile Troyon
Bistrot de Paris
Bon Accueil
Bookinistes
Butte Chaillot
C'Amelot
Connivence
Detourbe Duret
Epi Dupin
Michel Courtalhac
O à la Bouche
Os à Moelle
Philippe Detourbe
Réconfort
Régalade
Rest. d'Eric Fréchon
Saint Amarante
Troyon
Violon d'Ingres

French: Bistro (Traditional)
Allard
Allobroges
Ami Louis
André
Armoise
Assassins
Astier
Bacchantes
Bar des Théâtres

Batifol
Benoît
Berry's
Berthoud
Biche au Bois
Bistro de la Grille
Bistro des Deux Théâtres
Bistrot d'à Côté Flaubert
Bistrot d'à Côté Neuilly
Bistrot d'à Côté St-Germain
Bistrot d'à Côté Villiers
Bistrot d'André
Bistrot de Breteuil
Bistrot d'Henri
Bistrot du Cochon d'Or
Bistrot Mazarin
Boeuf Couronné
Boeuf Gros Sel
Bofinger
Bouchons de Fr. Clerc
Café Bennett
Café des Théâtres
Café Louis Philippe
Cafe Pancrace
Caméléon
Caves Pétrissans
Caves Solignac
Cercle Ledoyen
Chardenoux
Clémentine
Cloche d'Or
Contre-Allée
Crus de Bourgogne
Denise
Dos de la Baleine
Driver's
Drugstore Publicis
Ebauchoir
Elle
Filoche
Fred
Galopin
Gauloise
Georges
Germaine
Gigot Fin
Grandes Marches
Grille
Grille St-Honoré
Guinguette de Neuilly
Hangar
Impatient
Jean
Je Thé...Me...
Joséphine

151

Languedoc
Lescure
Marcel
Marie Louise
Mathusalem
Maupertu
Nénesse
Noces de Jeannette
Oeillade
Paul
Pento
Père Claude
Perraudin
Petites Sorcières
Petit Gavroche
Petit Keller
Petit Marguery
Petit St-Benoît
Petit Zinc
Polidor
Poule au Pot
P'tit Troquet
Relais de Venise
Réminet
Rendez-vous/Camionneurs
Rendez-vous des Chauffeurs
René
Rest. des Beaux Arts
Rest. des Chauffeurs
Ribe
Rond de Serviette
Rôtisserie d'Armaillé
Rôtisserie d'en Face
Rôtisserie du Beaujolais
Rôtisserie Monsigny
Scheffer
Table du Marché
Temps des Cerises
Terroir
Vieille
Vieux Bistro
Voltaire
Yvan
Yvan, Petit

French: Brasserie

Arbuci
Auberge Dab
Ballon des Ternes
Baumann Ternes
Boeuf sur le Toit
Bofinger
Bouillon Racine
Brasserie Balzar
Brasserie de la Poste

Brasserie de l'Isle St-Louis
Brasserie du Louvre
Brasserie Flo
Brasserie Le Stella
Brasserie Lipp
Brasserie Lorraine
Brasserie Lutétia
Brasserie Mollard
Brasserie Munichoise
Café de la Paix
Cap Vernet
Chope d'Alsace
Congrès
Coupole
Dôme
Francis
Gallopin
Grand Café Capucines
Grand Colbert
Grandes Marches
Jenny
Julien
Maison d'Alsace
Marty
Muniche
Petit Victor Hugo
Pichet
Pied de Cochon
Ruc Univers
Sébillon Neuilly
Taverne Kronenbourg
Terminus Nord
Thoumieux
Train Bleu
Vagenende
Vaudeville
Wepler
Zéphyr
Zeyer

French: Cheeses

Ambassade d'Auvergne
Androuët
Astier
Berthoud
Bistro d'Hubert
Boeuf Couronné
Fernand/Les Fernandises
Maison du Valais
Montparnasse 25
Rech
René
Soufflé
Taillevent
Val d'Isère

French: Classic

A et M Le Bistrot
Agape
Alain Ducasse
Alisier
Allard
Ambassadeurs
Ambroisie
Amognes
Amphyclès
Anacréon
André
Androuët
Appart'
Ardoise
Armand au Palais Royal
Assiette
Astor
Atelier Maître Albert
Auberge
Auberge du Champ de Mars
Augusta
Avenue
Bains
Bar à Huîtres
Barfly
Barrail
Bar Vendôme
Basilic
Béatilles
Beaujolais d'Auteuil
Beauvilliers (A.)
Bermuda Onion
Beudant
Bistro de Gala
Bistro du 17
Bistro Melrose
Bistrot du Sommelier
Bistrot Gambas
Bistrot Papillon
Bistrot St-James
Boeuf sur le Toit
Bon St. Pourçain
Boule d'Or
Braisière
Bûcherie
Café Beaubourg
Café Bleu Lanvin
Café de Flore
Café de la Musique
Café de l'Industrie
Café de Mars
Café du Commerce
Café du Passage
Café la Jatte

Café Les Deux Magots
Café Marly
Calèche
Camille
Cap Seguin
Carpe Diem
Cartes Postales
Catounière
Caveau du Palais
Cazaudehore La Forestière
Célébrités
Chalet des Iles
Champ de Mars
Charpentiers
Chartier
Châteaubriant
Chaumière des Gourmets
Christine
Cigale
Clément
Clocher Saint-Germain
Closerie des Lilas
Club Matignon
Cochon d'Or
Coco et sa Maison
Coconnas
Comptoir des Sports
Coq de la Maison Blanche
Corniche
Cote d'Amour
Côté 7ème
Cottage Marcadet
Couronne
Cuisinier François
Dagorno
Dame Jeanne
Dariole de Viry
Débarcadère
Deux Canards
Domarais
Drouant
Durand Dupont
Echaudé St-Germain
Entrepôt
Epicure 108
Escargot Montorgueil
Espadon
Etoile d'Or
Excuse
Faucher
Fauchon - Le 30
Faugeron
Ferme de Boulogne
Ferme St-Simon
Fermette Marbeuf

Feuilles Libres	Michel Rostang
Flandrin	Mille Colonnes
Fond de Cour	Miravile
Fontaines	Monde des Chimères
Fouquet's	Moniage Guillaume
Fous d'en Face	Monsieur Lapin
Françoise	Montalembert
Frézet	Moulin à Vent "Chez Henri"
Gabriel	Muniche
Gare	Muses
Gastroquet	Napoléon Chaix
Georges Porte Maillot	Navarin
Géorgiques	Nénesse
Gérard	Obélisque
Gérard Besson	Opium Café
Géraud	Orangerie
Gitane	Oulette
Gourmet de l'Isle	Pactole
Gourmets des Ternes	Papillote
Grande Cascade	Paris
Grand Louvre	Paul Chêne
Grand Véfour	Pauline
Grange Batelière	Pavillon des Princes
Guirlande de Julie	Pavillon Montsouris
Hôtel du Nord	Pavillon Panama
Hulotte	Père Claude
Iles Marquises	Pergolèse
Jacky	Perraudin
Jamin	Petite Chaise
Jardin des Cygnes	Petite Cour
Jardins de Bagatelle	Petite Tour
Ladurée	Petit Laurent
Lapérouse	Petit Lutétia
Lasserre	Petit Plat
Laurent	Petit Poucet
Ledoyen	Petit Prince de Paris
Luna	Petit Rétro
Magnolias	Pichet
Maison	Pied de Fouet
Maison de l'Amérique	"Pierre" à la Fontaine
Maison du Caviar	Pierre au Palais Royal
Maître Paul	Pierre Vedel
Mandragore	Port du Salut
Manufacture	Porte Océane
Marcande	Pré Carré
Marée	Pré Catelan
Marie et Fils	Pressoir
Marius	Procope
Marius (Chez)	Rech
Marlotte	Régence
Marronniers d'Auteuil	Relais du Parc
Maupertu	Relais Louis XIII
Mauzac	Relais Plaza
Maxim's	Réminet
Meurice	Repaire de Cartouche

Réservoir
Restaurant
Rest. du Musée d'Orsay
Rest. du Palais Royal
Rest. Opéra
Rest. Toutoune
River Café
Rond de Serviette
Saint Amour
Salle à Manger
Saveurs
Scheffer
Soufflé
Soupière
Square Trousseau
Stella Maris
Taillevent
Tante Louise
Télégraphe
Terroir
Timonerie
Toque
Totem
Toupary
Tour d'Argent
Train Bleu
Trois Marches
Truffe Noire
Venantius
Vendanges
Viaduc Café
Vieux Métiers de France
Villaret
Violon d'Ingres
Virgin Café
Yvan sur Seine
Zeyer
Zygomates

French: New
Affriolé
Alisier
Amuse Bouche
Apicius
Arpège
Astor
Atelier Gourmand
Bamboche
Barrière de Clichy
Bar Vendôme
Bristol
Café Bleu Lanvin
Caffé Foy
Camélia
Cantine des Gourmets

Carré des Feuillants
Céladon
Chiberta
Clos Morillons
Clovis
Cottage Marcadet
Cuisinier François
Dînée
Epopée
Fabrice
Fauchon - Le 30
Flèche d'Or Café
Fontaine d'Auteuil
Friends
Galerie
Grange Batelière
Grenadin
Guy Savoy
Hédiard
Jacques Cagna
Jardin des Cygnes
Jules Verne
Ladurée
Lucas Carton
Macéo
Maison Blanche
Manoir Detourbe
Manufacture
Marines
Montparnasse 25
Morot-Gaudry
Pactole
Pavillon des Princes
Petite Bretonnière
Petite Cour
Pierre Gagnaire
Pile ou Face
Poquelin
Quai Ouest
Régence
Relais d'Auteuil
Relais de Sèvres
Restaurant
Rest. Opéra
Shozan
Spicy Restaurant
Stella Maris
Table d'Anvers
Taïra
Timonerie
Toque
Trois Marches
Vivarois
Yves Quintard
Zebra Square

French: Regional

Alsace/Jura
Alsaco
Café Runtz
Chope d'Alsace
Dame Tartine
Epicure 108
Jenny
Kiosque
Maison d'Alsace
Maître Paul
Taverne Kronenbourg

Brittany
Crêperie de Josselin
Michel
Ty Coz

Burgundy
Bourguignon
Ferme des Mathurins
Ma Bourgogne
Petite Auberge
Pierre
Récamier
6 Bosquet

Lyons
Auberge Bressane
Bellecour
Bistrot d'Alex
Bouchon Beaujolais
Cartet
Fred
Marcel
Moissonnier
Monttessuy
Parc aux Cerfs
Petit Mâchon
Rôtisserie du Beaujolais
Saint Amour
Saint Vincent

Normandy
Fernand/Les Fernandises
Pharamond

Provence
Bastide Odéon
Bistrot d'Alex
Bistrot Gambas
Café Louis Philippe
Campagne et Provence
Carré Kléber
Casa Olympe
Charlot - Roi Coquillages
Chat Grippé
Elysées du Vernet

Janou
Jardin
Maison
Olivades
Pavillon Panama
Pavillon Puebla
Petit Niçois
Pierre Vedel
Senteurs de Provence
Sologne
Sud
Table du Marché
Vivario

Southwest
Ambassade du Sud-Ouest
Ami Pierre
Auberge Etchégorry
Auberge Landaise
Baracane
Bascou
Bistro de Gala
Cave Drouot
Chez Eux
Comte de Gascogne
Espace Sud-Ouest
Flambée/Bistrot du Sud
Fontaine de Mars
Gigot Fin
Grand Louvre
Grizzli
Languedoc
Lous Landès
Oie Cendrée
Oulette
Petit Robert
Plancha
Quercy
Rest. du Marché
Sarladais
Sousceyrac
Table de Pierre
Thoumieux
Trou Gascon
Truffière
Vagenende

Other
Altitude 95
Ambassade d'Auvergne
Auberge des Dolomites
Bernica
Berry's
Chantairelle
Coupe-Chou
Deux Canards

Epi d'Or
Galoche d'Aurillac
Jacky
Jacques Mélac
Kiosque
Lozère
Petit Colombier
Petite Bretonnière
Petit Riche
Quincy
Saint Pourçain
Savy
Tonnelle Saintongeaise
Val d'Isère

French: Seafood
Auberge Dab
Augusta
Ballon des Ternes
Bar à Huîtres
Bar au Sel
Baumann Ternes
Bistrot de Marius
Bistrot du Dôme
Boeuf sur le Toit
Brasserie du Louvre
Brasserie Flo
Brasserie Le Stella
Brasserie Lorraine
Brasserie Lutétia
Brasserie Mollard
Cagouille
Cap Vernet
Charlot - Roi Coquillages
Cochon d'Or
Coupole
Dessirier
Divellec
Dôme
Duc (Le)
Ecaille de PCB
Ecaille et Plume
Filoche
Francis
Frézet
Gaya, Estaminet
Gaya Rive Gauche
Glénan
Goumard
Huîtrier
Iles Marquises
Jarasse
Luna
Magnolias
Maison d'Alsace

Maison Prunier
Marée
Marines
Marius
Marius et Janette
Méditerranée
Moniage Guillaume
Ostréade
Paul Minchelli
Petit Navire
Petit Niçois
Pétrus
Pichet
Port Alma
Porte Océane
Procope
Rech
Rosimar
Sébillon Neuilly
Taverne Kronenbourg
Timonerie
Vaudeville
Venantius
Vin et Marée
Wepler

French: Shellfish
André
Auberge Dab
Baumann Ternes
Boeuf sur le Toit
Bofinger
Brasserie du Louvre
Brasserie Flo
Brasserie Le Stella
Brasserie Lorraine
Brasserie Lutétia
Brasserie Mollard
Clément
Coupole
Francis
Maison d'Alsace
Michel
Procope
Sébillon Neuilly
Taverne Kronenbourg
Trois Marches
Ty Coz

French: Steakhouse
Bistrot du Cochon d'Or
Boeuf Couronné
Cochon d'Or
Dagorno
Denise
Gavroche

Gigot Fin
Hippopotamus
Relais de Venise
Rôtisserie d'Armaillé
Rôtisserie d'en Face
Rôtisserie du Beaujolais
Rôtisserie Monsigny

French: Tearooms

Angelina
Deux Abeilles
Ladurée
Mariage Frères

French: Wine Bar/Bistro

Ange Vin
Bacchantes
Bourguignon
Cave Drouot
Clown Bar
Ecluse
Enotéca
Gavroche
Juvenile's
Ma Bourgogne
Mauzac
Moulin à Vins
Oenothèque
Vendanges
Verre Bouteille
Vin sur Vin
Willi's Wine Bar

German

Brasserie Munichoise

Greek

Délices d'Aphrodite
Diamantaires
Mavrommatis

Hamburgers

Drugstore Publicis
Hippopotamus
Joe Allen
Planet Hollywood

Health Food

Grenier de Notre Dame

Indian

Annapurna
Indra
Ravi
Vishnou
Yugaraj

Indochinese

Café Indochine
Kambodgia

Irish

Carr's

Italian

Bauta
Beato
Bellini
Cafetière
Caffé Bini
Casa Bini
Châteaubriant
Cherche Midi
Conti
Da Mimmo
Emporio Armani Caffé
Enotéca
Fellini
Finzi
Gildo
Giulio Rebellato
Grand Venise
I Golosi
Il Barone
Il Carpaccio
Il Cortile
Il Ristorante
Il Vicolo
Livio
Marcello
Osteria
Paolo Petrini
Perron
Pinocchio
Romantica
Sormani
Stresa
Trentaquattro
Véranda
Verre Bouteille
Villa Vinci
Vincent

Japanese

Benkay
Inagiku
Isami
Issé
Kifuné
Kinugawa
Orient-Extrême
Osaka
Shozan

Suntory
Taka
Tsukizi

Jewish
Goldenberg Wagram
Jo Goldenberg

Lebanese
Al Dar
Al Diwan
Arthur
Fakhr el Dine
Noura

Malaysian
Yit Foong

Mexican
Anahuacalli
Ay!! Caramba!!

Moroccan
Al Mounia
Amazigh
Atlas
Caroubier
Etoile Marocaine
Hammam Café
Mansouria
Omar
Oum el Banine
Pied de Chameau
404
Taroudant II
Timgad

Pizza
Chicago Pizza Pie Factory
Da Mimmo
Planet Hollywood

Portuguese
Saudade

Russian
Daru
Dominique
Maroussia
Nikita

Scandinavian
Café des Lettres
Comptoir du Saumon Fumé

Copenhague
Flora Danica

Seychelles
Coco de Mer

South American
Anahï (Argentine)
Botequim Brasileiro
Milonga (Argentine)

Spanish
Casa Alcalde
Casa Tina
Fogón Saint Julien
Pavillon Puebla
Rosimar
San Valero

Swiss
Maison du Valais

Tex-Mex
Indiana Café
Studio

Thai
Bains
Blue Elephant
Chieng Mai
Erawan
Foch-An
Foc-Ly
Khun Akorn
Sawadee
Village d'Ung et Li Lam

Tunisian
Caroubier
Corniche

Vegetarian
Grenier de Notre Dame

Vietnamese
Baie d'Ha Long
Foch-An
Gastronomie Quach
Kim Anh
Lac Hong
Ngo
Tan Dinh
Tong Yen

NEIGHBORHOOD LOCATIONS
(by arrondissement)

1st Arrondissement

Absinthe
Angelina
Ardoise
Armand au Palais Royal
Bar Vendôme
Brasserie du Louvre
Brasserie Munichoise
Café Bennett
Café Marly
Caffé Foy
Carré des Feuillants
Carr's
Cartes Postales
Caveau du Palais
Chicago Meatpackers
Colette
Costes
Denise
Elle
Epi d'Or
Escargot Montorgueil
Espadon
Fabrice
Fellini
Fumoir
Gabriel
Gaya, Estaminet
Gérard Besson
Goumard
Grand Louvre
Grand Véfour
Grille St-Honoré
Hippopotamus
Il Cortile
Joe Allen
Juvenile's
Kinugawa
Lescure
Lina's
Macéo
Meurice
Osaka
Pauline
Pharamond
Pied de Cochon
Pierre au Palais Royal
Poquelin
Poule au Pot
Rest. du Palais Royal
Ruc Univers

Saudade
Soufflé
Toupary
Vieille
Vong
Willi's Wine Bar
Yvan sur Seine

2nd Arrondissement

Ange Vin
Bistrot Gambas
Café des Théâtres
Café Runtz
Céladon
Clément
Crus de Bourgogne
Drouant
Gallopin
Gavroche
Georges
Grand Colbert
Hippopotamus
Issé
Lina's
Noces de Jeannette
Passy Mandarin
"Pierre" à la Fontaine
Pile ou Face
Rôtisserie Monsigny
Saint Amour
Vaudeville

3rd Arrondissement

Alisier
Ambassade d'Auvergne
Ami Louis
Anahï
Bains
Bar à Huîtres
Bascou
Batifol
Camille
Guirlande de Julie
Hangar
Janou
Jenny
Marais-Cage
Nénesse
Omar
Opium Café
404
Réconfort

4th Arrondissement

Ambroisie
Baracane
Benoît
Bistrot du Dôme
Bofinger
Bourguignon
Brasserie de l'Isle St-Louis
Café Beaubourg
Café Louis Philippe
Clément
Coconnas
Comptoir du Saumon Fumé
Domarais
Dos de la Baleine
Enotéca
Excuse
Fond de Cour
Fous d'en Face
Gourmet de l'Isle
Grizzli
Hammam Café
Hippopotamus
Il Vicolo
Isami
Jo Goldenberg
Mariage Frères
Marianne
Miravile
Monde des Chimères
Orangerie
Osteria
Petit Gavroche
Pied de Chameau
Studio
Thanksgiving
Vieux Bistro
Woolloomooloo

5th Arrondissement

Al Dar
Anahuacalli
Atelier Maître Albert
Atlas
Bar à Huîtres
Batifol
Berthoud
Bistrot d'à Côté St-Germain
Botequim Brasileiro
Bouchons de Fr. Clerc
Brasserie Balzar
Bûcherie
Campagne et Provence
Chantairelle
Chieng Mai

Coco de Mer
Coin des Gourmets
Coupe-Chou
Délices d'Aphrodite
Fogón Saint Julien
Fontaines
Grenier de Notre Dame
Hippopotamus
Iles Philippines
Inagiku
Languedoc
Maison
Marty
Mauzac
Mavrommatis
Mirama
Moissonnier
Moulin à Vent "Chez Henri"
Pactole
Pento
Perraudin
Petit Navire
Petit Prince de Paris
Port du Salut
Réminet
René
Restaurant A
Rest. Toutoune
Rôtisserie du Beaujolais
Timonerie
Tour d'Argent
Truffière
Vivario

6th Arrondissement

Allard
Arbuci
Assassins
Bastide Odéon
Bauta
Bistro de la Grille
Bistrot d'Alex
Bistrot d'Henri
Bistrot Mazarin
Bon St. Pourçain
Bookinistes
Bouillon Racine
Brasserie Lipp
Brasserie Lutétia
Café de Flore
Café Les Deux Magots
Cafetière
Caméléon
Casa Bini
Casa del Habano

Charpentiers
Chat Grippé
Cherche Midi
Chope d'Alsace
Christine
Clocher Saint-Germain
Closerie des Lilas
Coffee Parisien
Comptoir des Sports
Cosi
Dominique
Ecaille de PCB
Echaudé St-Germain
Ecluse
Emporio Armani Caffé
Epi Dupin
Hippopotamus
Hulotte
Jacques Cagna
Joséphine
Lapérouse
Lina's
Lozère
Maître Paul
Marcel
Mariage Frères
Marie et Fils
Marlotte
Maroussia
Méditerranée
Milonga
Muniche
Noura
O à la Bouche
Orient-Extrême
Parc aux Cerfs
Paris
Petite Cour
Petit Lutétia
Petit St-Benoît
Petit Zinc
Polidor
Procope
Relais Louis XIII
Rest. des Beaux Arts
Rond de Serviette
Rôtisserie d'en Face
Tsukizi
Vagenende
Yugaraj

7th Arrondissement

Affriolé
Altitude 95
Ambassade du Sud-Ouest

Arpège
Auberge Bressane
Auberge du Champ de Mars
Bamboche
Bar au Sel
Basilic
Beato
Bellecour
Bistrot de Breteuil
Bistrot de Paris
Bon Accueil
Boule d'Or
Café de Mars
Café des Lettres
Caffé Bini
Calèche
Cantine des Gourmets
Champ de Mars
Chez Eux
Cigale
Clémentine
Côté 7ème
Deux Abeilles
Divellec
Ecaille et Plume
Ferme St-Simon
Foc-Ly
Fontaine de Mars
Françoise
Gaya Rive Gauche
Germaine
Gildo
Glénan
Jules Verne
Maison de l'Amérique
Marius (Chez)
Maupertu
Michel Courtalhac
Montalembert
Monttessuy
Oeillade
Olivades
Paul Minchelli
Perron
Petite Chaise
Petit Laurent
Petit Niçois
Pied de Fouet
P'tit Troquet
Ravi
Récamier
Rest. du Musée d'Orsay
Ribe
6 Bosquet
Tan Dinh

Télégraphe
Thoumieux
Trentaquattro
Vin sur Vin
Violon d'Ingres
Voltaire

8th Arrondissement

Ailleurs
Al Diwan
Ambassadeurs
André
Androuët
Annapurna
Appart'
Astor
Avenue
Bar des Théâtres
Barfly
Batifol
Berry's
Bistrot de Marius
Bistrot du Sommelier
Boeuf sur le Toit
Bouchons de Fr. Clerc
Brasserie Lorraine
Brasserie Mollard
Bristol
Buddha Bar
Café Bleu Lanvin
Café Indochine
Cap Vernet
Caviar Kaspia
Cercle Ledoyen
Champs-Elysées Mandarin
Chiberta
Chicago Pizza Pie Factory
Clément
Clovis
Club Matignon
Copenhague
Corniche
Cou de la Girafe
Couronne
Daru
Diep
Drugstore Publicis
Ecluse
Elysées du Vernet
Etoile Marocaine
Fakhr el Dine
Fauchon - Le 30
Ferme des Mathurins
Fermette Marbeuf
Finzi

Flora Danica
Fouquet's
Francis
Friends
Géorgiques
Gourmets des Ternes
Grenadin
Hédiard
Hippopotamus
Il Carpaccio
Indra
Jardin
Jardin des Cygnes
Kinugawa
Ladurée
Lasserre
Laurent
Ledoyen
Lina's
Lucas Carton
Luna
Ma Bourgogne
Maison Blanche
Maison d'Alsace
Maison du Caviar
Maison du Valais
Marcande
Marée
Mariage Frères
Marius et Janette
Maxim's
Obélisque
Pichet
Pierre Gagnaire
Planet Hollywood
Régence
Relais Plaza
Sarladais
Saveurs
Savy
Sébillon Neuilly
Shozan
Spicy Restaurant
Stella Maris
Stresa
Suntory
Table du Marché
Taillevent
Tante Louise
Tong Yen
Val d'Isère
Véranda
Village d'Ung et Li Lam
Virgin Café
Vong

Yvan
Yvan, Petit

9th Arrondissement
Alsaco
Auberge Landaise
Bacchantes
Batifol
Bistro de Gala
Bistro des Deux Théâtres
Bistrot Papillon
Café de la Paix
Casa Olympe
Cave Drouot
Charlot - Roi Coquillages
Chartier
Cloche d'Or
Diamantaires
Grand Café Capucines
Grange Batelière
I Golosi
Jean
Lina's
Muses
Oenothèque
Paprika
Petit Riche
Poste
Quercy
Rest. Opéra
Table d'Anvers
Taverne Kronenbourg
Ty Coz
Venantius
Wally Le Saharien

10th Arrondissement
Batifol
Brasserie Flo
Canard Laqué Pékinois
Châteaubriant
China Town Belleville
Da Mimmo
Deux Canards
Galopin
Gigot Fin
Grille
Hippopotamus
Hôtel du Nord
Julien
Michel
Terminus Nord

11th Arrondissement
Ami Pierre
Amognes

Astier
Blue Elephant
Café de l'Industrie
Café du Passage
C'Amelot
Cartet
Chardenoux
Clown Bar
Dame Jeanne
Ecluse
Fernand/Les Fernandises
Galoche d'Aurillac
Jacques Mélac
Khun Akorn
Mansouria
Navarin
New Nioullaville
Paul
Petit Keller
Plancha
Président
Repaire de Cartouche
Réservoir
Sousceyrac
Villaret

12th Arrondissement
Biche au Bois
Bouchon Beaujolais
China Club
Connivence
Dame Tartine
Ebauchoir
Flambée/Bistrot du Sud
Grandes Marches
Lina's
Oulette
Pressoir
Quincy
Saint Amarante
Saint Pourçain
Sologne
Square Trousseau
Train Bleu
Trou Gascon
Viaduc Café
Zygomates

13th Arrondissement
Anacréon
Auberge Etchégorry
Avant Goût
Chinatown Olympiades
Entoto
Jacky
Nouveau Village Tao Tao

Petit Marguery
Temps des Cerises
Terroir
Vieux Métiers de France

14th Arrondissement

Amuse Bouche
Assiette
Bar à Huîtres
Batifol
Bernica
Bistrot du Dôme
Cagouille
Caroubier
Caves Solignac
Chaumière des Gourmets
Clément
Contre-Allée
Coupole
Crêperie de Josselin
Dôme
Duc (Le)
Entrepôt
Espace Sud-Ouest
Flamboyant
Hippopotamus
Il Barone
Iles Marquises
Indiana Café
Lous Landès
Mille Colonnes
Moniage Guillaume
Monsieur Lapin
Montparnasse 25
Natacha
Pavillon Montsouris
Petites Sorcières
Pinocchio
Régalade
Rendez-vous/Camionneurs
Vendanges
Vin et Marée
Vishnou
Zeyer

15th Arrondissement

Agape
Armoise
Arthur
Barrail
Batifol
Benkay
Bermuda Onion
Bistro 121
Bistro d'Hubert
Bistrot d'André

Bouchons de Fr. Clerc
Café du Commerce
Casa Alcalde
Célébrités
Chen
Clément
Clos Morillons
Dînée
Epopée
Erawan
Fellini
Filoche
Gastroquet
Gauloise
Gitane
Grand Venise
Hippopotamus
Je Thé...Me..
Kim Anh
Morot-Gaudry
Napoléon Chaix
Oie Cendrée
Os à Moelle
Ostréade
Papillote
Pavillon Panama
Père Claude
Petite Bretonnière
Petit Mâchon
Petit Plat
Philippe Detourbe
Pierre
Pierre Vedel
Porte Océane
Relais de Sèvres
Rest. de la Tour
Rest. du Marché
Saint Vincent
Sawadee
Senteurs de Provence
Yit Foong
Yves Quintard

16th Arrondissement

A et M Le Bistrot
Alain Ducasse
Al Dar
Al Mounia
Amazigh
Auberge Dab
Baie d'Ha Long
Beaujolais d'Auteuil
Bellini
Bertie's
Bistrot de l'Etoile Lauriston

Brasserie de la Poste
Brasserie Le Stella
Butte Chaillot
Carré Kléber
Casa Tina
Chalet des Iles
Conti
Cuisinier François
Detourbe Duret
Driver's
Fakhr el Dine
Faugeron
Flandrin
Fontaine d'Auteuil
Gare
Gastronomie Quach
Géraud
Giulio Rebellato
Grand Chinois
Grande Cascade
Jamin
Jardins de Bagatelle
Kambodgia
Kiosque
Lac Hong
Maison Prunier
Marius
Marronniers d'Auteuil
Mathusalem
Ngo
Nikita
Noura
Oum el Banine
Passy Mandarin
Paul Chêne
Pavillon des Princes
Pergolèse
Petite Tour
Petit Rétro
Petit Victor Hugo
Port Alma
Pré Catelan
Relais d'Auteuil
Relais du Parc
Rest. des Chauffeurs
Rosimar
Salle à Manger
Scheffer
Table de Babette
Totem
Tsé-Yang
Villa Vinci
Vin et Marée
Vivarois
Zebra Square

17th Arrondissement
Amphyclès
Apicius
Atelier Gourmand
Auberge des Dolomites
Augusta
Ballon des Ternes
Batifol
Baumann Ternes
Béatilles
Beudant
Bistro du 17
Bistro Melrose
Bistrot d'à Côté Flaubert
Bistrot d'à Côté Villiers
Bistrot de l'Etoile Niel
Bistrot de l'Etoile Troyon
Bistrot Gambas
Bouchons de Fr. Clerc
Braisière
Caves Pétrissans
Clément
Coco et sa Maison
Congrès
Cote d'Amour
Débarcadère
Dessirier
Ecluse
Epicure 108
Etoile d'Or
Faucher
Fred
Georges Porte Maillot
Goldenberg Wagram
Graindorge
Guy Savoy
Huîtrier
Il Ristorante
Impatient
Kifuné
Lina's
Manoir Detourbe
Marcello
Marines
Michel Rostang
Paolo Petrini
Petit Colombier
Petite Auberge
Pétrus
Pré Carré
Rech
Relais de Venise
Rôtisserie d'Armaillé
Sormani
Soupière
Sud
Table de Pierre
Taïra

Timgad
Tonton Yang
Toque
Troyon
Verre Bouteille

18th Arrondissement

Beauvilliers (A.)
Cottage Marcadet
Frézet
Galerie
Marie Louise
Moulin à Vins
Petit Robert
Rendez-vous des Chauffeurs
Restaurant
Taka
Taroudant II
Wepler

19th Arrondissement

Ay!! Caramba!!
Batifol
Bistrot du Cochon d'Or
Boeuf Couronné
Café de la Musique
Cochon d'Or
Dagorno
Mandragore
Pavillon Puebla
Rest. d'Eric Fréchon
Vincent

20th Arrondissement

Allobroges
Boeuf Gros Sel
Flèche d'Or Café
Zéphyr

OUTLYING AREAS

Bougival
Camélia

Boulogne
Auberge
Batifol
Cafe Pancrace
Cap Seguin
Comte de Gascogne
Ferme de Boulogne

Chatillon
Dariole de Viry

Clichy
Barrière de Clichy
Romantica

Défense (La)
Lina's

Issy-Les-Moulineaux
Manufacture
River Café

Levallois
Petit Poucet

Neuilly
Bistrot d'à Côté Neuilly
Bistrot St-James
Café la Jatte

Carpe Diem
Catounière
Coco d'Isles
Durand Dupont
Feuilles Libres
Foch-An
Foc-Ly
Gérard
Guinguette de Neuilly
Jarasse
Lina's
Livio
San Valero
Sébillon Neuilly
Tonnelle Saintongeaise
Truffe Noire

Perreux-sur-Marne
Magnolias

Saint-Cloud
Quai Ouest

Saint-Ouen
Coq de la Maison Blanche

Saint-Germain-en-Laye
Cazaudehore La Forestière

Versailles
Trois Marches

SPECIAL FEATURES AND APPEALS

Breakfast
(All hotels and the
following standouts)
Angelina
Avenue
Bar des Théâtres
Benkay
Bertie's
Bofinger
Brasserie Balzar
Brasserie du Louvre
Brasserie Flo
Brasserie Le Stella
Brasserie Lipp
Brasserie Lutétia
Café Beaubourg
Café Bleu Lanvin
Café de Flore
Café des Lettres
Café Les Deux Magots
Café Marly
Cave Drouot
Cazaudehore La Forestière
Clément
Closerie des Lilas
Clovis
Coq de la Maison Blanche
Costes
Deux Abeilles
Dôme
Drugstore Publicis
Flandrin
Fontaines
Fouquet's
Il Cortile
Janou
Jardins de Bagatelle
Jenny
Ladurée
Maison d'Alsace
Marius
Marty
Mille Colonnes
Muses
Pied de Cochon
Procope
Ruc Univers
Savy
Sébillon
Taverne Kronenbourg
Thoumieux
Train Bleu

Viaduc Café
Virgin Café
Voltaire
Wepler
Zebra Square
Zeyer

Brunch
(Best of many)
Bar des Théâtres
Barfly
Bermuda Onion
Brasserie Lutétia
Café Beaubourg
Café Bleu Lanvin
Café de Flore
Café de la Musique
Café de l'Industrie
Café des Lettres
Carr's
Coffee Parisien
Débarcadère
Deux Abeilles
Durand Dupont
Jardin des Cygnes
Joe Allen
Jo Goldenberg
Quai Ouest
River Café
Studio
Thanksgiving
Viaduc Café
Virgin Café
Zebra Square

Business Dining
Alain Ducasse
Ambassadeurs
Ambroisie
Amognes
André
Annapurna
Apicius
Armand au Palais Royal
Arpège
Assiette
Astor
Avenue
Ballon des Ternes
Bar au Sel
Bar Vendôme
Béatilles
Beato

Bellecour	Faucher
Bellini	Faugeron
Benkay	Ferme des Mathurins
Benoît	Ferme St-Simon
Bertie's	Finzi
Beudant	Fontaine d'Auteuil
Bistrot d'à Côté Flaubert	Fouquet's
Bistrot d'à Côté Villiers	Francis
Bistrot de l'Etoile Lauriston	Gaya Rive Gauche
Bistrot de l'Etoile Niel	Georges
Bistrot de l'Etoile Troyon	Gérard Besson
Bistrot de Marius	Goumard
Blue Elephant	Graindorge
Boeuf sur le Toit	Grande Cascade
Bouchons de Fr. Clerc	Grand Véfour
Boule d'Or	Grenadin
Braisière	Guy Savoy
Brasserie du Louvre	Huîtrier
Brasserie Lipp	Il Carpaccio
Brasserie Lorraine	Il Cortile
Brasserie Mollard	Issé
Bristol	Jacques Cagna
Bûcherie	Jamin
Café de la Paix	Jarasse
Cagouille	Jardin
Camélia	Jardin des Cygnes
Cantine des Gourmets	Jules Verne
Cap Vernet	Kinugawa
Carpe Diem	Lapérouse
Carré des Feuillants	Lasserre
Carré Kléber	Laurent
Cartes Postales	Ledoyen
Céladon	Lous Landès
Célébrités	Lucas Carton
Cercle Ledoyen	Magnolias
Charlot - Roi Coquillages	Maison Blanche
Chiberta	Maison d'Alsace
Cloche d'Or	Maison Prunier
Clovis	Manoir Detourbe
Conti	Marée
Copenhague	Marines
Coq de la Maison Blanche	Marius
Coupole	Marius (Chez)
Daru	Marius et Janette
Dessirier	Maxim's
Detourbe Duret	Meurice
Dînée	Michel Rostang
Divellec	Mille Colonnes
Dôme	Miravile
Drouant	Montalembert
Duc (Le)	Montparnasse 25
Ecaille de PCB	Morot-Gaudry
Elysées du Vernet	Muniche
Espadon	Muses
Fakhr el Dine	Obélisque

Oulette
Oum el Banine
Paolo Petrini
Parc aux Cerfs
Paris
Pauline
Pergolèse
Petit Colombier
Petite Bretonnière
Petit Marguery
Pétrus
Pharamond
Philippe Detourbe
Pichet
Pierre au Palais Royal
Pierre Gagnaire
Pierre Vedel
Pile ou Face
Port Alma
Pré Carré
Pré Catelan
Pressoir
Quercy
Rech
Régence
Relais d'Auteuil
Relais de Sèvres
Relais du Parc
Relais Louis XIII
Relais Plaza
Rest. du Marché
Rest. Opéra
Romantica
Rôtisserie d'Armaillé
Rôtisserie Monsigny
Salle à Manger
Savy
Sébillon Neuilly
Shozan
Sormani
Sousceyrac
Stresa
Sud
Table d'Anvers
Table de Pierre
Taillevent
Taïra
Tante Louise
Timgad
Timonerie
Tour d'Argent
Train Bleu
Trois Marches
Trou Gascon
Troyon

Truffe Noire
Ty Coz
Vieille
Vieux Métiers de France
Violon d'Ingres
Vivarois
Voltaire
Vong

Caters
(Best of many)
Affriolé
Al Dar
Al Diwan
Amazigh
Anahuacalli
Ardoise
Armand au Palais Royal
Atlas
Bamboche
Bar à Huîtres
Bernica
Bistro 121
Bistro de la Grille
Bistrot de l'Etoile Niel
Casa Tina
Caviar Kaspia
Coco de Mer
Dînée
Driver's
Fabrice
Fakhr el Dine
Glénan
Hédiard
Inagiku
Jacky
Joe Allen
Jo Goldenberg
Kinugawa
Livio
Magnolias
Maison Prunier
Marianne
Milonga
Noura
Oenothèque
Olivades
Paprika
Petite Tour
Relais Louis XIII
Rond de Serviette
Table du Marché
Thanksgiving
Tong Yen

Vendanges
Vong
Wally Le Saharien

Dancing/Entertainment
(Check days, times and
performers for entertainment;
D=dancing; best of many)
Arbuci (jazz)
Assassins (piano)
Ay!! Caramba!! (musicians)
Barfly (DJ)
Bar Vendôme (piano)
Bernica (singer)
Bistrot de l'Etoile Niel (magician)
Boeuf sur le Toit (jazz/piano)
Bouillon Racine (jazz)
Café de la Musique (jazz)
Café des Théâtres (karaoke)
Caffé Foy (theme evenings)
Cap Seguin (jazz/piano)
Carr's (Irish)
Céladon (piano bar)
China Club (jazz)
China Town Belleville (karaoke)
Closerie des Lilas (piano bar)
Clovis (piano)
Coupole (D/disco)
Débarcadère (varies)
Diamantaires (orchestra)
Domarais (cabaret/gospel)
Dominique (Russian)
Durand Dupont (DJ)
Elle (swing)
Elysées du Vernet (piano)
Espadon (violins)
Flèche d'Or Café (D/rock)
Françoise (D/piano)
Friends (DJ)
Georges Porte Maillot (piano)
Grille (orchestra)
Hammam Café (music)
Hôtel du Nord (jazz/swing)
Jardin des Cygnes (piano)
Jardins de Bagatelle (D)
Jenny (musical evenings)
Jo Goldenberg (music)
Kiosque (sports TV)
Maxim's (D/music)
Milonga (tango)
Nikita (orchestra)
Paprika (Hungarian)
Pavillon des Princes (D)
Pavillon Puebla (piano)
Planet Hollywood (bands/videos)

Poste (orchestra)
Régence (piano)
Relais Plaza (theme evenings)
Réservoir (rock)
Rest. du Musée d'Orsay (piano)
Saudade (Fado)
Table de Babette (piano)
Totem (theme evenings)
Véranda (D/musicians)
Viaduc Café (jazz brunch)

Dining Alone
(Other than hotels)
Affriolé
Alain Ducasse
Alisier
Allard
Al Mounia
Alsaco
Ambassade d'Auvergne
Ambassade du Sud-Ouest
Ambassadeurs
Ami Louis
Amphyclès
Anacréon
Anahuacalli
André
Androuët
Annapurna
Arbuci
Armand au Palais Royal
Arpège
Astor
Avenue
Bacchantes
Bamboche
Baracane
Bar à Huîtres
Bar des Théâtres
Bar Vendôme
Basilic
Bastide Odéon
Baumann Ternes
Béatilles
Bellecour
Benkay
Benoît
Berthoud
Bertie's
Beudant
Biche au Bois
Bistro 121
Bistro de Gala
Bistro de la Grille
Bistro d'Hubert

Bistrot d'à Côté Neuilly
Bistrot d'à Côté Villiers
Bistrot de l'Etoile Lauriston
Bistrot de l'Etoile Niel
Bistrot de l'Etoile Troyon
Bistrot de Paris
Bistrot Mazarin
Boeuf sur le Toit
Bon St. Pourçain
Boule d'Or
Bourguignon
Braisière
Brasserie Balzar
Brasserie de la Poste
Brasserie du Louvre
Brasserie Flo
Brasserie Le Stella
Brasserie Lorraine
Brasserie Lutétia
Brasserie Mollard
Bristol
Café Beaubourg
Café de Flore
Café de la Paix
Café de l'Industrie
Café des Lettres
Café Indochine
Café Les Deux Magots
Café Marly
Café Runtz
Caffé Bini
Cagouille
Calèche
Caméléon
Camille
Campagne et Provence
Cantine des Gourmets
Cap Vernet
Carré Kléber
Carr's
Cartes Postales
Cartet
Caves Solignac
Céladon
Célébrités
Cercle Ledoyen
Champs-Elysées Mandarin
Chardenoux
Charlot - Roi Coquillages
Charpentiers
Chat Grippé
Chen
Chez Eux
Chiberta
Chieng Mai

Chope d'Alsace
Clément
Cloche d'Or
Clocher Saint-Germain
Closerie des Lilas
Clos Morillons
Clovis
Clown Bar
Coconnas
Congrès
Conti
Coq de la Maison Blanche
Cosi
Coupole
Dame Tartine
Daru
Dessirier
Deux Abeilles
Deux Canards
Diep
Dînée
Divellec
Dôme
Drouant
Drugstore Publicis
Duc (Le)
Ebauchoir
Ecaille et Plume
Ecluse
Elysées du Vernet
Enotéca
Epi d'Or
Epi Dupin
Escargot Montorgueil
Espadon
Fakhr el Dine
Faugeron
Fellini
Ferme des Mathurins
Ferme St-Simon
Fernand/Les Fernandises
Flora Danica
Fontaines
Fouquet's
Galoche d'Aurillac
Gavroche
Gaya, Estaminet
Gaya Rive Gauche
Georges
Gérard Besson
Germaine
Gigot Fin
Gitane
Glénan
Goumard

172

Graindorge
Grand Colbert
Grand Véfour
Grenadin
Grenier de Notre Dame
Grille
Grille St-Honoré
Guy Savoy
Hammam Café
Huîtrier
Il Barone
Il Cortile
Il Vicolo
Indiana Café
Indra
Issé
Jardin
Jardin des Cygnes
Jean
Jenny
Joe Allen
Joséphine
Julien
Juvenile's
Khun Akorn
Laurent
Ledoyen
Lina's
Lous Landès
Macéo
Maison du Valais
Maison Prunier
Mandragore
Mansouria
Marcel
Marée
Marines
Marius (Chez)
Marlotte
Marty
Meurice
Michel
Michel Courtalhac
Michel Rostang
Mille Colonnes
Mirama
Miravile
Moissonnier
Montalembert
Montparnasse 25
Monttessuy
Moulin à Vins
Muniche
Muses
Noura

Obélisque
Oie Cendrée
Olivades
Ostréade
Oulette
Oum el Banine
Pactole
Paolo Petrini
Parc aux Cerfs
Paris
Pauline
Paul Minchelli
Pergolèse
Perraudin
Perron
Petite Bretonnière
Petite Chaise
Petit Laurent
Petit Lutétia
Petit Marguery
Petit Niçois
Petit Plat
Petit St-Benoît
Petit Zinc
Pétrus
Pichet
Pied de Cochon
Pied de Fouet
Pierre
Pierre Gagnaire
Pierre Vedel
Pinocchio
Poquelin
Port Alma
Porte Océane
Poule au Pot
Pré Carré
Procope
Quercy
Quincy
Ravi
Régence
Relais d'Auteuil
Relais de Sèvres
Relais du Parc
Relais Plaza
Réminet
René
Repaire de Cartouche
Rest. de la Tour
Rest. d'Eric Fréchon
Rest. des Beaux Arts
Rest. des Chauffeurs
Rest. du Marché
Rest. du Musée d'Orsay

Rest. Opéra
Rest. Toutoune
Ribe
Rôtisserie d'Armaillé
Rôtisserie du Beaujolais
Ruc Univers
Saint Amarante
Saint Pourçain
Salle à Manger
Saudade
Savy
Scheffer
Sébillon Neuilly
Sormani
Soufflé
Soupière
Sousceyrac
Suntory
Taillevent
Taïra
Tan Dinh
Tante Louise
Taverne Kronenbourg
Terminus Nord
Thanksgiving
Timgad
Timonerie
Toupary
Train Bleu
Troyon
Tsé-Yang
Tsukizi
Ty Coz
Vagenende
Viaduc Café
Vieille
Vieux Bistro
Vieux Métiers de France
Vin et Marée
Virgin Café
Vivarois
Vong
Wepler
Zeyer

Family Style

Agape
Alisier
Allard
Allobroges
Altitude 95
Ambassade d'Auvergne
Ambassade du Sud-Ouest
Anacréon
Anahuacalli

Baracane
Batifol
Biche au Bois
Bistro de la Grille
Bistro d'Hubert
Bistrot d'André
Bouchon Beaujolais
Brasserie de l'Isle St-Louis
Café de Mars
Café du Commerce
Café Runtz
C'Amelot
Campagne et Provence
Casa Alcalde
Caves Solignac
Cazaudehore La Forestière
Chantairelle
Charpentiers
Chicago Meatpackers
Chinatown Olympiades
Cigale
Clément
Clocher Saint-Germain
Crus de Bourgogne
Da Mimmo
Denise
Deux Canards
Ebauchoir
Epi d'Or
Epi Dupin
Escargot Montorgueil
Espace Sud-Ouest
Fakhr el Dine
Fellini
Fernand/Les Fernandises
Flandrin
Fontaine de Mars
Fontaines
Galoche d'Aurillac
Germaine
Gigot Fin
Grille
Grizzli
Jenny
Joséphine
Lescure
Maison du Valais
Marcel
Michel
Michel Courtalhac
Moissonnier
Monttessuy
Nouveau Village Tao Tao
Oie Cendrée
Olivades

Omar
Os à Moelle
Perraudin
Petite Chaise
Petit Keller
Petit Niçois
Petit St-Benoît
Pied de Fouet
Pinocchio
Poquelin
Porte Océane
Poule au Pot
Quincy
Régalade
Relais de Venise
Réminet
Rendez-vous/Camionneurs
Repaire de Cartouche
Rest. Toutoune
Saint Amarante
Scheffer
Soupière
Sousceyrac
Temps des Cerises
Terroir
Thanksgiving
Thoumieux
Val d'Isère
Vieux Bistro
Zygomates

Fireplaces

Amazigh
Ambassadeurs
Atelier Maître Albert
Brasserie Munichoise
Bûcherie
Cap Seguin
Carr's
Cazaudehore La Forestière
China Club
Clovis
Comptoir des Sports
Coq de la Maison Blanche
Coupe-Chou
Elysées du Vernet
Flambée/Bistrot du Sud
Frézet
Jarasse
Je Thé...Me...
Moniage Guillaume
Montalembert
Orangerie
Pactole
Pavillon Montsouris

Petit Colombier
Petit Poucet
Petit Victor Hugo
Pré Catelan
Procope
Quai Ouest
Rest. du Musée d'Orsay
River Café
Romantica
Truffière

Game in Season

Affriolé
Alain Ducasse
Ambassadeurs
Assiette
Bellecour
Benoît
Bertie's
Biche au Bois
Bristol
Bûcherie
Carré des Feuillants
Chardenoux
Ecaille et Plume
Ferme St-Simon
Fontaine de Mars
Grand Véfour
Grenadin
Grizzli
Guy Savoy
Lous Landès
Michel Rostang
Moissonnier
Oulette
Petit Marguery
Pierre Vedel
Pressoir
Régalade
René
Repaire de Cartouche
Rest. du Marché
Saint Amarante
Sologne
Sousceyrac
Taillevent
Trois Marches
Trou Gascon
Troyon
Vieux Bistro
Vieux Métiers de France
Villaret
Vivarois

Historic Interest

(Date of building and/or restaurant)

1292 Escargot Montorgueil	1900 Rest. des Beaux Arts
1582 Tour d'Argent	1900 Rest. du Musée d'Orsay
1600 Ambroisie	1900 Trou Gascon
1600 Monde des Chimères	1901 Petit St-Benoît
1605 Coconnas	1901 Train Bleu
1650 Petit Prince de Paris	1902 Grizzli
1680 Petite Chaise	1904 Chardenoux
1680 Relais Louis XIII	1904 Vagenende
1686 Procope	1905 Bouillon Racine
1750 Lapérouse	1906 Rendez-vous des Chauffeurs
1760 Grand Véfour	1907 Clovis
1780 Rest. du Palais Royal	1908 Bouchon Beaujolais
1807 Rest. Opéra	1909 Zygomates
1832 Pharamond	1910 Brasserie Lutétia
1845 Polidor	1910 Janou
1850 Coq de la Maison Blanche	1910 Pauline
1854 Charpentiers	1910 Rest. des Chauffeurs
1854 Petit Riche	1910 Trois Marches
1855 Ambassadeurs	1912 Benoît
1860 Poste	1912 Hôtel du Nord
1865 Dagorno	1914 Café Les Deux Magots
1867 Brasserie Mollard	1918 Daru
1870 Boeuf Couronné	1919 Clown Bar
1872 Goumard	1919 Lescure
1875 Cercle Ledoyen	1920 Closerie des Lilas
1875 Ledoyen	1921 Café du Commerce
1875 Pré Catelan	1923 Sousceyrac
1876 Gallopin	1923 Thoumieux
1880 Brasserie Lipp	1924 Ami Louis
1880 Drouant	1925 Allard
1880 "Pierre" à la Fontaine	1925 Biche au Bois
1886 Julien	1925 Boeuf sur le Toit
1889 Fouquet's	1925 Maison Prunier
1889 Jules Verne (Eiffel Tower)	1925 Salle à Manger
1890 Brasserie Flo	1925 Terminus Nord
1890 Café de Flore	1926 Georges
1892 Wepler	1927 Brasserie Lorraine
1893 Maxim's	1928 Cloche d'Or
1896 Chartier	1928 Dominique
1898 Brasserie de l'Isle St-Louis	1928 Jardin des Cygnes
1898 Dôme	1929 Tante Louise
1898 Fermette Marbeuf	1930 Ballon des Ternes
1898 Pavillon Montsouris	1930 Brasserie Balzar
1900 Congrès	1930 Diamantaires
1900 Elysées du Vernet	1930 Vaudeville
1900 Gauloise	1930 Zéphyr
1900 Géraud	1935 Poule au Pot
1900 Grande Cascade	1936 Cartet
1900 Grille St-Honoré	1936 Relais Plaza
1900 Joséphine	1940 Brasserie Le Stella
1900 Lucas Carton	1945 Lasserre
1900 Petit Gavroche	1945 Méditerranée
1900 Petit Lutétia	1946 Angelina
1900 Petit Rétro	
1900 Pierre	

Hotel Dining

Bourdonnais Hôtel
Cantine des Gourmets
Grand Hotel Intercontinental
Rest. Opéra
Hôtel Ambassador
Venantius
Hôtel Astor
Astor
Hôtel Baltimore
Bertie's
Hôtel Balzac
Pierre Gagnaire
Hôtel Bristol
Bristol
Hôtel Castille
Il Cortile
Hôtel Concorde-La Fayette
Etoile d'Or
Hôtel Costes
Costes
Hôtel de Crillon
Ambassadeurs
Obélisque
Hôtel du Louvre
Brasserie du Louvre
Hôtel Lutétia
Brasserie Lutétia
Paris
Hôtel Mercure/Val de Loire
Mille Colonnes
Hôtel Méridien-Montparnasse
Montparnasse 25
Hôtel Meurice
Meurice
Hôtel Montalembert
Montalembert
Hôtel Nikko
Benkay
Célébrités
Hôtel Plaza-Athénée
Régence
Relais Plaza
Hôtel Prince de Galles
Jardin des Cygnes
Hôtel Raphaël
Salle à Manger
Hôtel Ritz
Bar Vendôme
Espadon
Hôtel Royal Monceau
Il Carpaccio
Jardin
Hôtel Scribe
Muses

Hôtel Splendid Étoile
Pré Carré
Hôtel Vernet
Elysées du Vernet
Hôtel Warwick
Couronne
Hôtel Westminster
Céladon
Parc Westin Demeure Hôtel
Relais du Parc
Paris K. Palace
Carré Kléber
Sofitel Arc de Triomphe
Clovis
Sofitel Maison des Centraliens
Saveurs
Sofitel Porte de Sèvres
Relais de Sèvres

"In" Places

Absinthe
A et M Le Bistrot
Ailleurs
Alain Ducasse
Allobroges
Ami Louis
Anahï
Appart'
Arpège
Assiette
Avenue
Bains
Bamboche
Bar au Sel
Bar des Théâtres
Barfly
Bascou
Bellini
Bermuda Onion
Berry's
Bistro d'Hubert
Bistrot d'à Côté Villiers
Bistrot de l'Etoile Lauriston
Bistrot de l'Etoile Niel
Bistrot de l'Etoile Troyon
Bistrot de Paris
Bistrot du Dôme
Blue Elephant
Bon Accueil
Bookinistes
Bouillon Racine
Brasserie Balzar
Brasserie Le Stella
Brasserie Lipp
Bristol

177

Buddha Bar
Butte Chaillot
Café Beaubourg
Café Bleu Lanvin
Café de la Musique
Café de l'Industrie
Café de Mars
Café la Jatte
Café Marly
Cafetière
Caffé Bini
C'Amelot
Casa Bini
Casa del Habano
Caviar Kaspia
Cercle Ledoyen
Cherche Midi
China Club
Clown Bar
Coffee Parisien
Contre-Allée
Costes
Cou de la Girafe
Da Mimmo
Débarcadère
Detourbe Duret
Emporio Armani Caffé
Enotéca
Epi Dupin
Finzi
Fontaine de Mars
Fouquet's
Friends
Gare
Gaya Rive Gauche
Hammam Café
Hôtel du Nord
I Golosi
Il Barone
Il Cortile
Il Vicolo
Isami
Issé
Janou
Joséphine
Kiosque
Macéo
Maison
Maison Blanche
Manufacture
Marie et Fils
Marines
Natacha
Nénesse
O à la Bouche

Oeillade
Olivades
Omar
Orangerie
Orient-Extrême
Os à Moelle
Osteria
Pergolèse
Pétrus
Philippe Detourbe
Pierre au Palais Royal
Pierre Gagnaire
Poste
404
Réconfort
Régalade
Relais du Parc
Relais Plaza
Repaire de Cartouche
Réservoir
Restaurant
Rest. d'Eric Fréchon
Rest. du Palais Royal
River Café
Saint Amarante
Scheffer
Shozan
6 Bosquet
Sormani
Spicy Restaurant
Square Trousseau
Stresa
Télégraphe
Totem
Val d'Isère
Vaudeville
Véranda
Viaduc Café
Vincent
Vin sur Vin
Violon d'Ingres
Voltaire
Vong
Willi's Wine Bar
Yvan
Yvan sur Seine
Zebra Square

Jacket/Tie Recommended
Astor
Beauvilliers (A.)
Bristol
Carré des Feuillants
Drouant
Faugeron

Gérard Besson
Guy Savoy
Jules Verne
Laurent
Ledoyen
Lucas Carton
Maison Blanche
Orangerie
Pierre Gagnaire
Pré Catelan

Jacket/Tie Required

Alain Ducasse (dinner)
Ambassadeurs
Ambroisie
Espadon
Grand Véfour
Lasserre
Maxim's
Régence
Taillevent
Tour d'Argent

Late Late — After 12:30

(All hours are AM)
Arbuci (1)
Bar à Huîtres (2)
Bistro Melrose (1)
Bofinger (1)
Brasserie Flo (1:30)
Brasserie Lutétia (7)
Brasserie Munichoise (2)
Café Beaubourg (12:45)
Café du Passage (1:30)
Caviar Kaspia (1)
Chicago Meatpackers (1)
China Town Belleville (1:30)
Cloche d'Or (4)
Coupe-Chou (1)
Coupole (2)
Denise (7)
Dôme (12:45)
Dominique (1)
Drugstore Publicis (2)
Ecluse (1)
Espace Sud-Ouest (2)
Fouquet's (1)
Gavroche (2)
Hippopotamus (5)
Indiana Café (2)
Joe Allen (1)
Julien (1:30)
Ladurée (1)
Muniche (2)
Natacha (1)
New Nioullaville (1)
Petit Zinc (2)

Pied de Chameau (1)
Plancha (1:30)
Planet Hollywood (1)
Poste (3)
Président (1:30)
Procope (1)
Réservoir (1)
Taverne Kronenbourg (3)
Vagenende (1)
Vaudeville (2)
Villaret (1)
Wepler (1)
Yvan sur Seine (1)
Zeyer (1)

Meet for a Drink

(Most top hotels and the
following standouts)
Alain Ducasse
Alsaco
Barfly
Bar Vendôme
Bistrot Mazarin
Bourguignon
Brasserie Balzar
Brasserie Lipp
Brasserie Lorraine
Buddha Bar
Café Beaubourg
Café de Flore
Café de l'Industrie
Café du Passage
Café la Jatte
Café Les Deux Magots
Café Marly
Carr's
Casa del Habano
Cave Drouot
China Club
Clown Bar
Cosi
Débarcadère
Ecluse
Enotéca
Entrepôt
Fouquet's
Gavroche
Jacques Mélac
Juvenile's
Ma Bourgogne
Macéo
Montalembert
Moulin à Vins
Oenothèque
River Café

Studio
Trois Marches
Viaduc Café
Voltaire
Willi's Wine Bar
Zebra Square

Outdoor Dining
(G=garden; S=sidewalk;
T=terrace; W=waterside;
best of many)
Absinthe (T)
A et M Le Bistrot (T)
Ambassadeurs (G)
Arbuci (T)
Auberge Bressane (T)
Auberge Etchégorry (G,T)
Bar Vendôme (G)
Basilic (T)
Beauvilliers (A.) (T)
Bellecour (T)
Bermuda Onion (T)
Bernica (S)
Berthoud (T)
Bistro d'Hubert (T)
Bistrot d'à Côté Flaubert (T)
Bistrot d'à Côté St-Germain (T)
Bistrot de l'Etoile Niel (T)
Bouchons de Fr. Clerc (T)
Brasserie de l'Isle St-Louis (T)
Brasserie du Louvre (T)
Brasserie Lipp (T)
Bristol (G,T)
Café Beaubourg (T)
Café de Flore (T)
Café de la Musique (T)
Café de la Paix (T)
Café des Lettres (G)
Café Les Deux Magots (T)
Café Louis Philippe (T)
Café Marly (T)
Cagouille (T)
Cap Seguin (T,W)
Carré Kléber (T)
Caveau du Palais (T)
Cazaudehore La Forestière (G)
Chalet des Iles (T)
Champ de Mars (T)
Chantairelle (G,T)
Chicago Meatpackers (T)
Closerie des Lilas (T)
Coconnas (T)
Contre-Allée (T)
Coupe-Chou (G,T)
Crus de Bourgogne (T)

Deux Abeilles (T)
Dôme (T)
Durand Dupont (T)
Entrepôt (G)
Epopée (T)
Espadon (G)
Fauchon - Le 30 (T)
Fermette Marbeuf (T)
Flèche d'Or Café (T)
Flora Danica (G)
Foc-Ly (T)
Fond de Cour (T)
Fontaine de Mars (T)
Fouquet's (T)
Francis (T)
Fred (T)
Gallopin (T)
Georges Porte Maillot (T)
Grande Cascade (G,T)
Grenier de Notre Dame (T)
Guinguette de Neuilly (G,T,W)
Guirlande de Julie (T)
Hangar (T)
Il Cortile (G)
Jardin (G)
Jardin des Cygnes (G)
Jardins de Bagatelle (T)
Jenny (T)
Je Thé...Me... (G,T)
Khun Akorn (T)
Kiosque (T)
Ladurée (T)
Laurent (G)
Ledoyen (G)
Lescure (T)
Maison (T)
Maison d'Alsace (T)
Maison de l'Amérique (G,T)
Maison du Valais (T)
Manufacture (T)
Marcande (G)
Marcello (T)
Marie et Fils (T)
Marines (T)
Marius (T)
Marius et Janette (T)
Mavrommatis (T)
Méditerranée (T)
Mille Colonnes (T)
Moniage Guillaume (T)
Montalembert (T)
Morot-Gaudry (T)
Olivades (T)
Oulette (T)
Parc aux Cerfs (G,T)

Pavillon des Princes (G,T)
Pavillon Montsouris (G,T)
Pavillon Panama (T,W)
Pavillon Puebla (T)
Petite Cour (G,T)
Petites Sorcières (T)
Petit Poucet (W)
Petit Zinc (T)
Pharamond (T)
"Pierre" à la Fontaine (T)
Pré Carré (T)
Pré Catelan (G)
Quai Ouest (T,W)
Récamier (T)
Rech (T)
Régence (S,T)
Relais du Parc (G,T)
Rest. du Palais Royal (G)
River Café (W)
Romantica (T)
Salle à Manger (T)
Saveurs (T)
Shozan (T)
Sormani (G,T)
Square Trousseau (T)
Studio (T)
Sud (G,T)
Table de Babette (T)
Table de Pierre (T)
Tonnelle Saintongeaise (T)
Totem (T)
Trois Marches (G,T)
Vagenende (T)
Vaudeville (S,T)
Viaduc Café (T)
Zebra Square (T)
Zéphyr (T)

Outstanding Views

Altitude 95
Bermuda Onion
Café Marly
Camélia
Cap Seguin
Jules Verne
Lapérouse
Maison Blanche
Morot-Gaudry
Pavillon Montsouris
Pré Catelan
Quai Ouest
Rest. du Musée d'Orsay
Toupary
Tour d'Argent
Trois Marches

Parking/Valet

A et M Le Bistrot
Alain Ducasse
Al Diwan
Ambassadeurs
Ambroisie
Amphyclès
Apicius
Astor
Bains
Bar au Sel
Barfly
Bar Vendôme
Benkay
Bertie's
Bistro 121
Bistrot d'à Côté Flaubert
Bistrot d'à Côté Neuilly
Bistrot de l'Etoile Niel
Bistrot de l'Etoile Troyon
Bistrot du Cochon d'Or
Boeuf sur le Toit
Bouchons de Fr. Clerc
Brasserie Flo
Brasserie Lorraine
Brasserie Lutétia
Bristol
Buddha Bar
Café la Jatte
Cap Seguin
Céladon
Célébrités
Cercle Ledoyen
Champs-Elysées Mandarin
Closerie des Lilas
Clovis
Cochon d'Or
Coco et sa Maison
Comte de Gascogne
Coq de la Maison Blanche
Corniche
Costes
Cou de la Girafe
Couronne
Dagorno
Débarcadère
Dessirier
Diep
Dînée
Divellec
Drouant
Elysées du Vernet
Espadon
Fakhr el Dine
Faucher

Fauchon - Le 30
Faugeron
Finzi
Flandrin
Fouquet's
Francis
Françoise
Friends
Georges Porte Maillot
Gérard Besson
Goumard
Grand Colbert
Grande Cascade
Grand Véfour
Grand Venise
Grille
Guy Savoy
Hammam Café
Hédiard
Il Carpaccio
Il Cortile
Jacques Cagna
Jamin
Jarasse
Jardin
Jardin des Cygnes
Jenny
Jules Verne
Julien
Kiosque
Ladurée
Lapérouse
Lasserre
Laurent
Ledoyen
Lucas Carton
Maison Blanche
Maison du Caviar
Maison Prunier
Marcello
Marée
Marius
Marius et Janette
Maxim's
Méditerranée
Meurice
Michel
Michel Rostang
Moniage Guillaume
Montalembert
Montparnasse 25
Muses
Noura
Obélisque
Paolo Petrini

Paris
Paul
Paul Chêne
Pauline
Pavillon Montsouris
Pavillon Panama
Pergolèse
Petit Colombier
Petite Bretonnière
Petit Poucet
Pétrus
Pied de Cochon
Pierre au Palais Royal
Pierre Gagnaire
Poste
Pré Catelan
Pressoir
Quai Ouest
Régence
Relais d'Auteuil
Relais de Sèvres
Relais du Parc
Relais Louis XIII
Relais Plaza
Rest. d'Eric Fréchon
River Café
Romantica
Rôtisserie d'en Face
Salle à Manger
Saveurs
Sébillon Neuilly
Shozan
Sormani
Table de Babette
Table du Marché
Taillevent
Toupary
Tour d'Argent
Trois Marches
Trou Gascon
Truffe Noire
Tsé-Yang
Véranda
Vin et Marée
Violon d'Ingres
Vivarois
Vong
Zebra Square

Parties & Private Rooms
(Any nightclub or restaurant
charges less at off-times;
* indicates private rooms
available; best of many)
A et M Le Bistrot
Allard*

Amazigh
Ambassade d'Auvergne*
Ambassadeurs
Amphyclès*
Annapurna*
Armoise
Arpège*
Auberge Landaise*
Avenue*
Baie d'Ha Long*
Bains
Ballon des Ternes*
Barrail*
Bastide Odéon*
Baumann Ternes
Benkay*
Bertie's*
Bistro 121
Bistrot d'Alex
Bistrot de l'Etoile Niel*
Bistrot de l'Etoile Troyon
Bistrot de Paris*
Bistrot du Sommelier*
Bistrot St-James
Boeuf Couronné*
Boeuf sur le Toit
Bofinger*
Bouillon Racine*
Boule d'Or
Bristol*
Butte Chaillot
Café Bennett*
Café Runtz*
Cafetière*
Caffé Foy
Cagouille*
Calèche*
Camélia*
Cap Seguin*
Cap Vernet*
Carré des Feuillants*
Carré Kléber*
Caveau du Palais*
Cave Drouot*
Céladon*
Célébrités*
Champ de Mars*
Chaumière des Gourmets*
Chez Eux*
Chiberta*
China Club
Clémentine*
Cloche d'Or*
Closerie des Lilas*
Clovis*

Cochon d'Or*
Coco et sa Maison*
Coconnas
Contre-Allée*
Copenhague*
Coq de la Maison Blanche*
Coupe-Chou*
Coupole*
Couronne*
Crus de Bourgogne*
Diamantaires*
Dînée*
Dôme*
Dominique*
Drouant*
Durand Dupont*
Ecaille de PCB*
Ecaille et Plume*
Ecluse*
Elysées du Vernet*
Enotéca*
Etoile d'Or*
Fakhr el Dine*
Faucher
Fauchon - Le 30
Faugeron*
Ferme St-Simon
Foch-An*
Foc-Ly*
Fond de Cour*
Fontaine d'Auteuil*
Fouquet's*
Françoise*
Gabriel*
Gallopin*
Gauloise*
Georges Porte Maillot*
Géorgiques*
Glénan*
Goumard*
Grand Chinois*
Grand Colbert
Grande Cascade*
Grandes Marches
Grand Louvre*
Grand Véfour*
Grenadin*
Grenier de Notre Dame
Grille St-Honoré*
Grizzli*
Guy Savoy*
Hédiard*
Hôtel du Nord
Il Carpaccio*
Il Cortile*

Indiana Café
Indra*
Jacques Cagna*
Jamin*
Jardin*
Jardin des Cygnes*
Jardins de Bagatelle*
Jenny*
Joséphine*
Kambodgia*
Kinugawa*
Ladurée
Lapérouse*
Lasserre*
Laurent
Livio*
Lucas Carton*
Macéo*
Maison Blanche
Maison de l'Amérique*
Maison du Valais*
Maison Prunier*
Mansouria*
Marée*
Marius et Janette*
Marty*
Mavrommatis*
Maxim's*
Méditerranée*
Meurice*
Michel Rostang*
Mille Colonnes*
Miravile*
Montalembert*
Muniche*
Ngo
Noces de Jeannette*
Noura*
Passy Mandarin*
Pauline*
Paul Minchelli*
Pavillon des Princes*
Pavillon Montsouris*
Pavillon Puebla*
Pergolèse*
Petit Colombier*
Petite Auberge
Petite Bretonnière*
Petit Riche*
Pétrus*
Pharamond*
Philippe Detourbe
Pied de Cochon*
"Pierre" à la Fontaine*
Pierre Gagnaire*

Pierre Vedel*
Pile ou Face*
Port Alma*
Poste*
Poule au Pot*
Pré Carré*
Pressoir*
P'tit Troquet*
Quercy*
Récamier*
Rech*
Réconfort*
Relais Louis XIII*
Réminet*
Rest. du Musée d'Orsay*
Rest. du Palais Royal
Romantica*
Sarladais
Saudade*
Saveurs*
Shozan
Sologne
Sormani*
Soufflé*
Square Trousseau*
Stella Maris*
Suntory*
Table d'Anvers*
Table du Marché*
Taillevent*
Tan Dinh*
Tante Louise*
Taverne Kronenbourg*
Terminus Nord*
Thoumieux*
Tour d'Argent*
Train Bleu*
Truffe Noire
Truffière*
Tsé-Yang*
Vagenende*
Véranda
Viaduc Café*
Vieux Métiers de France*
Vin et Marée*
Vishnou*
Vong*
Wally Le Saharien*
Yugaraj*
Zebra Square*
Zeyer

People-Watching
Absinthe
Ailleurs

Ami Louis
Anahï
Appart'
Arpège
Assiette
Avenue
Bains
Barfly
Bar Vendôme
Bellini
Bistro des Deux Théâtres
Bistrot Mazarin
Blue Elephant
Boeuf sur le Toit
Bookinistes
Brasserie Balzar
Brasserie Le Stella
Brasserie Lipp
Buddha Bar
Café Beaubourg
Café Bleu Lanvin
Café de Flore
Café de l'Industrie
Café la Jatte
Café Les Deux Magots
Cercle Ledoyen
China Club
Contre-Allée
Costes
Cou de la Girafe
Da Mimmo
Débarcadère
Duc (Le)
Emporio Armani Caffé
Espadon
Ferme St-Simon
Finzi
Fouquet's
Fumoir
Gare
Grand Colbert
Il Barone
Il Cortile
Il Vicolo
Issé
Kiosque
Ladurée
Ledoyen
Macéo
Maison
Maison Blanche
Marie et Fils
Natacha
Omar
Orangerie

Paul Minchelli
Pétrus
Pichet
Pierre au Palais Royal
Poste
Réconfort
Relais du Parc
Relais Plaza
Restaurant
Rest. du Marché
River Café
Scheffer
Stresa
Table du Marché
Taillevent
Télégraphe
Tong Yen
Véranda
Voltaire
Vong
Yvan sur Seine
Zebra Square

Power Scenes
Alain Ducasse
Ambassadeurs
Ami Louis
Amphyclès
Apicius
Arpège
Assiette
Astor
Avenue
Bar au Sel
Bastide Odéon
Beato
Bellini
Benoît
Bistrot d'à Côté Flaubert
Bistrot d'à Côté Neuilly
Bistrot de l'Etoile Lauriston
Bistrot de l'Etoile Niel
Bistrot de Marius
Bistrot de Paris
Boeuf sur le Toit
Brasserie Balzar
Brasserie Le Stella
Brasserie Lipp
Bristol
Café de Flore
Café de Mars
Café Les Deux Magots
Carré des Feuillants
Cartet
Casa Bini

185

Casa del Habano
Caviar Kaspia
Céladon
Cercle Ledoyen
Chen
Chiberta
Conti
Daru
Dessirier
Divellec
Dôme
Drouant
Duc (Le)
Elysées du Vernet
Espadon
Faucher
Faugeron
Ferme St-Simon
Finzi
Fouquet's
Francis
Gaya, Estaminet
Gaya Rive Gauche
Georges
Gérard Besson
Glénan
Goumard
Grenadin
Guy Savoy
Il Cortile
Jamin
Jardin
Joséphine
Lasserre
Laurent
Ledoyen
Lous Landès
Lucas Carton
Maison Blanche
Maison Prunier
Marée
Marie et Fils
Marius
Marius (Chez)
Marius et Janette
Maxim's
Meurice
Michel Rostang
Miravile
Montalembert
Obélisque
Orangerie
Oulette
Paris
Pauline

Paul Minchelli
Pergolèse
Petit Marguery
Pétrus
Pichet
Pierre au Palais Royal
Pierre Gagnaire
Port Alma
Pré Carré
Pré Catelan
Récamier
Rech
Régalade
Régence
Relais d'Auteuil
Relais Plaza
Rest. des Chauffeurs
Rest. du Marché
Salle à Manger
Savy
Sébillon Neuilly
Stella Maris
Stresa
Table d'Anvers
Taillevent
Tan Dinh
Télégraphe
Tong Yen
Tour d'Argent
Trois Marches
Troyon
Vieille
Vieux Bistro
Vin sur Vin
Violon d'Ingres
Vivarois
Voltaire

Quick Fix
Angelina
Bacchantes
Bar des Théâtres
Café Beaubourg
Café Bleu Lanvin
Café de Flore
Café de la Musique
Café de la Paix
Café de l'Industrie
Café des Lettres
Café Marly
Caffé Bini
Chinatown Olympiades
Clocher Saint-Germain
Clown Bar
Comptoir du Saumon Fumé

Cosi
Dame Tartine
Drugstore Publicis
Ecluse
Fontaines
Fouquet's
Galoche d'Aurillac
Gavroche
Grenier de Notre Dame
Inagiku
Indiana Café
Jacques Mélac
Joe Allen
Ladurée
Lina's
Ma Bourgogne
Mariage Frères
Marianne
Mirama
Moulin à Vins
Nouveau Village Tao Tao
Oenothèque
Pied de Fouet
Planet Hollywood
Rest. du Musée d'Orsay
Ruc Univers
Studio
Terminus Nord
Thanksgiving
Viaduc Café
Virgin Café

Quiet Conversation
Affriolé
Agape
Alain Ducasse
Alisier
Allobroges
Al Mounia
Alsaco
Ambassadeurs
Ambroisie
Ami Louis
Amphyclès
Anacréon
Androuët
Annapurna
Apicius
Ardoise
Armand au Palais Royal
Arpège
Astor
Auberge Bressane
Avenue
Bamboche

Baracane
Bar Vendôme
Basilic
Beato
Beauvilliers (A.)
Bellecour
Bellini
Benkay
Benoît
Berthoud
Bertie's
Beudant
Bistro d'Hubert
Bistrot d'Alex
Bistrot de l'Etoile Lauriston
Bistrot de l'Etoile Troyon
Bistrot de Marius
Bistrot de Paris
Blue Elephant
Bon St. Pourçain
Boule d'Or
Bourguignon
Braisière
Bristol
Café Beaubourg
Café de Flore
Café de Mars
Café des Lettres
Café du Passage
Café Indochine
Café Les Deux Magots
Café Marly
Café Runtz
Cafetière
Calèche
Caméléon
Camélia
Cap Seguin
Carré des Feuillants
Carré Kléber
Cartes Postales
Cartet
Casa del Habano
Casa Olympe
Caves Solignac
Caviar Kaspia
Céladon
Cercle Ledoyen
Chantairelle
Chardenoux
Charpentiers
Chat Grippé
Chez Eux
Chiberta
Cigale

Pierre Gagnaire
Pierre Vedel
Pile ou Face
Poquelin
Port Alma
Poule au Pot
Pré Carré
Pré Catelan
Pressoir
Ravi
Récamier
Rech
Régence
Relais Plaza
Réminet
René
Repaire de Cartouche
Restaurant A
Rest. de la Tour
Rest. d'Eric Fréchon
Rest. du Marché
Rest. du Palais Royal
Rest. Opéra
Ribe
Romantica
Saudade
Savy
Sormani
Soupière
Sousceyrac
Taillevent
Taïra
Tan Dinh
Tante Louise
Timgad
Timonerie
Totem
Tour d'Argent
Trou Gascon
Troyon
Truffe Noire
Ty Coz
Venantius
Vieille
Vieux Bistro
Vivarois
Vong

Romantic Spots

Alain Ducasse
Allard
Altitude 95
Ambassadeurs
Ambroisie
Ami Louis

Anahï
Angelina
Annapurna
Armand au Palais Royal
Bamboche
Bar Vendôme
Bauta
Beauvilliers (A.)
Bellini
Benoît
Blue Elephant
Boeuf sur le Toit
Brasserie Flo
Brasserie Lipp
Bristol
Bûcherie
Café de Flore
Café Indochine
Café Les Deux Magots
Café Marly
Café Runtz
Cafetière
Caméléon
Camélia
Caviar Kaspia
Chardenoux
China Club
Closerie des Lilas
Coconnas
Conti
Coupe-Chou
Daru
Divellec
Dôme
Elysées du Vernet
Espadon
Fermette Marbeuf
Gérard Besson
Gitane
Goumard
Grand Colbert
Grande Cascade
Grand Véfour
Guinguette de Neuilly
Guirlande de Julie
Guy Savoy
Hôtel du Nord
Il Cortile
Il Vicolo
Jacques Cagna
Jamin
Jardin
Jardins de Bagatelle
Joséphine
Jules Verne

Julien
Kambodgia
Lapérouse
Lasserre
Laurent
Ledoyen
Lucas Carton
Maison Blanche
Maison de l'Amérique
Maison du Caviar
Maison du Valais
Maison Prunier
Mansouria
Marée
Maxim's
Meurice
Monde des Chimères
Morot-Gaudry
Nikita
Orangerie
Pactole
Paris
Paul Minchelli
Pavillon Montsouris
Pavillon Puebla
Petite Cour
Petit Prince de Paris
Petit Riche
Pharamond
"Pierre" à la Fontaine
Pile ou Face
Pré Catelan
Quai Ouest
Relais Louis XIII
Rest. du Palais Royal
Rest. Opéra
River Café
Romantica
Saudade
Shozan
Sousceyrac
Square Trousseau
Sud
Taillevent
Terminus Nord
Timgad
Toupary
Tour d'Argent
Train Bleu
Trois Marches
Trou Gascon
Truffière
Vagenende
Vaudeville
Vieux Bistro

Voltaire
Vong

Sleepers
(Good to excellent food,
but little known)

Alisier
Amazigh
Amuse Bouche
Avant Goût
Bistrot Papillon
Braisière
Camélia
C'Amelot
Cartes Postales
Cartet
Clos Morillons
Connivence
Cottage Marcadet
Cuisinier François
Dariole de Viry
Detourbe Duret
Epopée
Excuse
Galerie
Isami
Issé
Lac Hong
Mandragore
Michel Courtalhac
Mirama
Nikita
O à la Bouche
Oie Cendrée
Plancha
Pressoir
P'tit Troquet
Quercy
Quincy
Ravi
Repaire de Cartouche
Rest. Opéra
Saint Amarante
Suntory
Taïra
Timonerie
Troyon
Tsukizi
Yit Foong
Yves Quintard

Teflons

(Get lots of business, despite so-so food, i.e. they have other attractions that prevent criticism from sticking)

André
Angelina
Appart'
Auberge Dab
Avenue
Ballon des Ternes
Bar à Huîtres
Bar des Théâtres
Barfly
Baumann Ternes
Bermuda Onion
Bistrot de Marius
Boeuf sur le Toit
Brasserie Flo
Brasserie Le Stella
Brasserie Lipp
Brasserie Lorraine
Brasserie Lutétia
Buddha Bar
Butte Chaillot
Café du Commerce
Café Indochine
Café la Jatte
Café Les Deux Magots
Café Marly
Cap Vernet
Charlot - Roi Coquillages
Chartier
Chicago Pizza Pie Factory
Closerie des Lilas
Costes
Coupole
Drugstore Publicis
Fermette Marbeuf
Flandrin
Fouquet's
Francis
Gare
Goldenberg Wagram
Grand Colbert
Hippopotamus
Jenny
Joe Allen
Jo Goldenberg
Julien
Lina's
Livio
Maison d'Alsace
Maison de l'Amérique
Mariage Frères

Maxim's
Noura
Petit Poucet
Petit Riche
Petit Zinc
Pied de Cochon
Planet Hollywood
Procope
Quai Ouest
River Café
Sébillon Neuilly
Terminus Nord
Thoumieux
Train Bleu
Val d'Isère
Vaudeville
Virgin Café
Zebra Square

Special Occasions

Alain Ducasse
Ambassadeurs
Ami Louis
Amphyclès
Apicius
Arpège
Astor
Bamboche
Bar Vendôme
Beauvilliers (A.)
Benoît
Blue Elephant
Boeuf sur le Toit
Bofinger
Boule d'Or
Brasserie Flo
Brasserie Lipp
Bristol
Buddha Bar
Café la Jatte
Café Marly
Camélia
Carré des Feuillants
Céladon
Cercle Ledoyen
Chardenoux
Chiberta
Daru
Diep
Dînée
Divellec
Dôme
Duc (Le)
Elysées du Vernet
Espadon

Faucher	**Sunday Dining – Best Bets**
Faugeron	(B=brunch; L=lunch;
Flandrin	D=dinner; plus all hotels
Georges	and most Asians)
Gérard Besson	Al Dar (L,D)
Goumard	Al Diwan (L,D)
Grande Cascade	Altitude 95 (L,D)
Grand Véfour	Ambassade d'Auvergne (L,D)
Guy Savoy	Ambassadeurs (L,D)
Il Cortile	Ami Louis (L,D)
Jacques Cagna	Anahï (D)
Janou	André (L,D)
Jules Verne	Angelina (L)
Julien	Appart' (B,L,D)
Lapérouse	Arbuci (L,D)
Lasserre	Arpège (D)
Laurent	Assiette (L,D)
Ledoyen	Atlas (L,D)
Lous Landès	Auberge Bressane (L,D)
Lucas Carton	Auberge Dab (L,D)
Maison Blanche	Avenue (L,D)
Marée	Ay!! Caramba!! (L,D)
Maxim's	Ballon des Ternes (L,D)
Meurice	Bar à Huîtres (L,D)
Michel Rostang	Bar au Sel (L,D)
Miravile	Bar des Théâtres (L,D)
Orangerie	Barfly (B)
Pauline	Basilic (L,D)
Paul Minchelli	Batifol (L,D)
Pavillon Montsouris	Baumann Ternes (L,D)
Pavillon Puebla	Beaujolais d'Auteuil (L,D)
Pergolèse	Beauvilliers (A.) (D)
Pétrus	Benkay (L,D)
Philippe Detourbe	Benoît (L)
Pierre Gagnaire	Bermuda Onion (B,D)
Port Alma	Bistro de la Grille (L,D)
Pré Catelan	Bistro des Deux Théâtres (L,D)
Récamier	Bistro d'Hubert (L,D)
Relais du Parc	Bistro du 17 (L,D)
Relais Louis XIII	Bistrot d'à Côté Flaubert (L,D)
Rest. du Palais Royal	Bistrot de Breteuil (L,D)
Rest. Opéra	Bistrot de l'Etoile Niel (D)
Sousceyrac	Bistrot de l'Etoile Troyon (D)
Table d'Anvers	Bistrot de Marius (L,D)
Taillevent	Bistrot de Paris (L,D)
Timonerie	Bistrot du Dôme (L,D)
Tour d'Argent	Bistrot Mazarin (L,D)
Trois Marches	Boeuf sur le Toit (L,D)
Trou Gascon	Bookinistes (D)
Violon d'Ingres	Botequim Brasileiro (D)
Vivarois	Bouillon Racine (L,D)
Voltaire	Boule d'Or (D)
	Brasserie Balzar (L,D)
	Brasserie de la Poste (L,D)
	Brasserie de l'Isle St-Louis (L,D)

Brasserie du Louvre (L,D)
Brasserie Flo (L,D)
Brasserie Le Stella (L,D)
Brasserie Lipp (L,D)
Brasserie Lorraine (D)
Brasserie Lutétia (B,L,D)
Brasserie Mollard (L,D)
Bristol (L,D)
Bûcherie (L,D)
Buddha Bar (D)
Butte Chaillot (L,D)
Café Beaubourg (L,D)
Café de Flore (B,L,D)
Café de la Musique (L,D)
Café de la Paix (L,D)
Café de l'Industrie (L,D)
Café de Mars (L)
Café des Lettres (B)
Café du Commerce (L,D)
Café du Passage (D)
Café la Jatte (L,D)
Café Les Deux Magots (L,D)
Café Marly (D)
Cagouille (L,D)
Camélia (L)
Camille (L,D)
Canard Laqué Pékinois (L,D)
Cantine des Gourmets (D)
Cap Vernet (L,D)
Caroubier (L,D)
Carr's (D)
Casa Bini (D)
Casa Tina (L,D)
Caveau du Palais (L,D)
Cazaudehore La Forestière (L,D)
Célébrités (L,D)
Chalet des Iles (L,D)
Champ de Mars (L,D)
Champs-Elysées Mandarin (L,D)
Charlot - Roi Coquillages (L,D)
Charpentiers (L,D)
Chartier (L,D)
Chat Grippé (L)
Cherche Midi (L,D)
Chicago Meatpackers (L,D)
Chicago Pizza Pie Factory (D)
Chieng Mai (L,D)
China Club (D)
China Town Belleville (L,D)
Chinatown Olympiades (L,D)
Chope d'Alsace (L,D)
Clément (L,D)
Closerie des Lilas (L,D)
Coffee Parisien (D)
Coin des Gourmets (L,D)

Congrès (L,D)
Connivence (L,D)
Contre-Allée (L)
Cosi (L,D)
Costes (L,D)
Côté 7ème (L,D)
Coupe-Chou (D)
Coupole (L,D)
Crêperie de Josselin (L,D)
Cuisinier François (L)
Dagorno (L)
Dame Tartine (L,D)
Débarcadère (B,L,D)
Denise (L,D)
Dessirier (L,D)
Diamantaires (L)
Diep (L,D)
Dôme (L,D)
Dos de la Baleine (D)
Drouant (D)
Drugstore Publicis (L,D)
Durand Dupont (B,L,D)
Echaudé St-Germain (L,D)
Enotéca (L)
Entrepôt (D)
Escargot Montorgueil (L,D)
Espace Sud-Ouest (L,D)
Espadon (L,D)
Etoile Marocaine (L,D)
Fakhr el Dine (L,D)
Fellini (L,D)
Fermette Marbeuf (L,D)
Flamboyant (L)
Flandrin (L,D)
Foch-An (L,D)
Foc-Ly (L,D)
Fond de Cour (B,D)
Fouquet's (L,D)
Fous d'en Face (L,D)
Francis (L,D)
Françoise (L,D)
Fred (L,D)
Frézet (L)
Friends (D)
Gare (L,D)
Gastronomie Quach (L,D)
Gauloise (L,D)
Georges Porte Maillot (L,D)
Géraud (L)
Goldenberg Wagram (L,D)
Graindorge (L)
Grand Café Capucines (L,D)
Grand Chinois (L,D)
Grand Colbert (L,D)
Grande Cascade (L,D)

Grandes Marches (L,D)
Grand Louvre (L,D)
Grenier de Notre Dame (L,D)
Guinguette de Neuilly (L,D)
Guirlande de Julie (D)
Hammam Café (L,D)
Hôtel du Nord (L)
Huîtrier (L)
Il Barone (D)
Il Carpaccio (L,D)
Il Vicolo (D)
Isami (D)
Janou (L,D)
Jardin des Cygnes (B,D)
Jardins de Bagatelle (L,D)
Jenny (L,D)
Jo Goldenberg (L,D)
Jules Verne (L,D)
Julien (D)
Khun Akorn (L,D)
Languedoc (L,D)
Livio (L,D)
Maison (L,D)
Maison d'Alsace (L,D)
Maison du Caviar (L,D)
Maître Paul (L,D)
Mandragore (L)
Mansouria (L,D)
Manufacture (L,D)
Marcello (B,D)
Mariage Frères (L)
Marianne (L,D)
Marius et Janette (D)
Marty (L,D)
Mavrommatis (L,D)
Méditerranée (L,D)
Meurice (L,D)
Milonga (D)
Mirama (L,D)
Monsieur Lapin (L,D)
Montalembert (L,D)
Muniche (L,D)
Navarin (L)
New Nioullaville (L,D)
Ngo (L,D)
Noces de Jeannette (L,D)
Noura (D,L)
Nouveau Village Tao Tao (L,D)
Obélisque (L,D)
Omar (D)
Orangerie (D)
Osaka (L,D)
Ostréade (L,D)
Paolo Petrini (L,D)
Parc aux Cerfs (L,D)

Passy Mandarin (L,D)
Pavillon des Princes (L,D)
Pavillon Montsouris (L,D)
Pavillon Panama (L,D)
Père Claude (L,D)
Perron (L,D)
Petite Chaise (L,D)
Petite Cour (L,D)
Petit Lutétia (L,D)
Petit Poucet (L,D)
Petit Prince de Paris (D)
Petit Zinc (L,D)
Pétrus (L,D)
Philippe Detourbe (L,D)
Pichet (D)
Pied de Chameau (L,D)
Pied de Cochon (L,D)
"Pierre" à la Fontaine (D)
Pierre Gagnaire (D)
Planet Hollywood (L,D)
Polidor (L,D)
Port du Salut (L)
Porte Océane (L,D)
Poste (D)
Poule au Pot (D)
Pré Catelan (L)
Président (L,D)
Procope (D)
Quai Ouest (B,L,D)
404 (L,D)
Régence (L,D)
Relais de Venise (L,D)
Relais du Parc (L,D)
Relais Plaza (L,D)
Réminet (L,D)
Rendez-vous des Chauffeurs (L,D)
Restaurant A (L,D)
Rest. des Beaux Arts (L,D)
Rest. des Chauffeurs (L,D)
Rest. du Musée d'Orsay (L)
Rest. Toutoune (L,D)
River Café (B,L,D)
Rôtisserie du Beaujolais (L,D)
Rôtisserie Monsigny (L,D)
Ruc Univers (L,D)
Salle à Manger (L,D)
Sébillon Neuilly (L,D)
Spicy Restaurant (L,D)
Square Trousseau (L,D)
Studio (D)
Suntory (L,D)
Table du Marché (L,D)
Taroudant II (L,D)
Taverne Kronenbourg (L,D)
Terminus Nord (L,D)

Thanksgiving (L)
Thoumieux (L,D)
Timgad (L,D)
Tong Yen (L,D)
Tour d'Argent (L,D)
Train Bleu (L,D)
Trentaquattro (D)
Trois Marches (L,D)
Tsé-Yang (L,D)
Tsukizi (D)
Vagenende (L,D)
Val d'Isère (L,D)
Vaudeville (L,D)
Venantius (L,D)
Verre Bouteille (L,D)
Viaduc Café (B,L,D)
Vieux Bistro (L,D)
Village d'Ung et Li Lam (L,D)
Vin et Marée (L,D)
Virgin Café (B,L,D)
Wepler (L,D)
Woolloomooloo (L,D)
Yugaraj (L,D)
Yvan sur Seine (D)
Zebra Square (L,D)
Zeyer (L,D)

Teenagers & Other Youthful Spirits

Agape
Ailleurs
Altitude 95
Anahuacalli
Angelina
Arbuci
Astier
Avant Goût
Ay!! Caramba!!
Bains
Baracane
Bascou
Batifol
Bermuda Onion
Berry's
Berthoud
Bistrot d'André
Bistrot d'Henri
Blue Elephant
Botequim Brasileiro
Bouchon Beaujolais
Bouillon Racine
Brasserie Balzar
Brasserie de l'Isle St-Louis
Brasserie Flo
Brasserie Lutétia

Buddha Bar
Butte Chaillot
Café Beaubourg
Café Bleu Lanvin
Café de la Musique
Café de la Paix
Café de l'Industrie
Café des Lettres
Café du Commerce
Café la Jatte
Café Marly
Caffé Bini
Caméléon
C'Amelot
Carr's
Casa Olympe
Cercle Ledoyen
Chantairelle
Chartier
Chicago Meatpackers
Chicago Pizza Pie Factory
China Club
Chinatown Olympiades
Clément
Clocher Saint-Germain
Clown Bar
Coco de Mer
Coffee Parisien
Coin des Gourmets
Comptoir des Sports
Cosi
Dame Tartine
Da Mimmo
Débarcadère
Délices d'Aphrodite
Denise
Deux Canards
Domarais
Dominique
Driver's
Ebauchoir
Entoto
Espace Sud-Ouest
Fernand/Les Fernandises
Finzi
Fontaines
Galoche d'Aurillac
Gare
Germaine
Grand Café Capucines
Grenier de Notre Dame
Guinguette de Neuilly
Hammam Café
Hôtel du Nord
Indiana Café

Janou
Jenny
Joe Allen
Khun Akorn
Lina's
Maison du Valais
Mandragore
Manufacture
Marianne
Marty
Milonga
Moulin à Vins
New Nioullaville
Nikita
Nouveau Village Tao Tao
Olivades
Omar
Orient-Extrême
Ostréade
Oum el Banine
Paul
Pento
Perraudin
Petit Gavroche
Petit Keller
Petit Lutétia
Petit Mâchon
Petit St-Benoît
Pied de Chameau
Pied de Cochon
Planet Hollywood
Polidor
Port du Salut
Président
Quai Ouest
404
Quincy
Réconfort
Relais de Venise
Réminet
Rendez-vous/Camionneurs
Rendez-vous des Chauffeurs
Réservoir
Restaurant A
Rest. des Beaux Arts
Rest. des Chauffeurs
River Café
Rôtisserie Monsigny
Ruc Univers
Scheffer
Square Trousseau
Studio
Table de Pierre
Taroudant II
Taverne Kronenbourg

Temps des Cerises
Thanksgiving
Thoumieux
Toupary
Tsukizi
Val d'Isère
Viaduc Café
Virgin Café
Wally Le Saharien
Wepler
Willi's Wine Bar
Yvan sur Seine
Zebra Square
Zéphyr
Zygomates

Transporting Experiences

Al Mounia
Alsaco
Androuët
Annapurna
Atlas
Benkay
Blue Elephant
Bouillon Racine
Café Indochine
Chinatown Olympiades
Coco de Mer
Délices d'Aphrodite
Denise
Diamantaires
Diep
Domarais
Dominique
Entoto
Fakhr el Dine
Fogón Saint Julien
Grande Cascade
Grand Louvre
Grand Véfour
Guinguette de Neuilly
Iles Philippines
Indra
Isami
Jardins de Bagatelle
Jules Verne
Kambodgia
Khun Akorn
Maison Blanche
Maison du Caviar
Mansouria
Manufacture
Pré Catelan
Président
404

Ravi
Restaurant A
Rest. d'Eric Fréchon
River Café
Saudade
Sud
Table de Babette
Taïra
Tan Dinh
Timgad
Tour d'Argent
Tsé-Yang
Vong
Wally Le Saharien
Yit Foong

Trendy Intelligentsia

A et M Le Bistrot
Affriolé
Ailleurs
Allobroges
Ami Louis
Amognes
Anahï
André
Appart'
Assiette
Astier
Avant Goût
Avenue
Bar des Théâtres
Barfly
Bascou
Bastide Odéon
Beato
Benoît
Berthoud
Bistro de la Grille
Bistro des Deux Théâtres
Bistro d'Hubert
Bistrot d'à Côté Neuilly
Bistrot d'à Côté St-Germain
Bistrot d'Alex
Bistrot de l'Etoile Lauriston
Bistrot de Paris
Bistrot d'Henri
Bistrot du Dôme
Bistrot Mazarin
Blue Elephant
Boeuf sur le Toit
Bon Accueil
Bon St. Pourçain
Bookinistes
Brasserie Balzar
Brasserie Le Stella

Brasserie Lipp
Buddha Bar
Butte Chaillot
Café Beaubourg
Café Bleu Lanvin
Café de Flore
Café de la Musique
Café de l'Industrie
Café de Mars
Café des Lettres
Café du Passage
Café la Jatte
Café Les Deux Magots
Café Marly
Cafetière
C'Amelot
Camille
Casa Bini
Casa del Habano
Cercle Ledoyen
Chantairelle
Chardenoux
Chen
Cherche Midi
Chieng Mai
China Club
Clown Bar
Coffee Parisien
Contre-Allée
Cosi
Costes
Cou de la Girafe
Da Mimmo
Débarcadère
Denise
Dôme
Dominique
Duc (Le)
Ebauchoir
Ecaille de PCB
Elle
Enotéca
Finzi
Fontaine de Mars
Fouquet's
Gare
Gaya Rive Gauche
Georges
Grand Colbert
Hammam Café
I Golosi
Il Barone
Il Vicolo
Inagiku
Isami

Issé
Janou
Jean
Joséphine
Juvenile's
Kambodgia
Kinugawa
Macéo
Maison Blanche
Manufacture
Marianne
Marie et Fils
Mavrommatis
Michel
Montalembert
Moulin à Vins
Natacha
Nénesse
O à la Bouche
Omar
Orangerie
Orient-Extrême
Osteria
Paul Minchelli
Petit Plat
Petit St-Benoît
Pichet
Pied de Chameau
Poste
Quai Ouest
404
Quincy
Réconfort
Régalade
Réminet
Rendez-vous des Chauffeurs
Repaire de Cartouche
Réservoir
Restaurant
Rest. d'Eric Fréchon
Rest. des Beaux Arts
Rest. des Chauffeurs
Rest. du Marché
Rôtisserie d'en Face
Ruc Univers
Saint Amarante
Saint Pourçain
Shozan
Square Trousseau
Taïra
Taka
Tan Dinh
Taroudant II
Temps des Cerises
Terroir

Tsukizi
Val d'Isère
Viaduc Café
Vieux Bistro
Villaret
Vincent
Voltaire
Vong
Wally Le Saharien
Willi's Wine Bar
Yvan sur Seine
Zebra Square
Zéphyr
Zygomates

Visitors on Expense Accounts
Alain Ducasse
Ambroisie
Ami Louis
Amphyclès
Apicius
Arpège
Assiette
Beauvilliers (A.)
Benoît
Bistrot du Sommelier
Braisière
Bristol
Bûcherie
Cantine des Gourmets
Carpe Diem
Carré des Feuillants
Caviar Kaspia
Céladon
Célébrités
Cercle Ledoyen
Charlot - Roi Coquillages
Chez Eux
Chiberta
Clovis
Couronne
Daru
Dessirier
Divellec
Dôme
Drouant
Duc (Le)
Elysées du Vernet
Espadon
Faucher
Gaya, Estaminet
Gérard Besson
Goumard
Grand Véfour

Grenadin
Guy Savoy
Il Carpaccio
Issé
Jacques Cagna
Jamin
Jarasse
Jardin
Jardin des Cygnes
Kinugawa
Lasserre
Laurent
Ledoyen
Lous Landès
Lucas Carton
Magnolias
Maison du Caviar
Maison Prunier
Marée
Marius
Marius (Chez)
Marius et Janette
Meurice
Michel Rostang
Miravile
Montparnasse 25
Muses
Orangerie
Parc aux Cerfs
Paris
Paul Minchelli
Pavillon Montsouris
Pergolèse
Pichet
Pierre Gagnaire
Pierre Vedel
Pré Catelan
Pressoir
Récamier
Relais d'Auteuil
Relais de Sèvres
Relais Louis XIII
Rest. Opéra
Romantica
Shozan
Sormani
Sousceyrac
Stresa
Table d'Anvers
Taillevent
Taïra
Tan Dinh
Timonerie
Tour d'Argent
Trois Marches

Troyon
Truffe Noire
Tsé-Yang
Ty Coz
Vin sur Vin
Vivarois
Voltaire

Wheelchair Access

(The following indicate that
they have easy access, but
it's best to call in advance
to check)

A et M Le Bistrot
Alain Ducasse
Al Dar
Allard
Ambassadeurs
Ambroisie
Ami Pierre
Anahuacalli
Androuët
Ange Vin
Ardoise
Armand au Palais Royal
Arthur
Astor
Atlas
Avant Goût
Ay!! Caramba!!
Batifol
Bermuda Onion
Bernica
Bistrot d'à Côté Flaubert
Bistrot de l'Etoile Niel
Bistrot du Cochon d'Or
Bistrot Gambas
Blue Elephant
Boeuf Gros Sel
Bouchon Beaujolais
Bouchons de Fr. Clerc
Boule d'Or
Braisière
Brasserie Flo
Buddha Bar
Café de Flore
Café de la Musique
Café de l'Industrie
Cagouille
Cantine des Gourmets
Céladon
Cercle Ledoyen
Chartier
Chiberta
Cigale

Clovis
Cochon d'Or
Coco d'Isles
Coffee Parisien
Comte de Gascogne
Connivence
Corniche
Crêperie de Josselin
Dame Tartine
Dariole de Viry
Débarcadère
Denise
Diamantaires
Divellec
Dominique
Durand Dupont
Emporio Armani Caffé
Entoto
Entrepôt
Escargot Montorgueil
Espadon
Etoile d'Or
Excuse
Faucher
Fauchon - Le 30
Ferme de Boulogne
Ferme des Mathurins
Ferme St-Simon
Flambée/Bistrot du Sud
Flèche d'Or Café
Flora Danica
Foch-An
Fogón Saint Julien
Fontaine d'Auteuil
Françoise
Fumoir
Gallopin
Géraud
Gildo
Grand Louvre
Grand Venise
Grenier de Notre Dame
Guirlande de Julie
Hammam Café
Hédiard
Il Cortile
Indra
Jarasse
Jardin
Jardin des Cygnes
Julien
Kinugawa
Kiosque
Ladurée
Lasserre

Livio
Lous Landès
Maxim's
Mille Colonnes
Montparnasse 25
Muses
Obélisque
Oie Cendrée
Oulette
Paolo Petrini
Paprika
Parc aux Cerfs
Passy Mandarin
Pavillon des Princes
Pavillon Panama
Petites Sorcières
Pied de Cochon
Pierre
Pierre Vedel
Planet Hollywood
Port Alma
Porte Océane
Pré Carré
Quercy
Ravi
Régence
Relais de Venise
Relais du Parc
Repaire de Cartouche
Rest. des Chauffeurs
Rest. du Musée d'Orsay
Romantica
Rosimar
Saveurs
Sousceyrac
Spicy Restaurant
Totem
Toupary
Troyon
Véranda
Verre Bouteille
Village d'Ung et Li Lam
Vin et Marée
Violon d'Ingres
Vishnou
Vivario
Vivarois
Zebra Square

Winning Wine Lists

Alain Ducasse
Alsaco
Ambroisie
Ami Louis
Ange Vin

Arpège
Bistrot du Sommelier
Bouchons de Fr. Clerc
Bourguignon
Café du Passage
Carré des Feuillants
Caveau du Palais
Cave Drouot
Caves Pétrissans
Ecluse
Enotéca
Espadon
Faugeron
Gérard Besson
Goumard
Grand Véfour
Guy Savoy
Jacques Cagna
Joséphine
Juvenile's
Lasserre
Laurent
Lucas Carton
Ma Bourgogne
Macéo
Marée
Maxim's
Michel Rostang
Moulin à Vins
Oenothèque
Pré Catelan
Pressoir
Quincy
Récamier
Rest. Opéra
Rôtisserie du Beaujolais
Taillevent
Tour d'Argent
Trois Marches
Vin sur Vin
Willi's Wine Bar

Worth a Trip
Bois de Boulogne
    Pré Catelan
Clichy
    Romantica

Issy-Les-Moulineaux
    Manufacture
St-Germain-en-Laye
    Cazaudehore La Forestière
Versailles
    Trois Marches

Young Children
Altitude 95
Angelina
Arbuci
Ay!! Caramba!!
Bermuda Onion
Brasserie de l'Isle St-Louis
Brasserie Lutétia
Café Beaubourg
Café Bleu Lanvin
Café de la Paix
Café du Commerce
Chicago Meatpackers
Chicago Pizza Pie Factory
Clément
Clocher Saint-Germain
Guinguette de Neuilly
Hippopotamus
Indiana Café
Lina's
Mandragore
Marty
Ostréade
Pied de Cochon
Pinocchio
Planet Hollywood
Porte Océane
Quai Ouest
Relais de Venise
Restaurant A
River Café
Studio
Taverne Kronenbourg
Thanksgiving
Val d'Isère
Viaduc Café
Virgin Café

NOTES

NOTES

NOTES